PENGUIN BOOKS

THE PENGUIN BOOK OF MYTHS & LEGENDS OF ANCIENT EGYPT

Dr Joyce Tyldesley has a degree in the archaeology of the eastern Mediterranean from Liverpool University and a doctorate from Oxford University. She is currently Lecturer in Egyptology at the University of Manchester, a Fellow of the Manchester Museum, and an Honorary Research Fellow at Liverpool University. She has worked on many excavations in Britain, Europe and Egypt, and is the author of several published works on Ancient Egypt including acclaimed biographies of Rameses the Great and Cleopatra (a Radio 4 Book of the Week), and *Egypt: How a Lost Civilization was Rediscovered*, which accompanied a major BBC television series.

The Penguin Book of
MYTHS & LEGENDS of
ANCIENT EGYPT

Joyce Tyldesley

PENGUIN BOOKS

PENGUIN BOOKS

Published by the Penguin Group
Penguin Books Ltd, 80 Strand, London WC2R ORL, England
Penguin Group (USA) Inc., 375 Hudson Street, New York, New York 10014, USA
Penguin Group (Canada), 90 Eglinton Avenue East, Suite 700, Toronto, Ontario, Canada M4P 2Y3
(a division of Pearson Penguin Canada Inc.)
Penguin Ireland, 25 St Stephen's Green, Dublin 2, Ireland (a division of Penguin Books Ltd)
Penguin Group (Australia), 250 Camberwell Road, Camberwell, Victoria 3124, Australia
(a division of Pearson Australia Group Pty Ltd)
Penguin Books India Pvt Ltd, 11 Community Centre, Panchsheel Park, New Delhi – 110 017, India
Penguin Group (NZ), 67 Apollo Drive, Rosedale, Auckland 0632, New Zealand
(a division of Pearson New Zealand Ltd)
Penguin Books (South Africa) (Pty) Ltd, 24 Sturdee Avenue, Rosebank, Johannesburg 2196, South Africa

Penguin Books Ltd, Registered Offices: 80 Strand, London WC2R ORL, England

www.penguin.com

First published as *Myths & Legends of Ancient Egypt* by Particular Books 2010
Published in Penguin Books 2011

015

Copyright © Joyce Tyldesley, 2011

The moral right of the author has been asserted

Typeset by Ellipsis Books Limited, Glasgow

Printed and bound in Great Britain by Clays Ltd, Elcograf S.p.A.

A CIP catalogue record for this book is available from the British Library

ISBN: 978-0-141-02176-8

www.greenpenguin.co.uk

MIX
Paper from
responsible sources
FSC
www.fsc.org   FSC™ C018179

Penguin Books is committed to a sustainable
future for our business, our readers and our planet.
This book is made from Forest Stewardship
Council™ certified paper.

For Philippa Anne Snape,
who has always wanted a book of her own

CONTENTS

CONTENTS

CONTENTS

LIST OF ILLUSTRATIONS

All photographs are copyright © Steven Snape

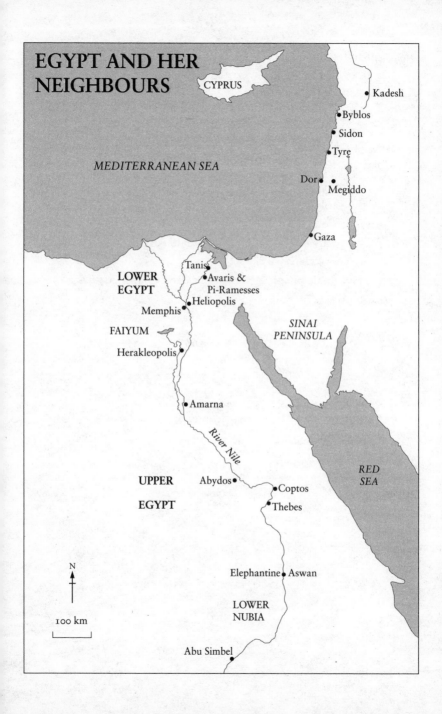

EGYPT AND HER NEIGHBOURS

CYPRUS

• Kadesh

MEDITERRANEAN SEA

• Byblos
• Sidon
• Tyre
Dor • • Megiddo

• Gaza

Tanis •
LOWER   • Avaris &
EGYPT   Pi-Ramesses
            • Heliopolis
Memphis •

SINAI
PENINSULA

FAIYUM

Herakleopolis •

• Amarna

River Nile

RED
SEA

UPPER   Abydos •
                        • Coptos
EGYPT   • Thebes

N

100 km

Elephantine • Aswan

LOWER
NUBIA

Abu Simbel •

INTRODUCTION

The work of the god is a joke to the heart of the fool.
The life of a fool is a burden to the god himself . . .
Fate does not look ahead, retaliation does not come wrongfully.
Great is the counsel of the god in putting one thing after another.
The fate and the fortune that come, it is the god who sends them.[1]

Ancient Egypt supplies some startling statistics: 3,000 years of dynastic rule by at least 300 heroic kings who recognized, at a conservative estimate, some 1,500 deities. This immense time span saw the development of a complex and frequently contradictory mythology peopled by a vast and ever-increasing pantheon, whose myriad members changed name, appearance and character with startling regularity, frequently splitting into different components or fusing to form a deity more powerful than the sum of his or her parts. Their stories, the science and history of their age, entertain while providing explanations for the mysteries of creation, existence and death that challenge every community. In so doing they provide a glimpse into the thoughts and fears of the ancient mind.

It would be a mistake to see the different explanations for specific phenomena – the many colourful creation myths, for example – as rival mythologies. Rivalry could never be an issue in a land with no single, correct answer to the mysteries of life.

Either/or logic is a relatively modern convention developed by the Greeks; the Egyptians, happily logic-free, had no difficulty in accepting the contradictions, inconsistencies and multiple interpretations within their stories, just as children today see little problem in accepting the parallel stories of Santa Claus and Baby Jesus as the *raison d'être* for Christmas. Their myths were not designed to be analysed, compared and contrasted by scholars; they were simply accepted as valid attempts to interpret the inexplicable for different people at different times and in different places. Each individual tale carried its own internal logic, and that was all that was needed. However, if we look closely enough we can identify one constant theme – the desire to justify and reinforce the divine rule of the king – underpinning and unifying the diverse tales.

DEFINITIONS AND SOURCES

Myth, like logic, is a word derived from the Greek world. The Egyptians had no equivalent word or concept, and they did not feel the need to separate their thoughts into 'fact' and 'fiction'. Nor, for that matter, did they have words for 'religion' or 'philosophy'. We therefore cannot rely on the Egyptians to define our area of study for us. I have chosen to define a myth as 'a traditional story set in the past, with a supernatural element, which is used to explain or justify the otherwise inexplicable'. I define a legend as simply 'a traditional, unverifiable story set in the past, concerning people or places that were, or were believed to be, real'. A purist might argue that these definitions are far too general, embracing as they do such diverse genres as fairy stories and royal propaganda. However, in the context of ancient Egypt, where there are no fairies and few heroes other than the divinely inspired king, a more restrictive definition seems unnecessarily exclusive. As Egypt has left us far more myths than legends, the first three sections of this book will be dedicated to myths, while the final section has both myths and legends.

Tomb and temple walls, statues, papyri and amulets make it clear that Egypt recognized many gods, demi-gods and supernatural beings. Yet few well-developed tales about these beings survive. We have no complete, or even partially complete, contemporary book of Egyptian myths. That book, if it ever existed (and this seems highly unlikely – Egyptian theology had no central dogma and no single book of divine revelation), was lost when the libraries attached to the great temples were destroyed in the turmoil that accompanied Egypt's compulsory conversion from paganism to Christianity in AD 391. Our canon of myths must therefore be constructed using a variety of sources that yield oblique references to myths, rather than the myths themselves. This is neither unusual nor unexpected: no ancient civilization has provided a full written record. However, the archaeological bias that has seen the preservation of many of Egypt's desert graves but the almost complete loss of her mud-brick domestic architecture means that our evidence will always veer towards the mythology of death. More particularly, it will veer towards the mythology of death accepted by those wealthy enough to invest in a decorated tomb.

With this caveat in mind, mythic elements and abstract concepts can be deduced from stone architecture and architectural fragments, and picked out from the writings and illustrations preserved on temple and tomb walls. They can be identified in, and occasionally read on, the grave-goods provided for the deceased, and in the literature, art and artefacts that have survived the now-vanished domestic sites. This randomly preserved evidence can be frustrating: a whole series of New Kingdom animal fables exists, for example, as pictures painted on papyri and ostraca.[2] We can see the animals performing human actions but, without any text, it is never going to be possible to comprehend the full story of the cats who are challenged by the fierce warrior mice. At the same time there is always the double-edged worry that we may be either missing something of significance, or misinterpreting or over-interpreting what we do see.

The principal textual sources that we will use to reconstruct the canon of Egyptian myth and legends are as follows:

Temples and tombs

Although Egypt's great palaces and cities have mostly vanished, several decorated stone temples have survived more or less intact. These, dating in the main to the Graeco-Roman Period at the very end of the dynastic age, present us with the final version of a constantly developing architecture that reflects 3,000 years of constantly developing theology. The temple was both the cosmos in miniature and the home of the god, and its wide courtyards and sacred lakes were used for public re-enactments of the myths underpinning the temple cult. Few papyri have survived to preserve details of the daily, annual and more irregular temple ceremonies. Fortunately, however, from the New Kingdom onwards, the stone temple walls were used as billboards to record in words and images some details of temple hymns and rituals (on the inner walls: hidden from the people) and pharaoh's legendary triumphs (on the outer walls: accessible to the people).

The state temples were, to all intents and purposes, out of bounds to the non-elite Egyptian. He, or she, would communicate with the divine via local temples and personal domestic rituals. Inscribed stelae,[3] prayers used as school texts and informal scribblings on ostraca preserve the petitions of these ordinary people. These, like the official hymns recited in the great temples, lack narrative structure, but they do include useful mythic references.

Here, for example, a New Kingdom prayer is addressed to Thoth, wise scribe of the gods:[4]

> *Come to me, Thoth, O noble Ibis . . .*
> *Come to me and give me counsel,*
> *Make me skilful in your calling;*
> *Better is your calling than all callings,*
> *It makes [men] great . . .*

Tombs, too, were designed to reflect the mythical world. The royal funerary complexes were first and foremost sacred land-scapes: the universe in miniature and a place where mortal life met the divine. Everything in the complex was designed for a specific ritual purpose, and nothing was included by chance. To take the most obvious example: the pyramids, the great stone tombs of the Old and Middle Kingdom pharaohs, may be inter-preted as ramps or stairways that will help the deceased king to achieve his star- or sun-based destiny in the sky. Hidden within the pyramid, the burial chamber may be interpreted as the womb from which the deceased king will be reborn, while the corridors leading to the outside world represent both the passageways through the underworld (leading to the birth of the god Re), and the birth canal of the goddess Nut (leading to the birth of the god Osiris). Although the pyramid form was abandoned at the start of the New Kingdom, the link between the tomb and the mechanisms of rebirth continued until the end of the dynastic age.

While funerary traditions varied from town to town, and from time to time, most non-royal mummies were buried on the west bank of the Nile in east-facing tombs. The geography of the tomb and the positioning of the mummy were important. Within the tomb, the mummy usually lay on a north–south axis on its left side, so that it might look east, towards the rising sun and towards the tomb entrance and false door (accessible only by the spirit of the deceased) whence the vital offerings would come. Royal mummies, anticipating a slightly different afterlife, lay on their backs, looking towards the sun and the stars.

Medical texts

More indirect references to myths can be gleaned from the writings compiled by the physicians, magicians and priests whose healing and protective remedies used a tried and tested combination of practical measures (physical examination, diagnosis and treatment) and myth-based magic (incantations and spells) to effect a cure. Many of the healing recipes identify the patient with the weak child-god Horus, who thus becomes an eternal invalid, while the physician may be identified either with healing deities such as Isis and Thoth, or with potentially lethal deities such as Sekhmet the lioness, the terrible mistress of plagues and pestilence, and Serket the scorpion who could both inflict and cure stings. Some of the recipes even incorporate a short myth (a *historiola*) which must be recited over the patient as the remedy is applied. For example, recipe 58 in the 18th Dynasty *Papyrus Ebers* deals with an eye-infection by providing a brief, and to modern eyes extremely confusing, story concerning the crew who sail in the sun boat of the god Re, and who will help the healer to cure the affliction. The story must be told as the eye is anointed with a healing mixture of gall of tortoise and honey:[5]

To expel white spots in the eyes: It is thundering in the southern sky since the evening, there is rough weather in the northern sky, as corpses fell into the water, and Re's crew were landing at the shore, because the heads fell into the water. Who shall bring them? [Who shall] find them? I shall bring them, I shall find them. I have brought your heads, I have attached [them to] your necks, I have fastened your cut-off [heads] in their place. I have brought you (i.e. Re's crew) to expel afflictions [caused] by a god, by dead man or woman, etc. It is recited over gall of tortoise, [which] is pounded with honey and applied to the eyelids.

The slightly older *Papyrus Edwin Smith*, a document largely concerned with traumatic injury, offers less mythology and more practical advice, yet still recommends this incantation against the unspecified epidemic known as 'the pest of the year', and, in so doing, references a whole host of mythological characters and events:[6]

O Flame-in-His-Face! Presider over the horizon, speak thou to the chief of the Hemesut-house, who makes Osiris, first of the land, to flourish. O Nekhbet, lifting the earth to the sky for her father, come thou, bind the two feathers around me, around me, that I may live and flourish because I possess the White One. The first is the Great One dwelling in Heliopolis; the second is Isis; the third is Nephthys; while I am subject to thee.

O Seizer-of-the-Great-One, son of Sekhmet, mightiest of the mighty, son of the Disease-Daemon, Dened, son of Hathor, mistress of the crown and flooder of the streams; when thou voyagest in the Celestial Ocean, when thou sailest in the morning boat, thou hast saved me from every sickness.

Fictional tales

In a land without any secular public entertainment – no theatres, sports arenas or circuses – storytelling was an important art at all levels of society. Kings, when bored, called upon their sons to entertain them with exciting tales of mystery and adventure, and even the gods enjoyed a good yarn; the loquacious Thoth was able to persuade the errant goddess Tefnut to return to Egypt by tempting her with a long string of fables. This tradition long outlasted the pharaohs, so that Amelia B. Edwards, visiting Egypt at the end of the nineteenth century, was able to enjoy a performance by a traditional storyteller.[7]

> *While the Writer was at work in the shade of the first pylon* (of Medinet Habu: the mortuary temple of Ramesses III), *an Arab storyteller took possession of that opposite doorway, and entertained the donkey-boys and sailors. Well-paid with a little tobacco and a few copper piastres, he went on for hours, his shrill chant rising every now and again to a quavering scream. He was a wizened, grizzled old fellow, miserably poor and tattered; but he had the* Arabian Nights *and hundreds of other tales by heart.*

Fifty years later, the anthropologist Winifred S. Blackman noted the Egyptian fondness for storytelling, with most villages boasting at least one acknowledged, semi-professional storyteller equipped with a good anthology of collected and inherited tales, all committed to memory. Performances were exciting and moving, as 'the peasant is an excellent *raconteur* possessed of great imagination, very dramatic, and entirely free from self consciousness'.[8] Hasan el-Shamy, interviewing a village storyteller in 1969, learned of a regular routine of daily work, evening prayers and night-time storytelling, with the longer tales – traditionally told during July and August when, in pre-Aswan-Dam times, the fields were flooded and work was light – taking one or two nights to complete.[9]

Spoken stories and dramas must have played a vital role in the development and transmission of Egypt's ancient culture but, with the performers long dead and their 'scripts' largely missing, it is a role that is very hard for us to recapture. As it has been estimated that no more than 5 per cent of the population was literate, with most, if not all, of these belonging to the male urban elite, we can guess with some confidence that the majority of people heard, subtly altered and passed on tales without ever consulting a papyrus scroll, just as they did in Egypt's pre-television-age, post-dynastic villages. We can speculate, but never prove, that the stories transmitted and eventually lost in the oral tradition were different from both the official history promoted through royal inscriptions and the official theology promoted and preserved by the undertakers and high priests. And, as the storytellers observed by Edwards, Blackman and el-Shamy were all men, and the few storytellers that we meet in the ancient texts are also male, we can push this speculation further by wondering if the stories transmitted by women as they went about their daily chores were different from, and perhaps more female-centred than those told by men.

A handful of contemporary tales have survived by chance on fragile papyri from the Middle Kingdom onwards. These papyri are today scattered in museums throughout the world. By convention they are referenced by their find-spot (e.g. the *Ramesseum Dramatic Papyrus* is part of the collection of the British Museum where it is more properly known as *Papyrus Ramesseum B*);[10] by the name of their museum (e.g. *Papyrus Berlin* 3008 is *The Lamentations of Isis and Nephthys*, housed in Berlin Museum under the museum accession number 3008); or by the name of their first western owner (e.g. *Papyrus Westcar* is a collection of magical tales which, originally acquired by Henry Westcar in 1839, is also housed in Berlin Museum where it bears the accession number 3033).

These fictional tales, just a fraction of the stories once told, are fundamental to our understanding of Egyptian mythology. But we need to be careful. In most cases we have a single papyrus giving one version of what we can assume to have been a widely told story. This can bring a false sense of completeness, freezing a tale that once enjoyed a more fluid telling while giving the one preserved version an unwarranted validity. In modern times, committing a traditional folktale to film can have a similar effect. Few, having seen the Disney cartoon version of Cinderella, remember the dark seventeenth-century French folktale that preceded it: even fewer realize that the French folktale is itself just one version of a rags-to-riches genre which stretches back to the Egyptian tale of the beautiful Rhodophis and her lost sandal. Children throughout the world now find it difficult, if not impossible, to imagine a Cinderella without long blonde hair, a glass slipper and a pale blue party dress worn with matching headband. In ancient Egypt, where both the spoken and the written word carried magical properties, this freezing effect was well understood. Committing a thought to writing made it permanent so that it became a form of truth; a viewpoint which encouraged kings to promote their own exaggerated and, on occasion, blatantly false, propaganda on stone walls throughout their land.

All our stories have to be read through the eyes of a translator who has to supply not only the words but also the underlying sentiments, subtleties and nuances that will make that story accessible to a modern reader. The difficulties inherent in translating complex thoughts from one modern language to another are legion: the difficulties in translating such thoughts from an ancient and long-dead language (a language, moreover, lacking any indication of punctuation, and with very different cultural references) to a modern one are even more daunting. It seems unlikely, however hard we try, that we will ever reach a full understanding of Egypt's literature. The majority of the stories told in this book have been adapted by me from original texts; readers wishing to read direct translations of the tales are directed first of all to the splendid works of Miriam Lichtheim listed in the bibliography which ends this book. Just occasionally, direct translations of original and classical texts have been quoted, in order to allow the Egyptians to speak for themselves: these are shown in italics. Within these direct translations, reconstructed omissions are given in square brackets [like this], explanations are given in curved brackets (like this).

Funerary texts

Funerary literature – writings prepared specifically for the grave, to protect and aid the deceased on his or her journey to the afterlife – has survived in far greater quantity. Within this genre we may detect two strong traditions: the solar myths of the creator god Atum and the life-giving sun god Re, and the myths of the divine king of the dead, Osiris, who promises eternal life to all. These twin traditions exist in parallel; both will ultimately contribute to the survival of the dead and neither can be fully separated from the other.

The earliest of the funerary writings are the Old Kingdom *Pyramid Texts*: a collection of at least 750 protective spells or utterances of varying length which, when combined, tell the story of the royal deceased as he ascends to the sky to join the sun god.[11] Selections from the *Pyramid Texts* were first carved on the internal walls of the pyramid built for the 5th Dynasty pharaoh Unas, but analysis of their language suggests that many of the spells reflect beliefs and rituals predating the pyramid age. Incorporating at least 200 divine beings, they are derived from a mixture of overlapping genres including myths, rituals, recitations, hymns and magical spells. They appear in all subsequent Old Kingdom kings', and some queens', pyramids, and are intended to be read in a specific order, although no one pyramid has every spell. The spells not only describe the difficult passage to eternity, but provide the specific knowledge of names, places and dangers that the deceased will need if he is to reach the afterlife. As they name the deceased, and as they are carved into the very fabric of the stone pyramid, they ensure that he or she will be protected forever. They are, however, both confusing and contradictory and they assume an in-depth knowledge of mythology, as spell 374, a spell intended to help the deceased king travel without hindrance, shows:[12]

> *Be great, O King! Ferry over, O King! May your name be*
> *notified to Osiris. Your foot is great, your foot is mighty, so*
> *traverse the Great Bed (the sky); you will [not] be seized by*
> *the earth-gods, you will not be opposed by the starry sky. The*
> *doors of the sky will be opened to you that you may go out*
> *from them as Horus and as the jackal beside him who hides*
> *his shape from his foes, [for] there is no father of yours among*
> *men who could beget you, for there is no mother of yours*
> *among men who could bear you.*

Woven among the obvious solar and Osirid traditions we may glimpse evidence for stellar belief plus remnants of other, less enduring mythologies: the suggestion that the dead king might transform into a grasshopper who leaps up into the sky, for example, or the idea, graphically expressed in the *Cannibal Hymn* (*Pyramid Texts* spells 273 and 274), that he might eat the gods to absorb their powers.

As the Old Kingdom pharaohs used their *Pyramid Texts* to achieve an afterlife away from the grave, their elite subjects remained trapped within their tombs, confined by walls decorated with scenes of a perfect Egypt – scenes of agriculture, markets, fishing and relaxation – which would provide a magical, eternal sustenance. Some added a blunt request for offerings, or an autobiography, a highly flattering composition detailing earthly achievements which, it was hoped, would prompt passers-by to leave a gift. Then, at the end of the Old Kingdom, the once exclusively royal afterlife was thrown open to the masses.

Now anyone who could afford the correct funerary rituals could reasonably hope to escape to a better life. Like the *Pyramid Texts* from which they were derived, the First Intermediate Period and Middle Kingdom *Coffin Texts* were a collection of spells designed to help the deceased to be reborn after death.[13] But, whereas the *Pyramid Texts* were restricted to the royal family, the 1,185 spells of the *Coffin Texts* were, in theory, available to everyone. Although they were occasionally written on tomb walls, stelae, papyri and canopic chests,[14] they were principally inscribed on the rectangular wooden outer coffins which now protected the mummies of the elite. These coffins, decorated with sacred texts and images, including maps detailing the route to the afterlife, and equipped with pairs of painted eyes which allowed the dead to peep into the land of the living, were themselves objects of great magical power. The *Coffin Texts* exhibit a strong solar mythology, but they also reflect local or regional traditions and, as most of the recovered *Coffin Texts* come from cemeteries in Middle Egypt, the Middle Egyptian god Thoth of Hermopolis Magna is accorded a prominent role. Once again, the spells are confusing and repetitive, and suffused with opaque mythic allusions:[15]

> Spell 119: *Twice he has placed [someone] behind me, so that he cannot reach me. He has placed Horus son of Isis behind me, so that he cannot reach me. He has placed Seth behind me, so that he cannot reach me. Twice he has placed [someone] behind me, so that he cannot reach me. He has placed Geb behind me, even he who went forth from his Eye, so that he cannot reach me on the great path which the Sole One inherited, the way to which is unknown to men and upon which the gods never go.*

By the New Kingdom the non-royal dead had abandoned their *Coffin Texts* in favour of the *Chapters of Going Forth by Day*, better known today as the *Book of the Dead*. The *Book* outlived the pharaohs, and was still in use during the Roman period. It was a personalized, practical guide to the afterlife written on a lengthy papyrus scroll (or, occasionally, on leather, linen, tomb furniture or tomb walls) and included either within the coffin or among the grave-goods. The scroll might be bespoke, or it could be purchased ready-written with gaps for the name of the deceased to be inserted: this occasionally led to mistakes when a scroll intended for a man was carelessly personalized with the name of a woman. In fact the vast majority of the surviving *Books* did belong to men, as did the vast majority of the tombs: women, it seems, were able to benefit from the afterlife provisions of their menfolk.

The *Book of the Dead* did not reach its finished form until the 26th Dynasty, by which time its 192 spells or chapters had been given an agreed order although, as with the earlier funerary texts, no individual *Book* included all the spells. Originally unillustrated, the *Book* soon acquired a series of standard vignettes that sometimes replaced the spells. It is from these curiously moving images, and their accompanying text, that we can gain an insight into the hopes and fears of an extraordinarily complex afterlife. Here, in Chapter 91, for example, the dead scribe Ani is provided with a spell to ensure that he is able to pass through the gates of the afterlife:[16]

> *O you who are on high, who are worshipped, whose power is great, a Ram greatly majestic, the dread of whom is put into the gods when you appear on your great throne: you shall make a way for me and my soul, my spirit and my shade, for I am equipped. I am a worthy spirit; make a way for me to the place where Re and Hathor are.*

As for him who knows this chapter, he shall become an equipped spirit in the God's Domain, he shall not be restrained at any gate of the West whether coming or going. A true matter.

Pyramids were out of fashion, and kings were now buried with greater secrecy in deep rock-cut tombs in the remote Valley of the Kings at Thebes. Here the walls of their tombs – which were essentially underground chambers linked by tunnels – were decorated with exclusively royal texts and scenes selected from a group of approximately twelve religious writings known collectively as the *Books of the Underworld* or *Guides to the Afterlife*. These, which include the *Book of the Hidden Chamber which is in the Underworld* (popularly known today as the *Amduat*), the *Book of Gates* and the *Book of Caverns*, aid the king's journey to the afterlife, and his ultimate union with the sun god, by telling the story of the dangerous night-journey of the sun god Re as he passes through the underworld to be reborn at dawn.

At the end of the 20th Dynasty the Valley of the Kings was abandoned and the royal funerary texts acquired a new life on the coffins and papyri of the elite.

The Classical authors

Evidence suggests that the stories told at the beginning of the dynastic age were very different – simpler, shorter, more disjointed and in many ways more violent – from the well-crafted, interlocking narratives recorded by the Classical authors at its end. Herodotus of Halicarnassus (writing at the time of the 27th Dynasty), Diodorus of Sicily (writing during the Ptolemaic Period) and the Greek/Roman Plutarch (writing during the Roman Period), each preserved versions of some of Egypt's better-known myths and legends, written in Greek for the entertainment and education of their non-Egyptian readers. In deference to those readers they tended to use Classical rather than Egyptian names for the gods, so that Thoth, for example, became the Greek Hermes. As none of the authors was fluent in the Egyptian language they could neither speak directly to the priests and storytellers nor read the scrolls stored in the temple libraries. All, therefore, had to collect their tales through interpreters and tour guides and, as a result, their tellings incorporate errors, misconceptions and their own personal and cultural biases. As the later Classical authors read the works of their predecessors, this distortion was magnified.

Flawed though their accounts undoubtedly are, the Classical authors are an invaluable resource to the Egyptologist. Here Herodotus, who is struck by the piety that he encounters, introduces his readers to the curious land of Egypt and her even more curious inhabitants:[17]

About Egypt I shall have a great deal more to relate because of the number of remarkable things which the country contains, and because of the fact that more monuments which beggar description are to be found there than anywhere else in the world ... Not only is the Egyptian climate peculiar to that country, and the Nile different in its behaviour from other rivers elsewhere, but the Egyptians themselves in their manners and customs seem to have reversed the ordinary practices of mankind.

EGYPT'S GODS

The gods evolved as independent, locally potent beings in the villages and towns of the prehistoric Nile Valley and Delta. Their cults served by local priests in local shrines, they developed myths to explain the mysteries of life and cultic rituals to reinforce their own divine authority. The question of which came first, the myth or the cult, is one that has sparked intense scholarly debate; it is a question which is unlikely ever to find a universally accepted answer. However, it is agreed that myth and cult quickly became mutually supportive: myths were used to justify the cults of the gods while cultic rituals re-enacted and so reinforced the mythology.

Generally speaking, the gods had geographically limited powers; each extended protection to those living in, or passing through, his or her particular territory so that a traveller embarking on a dangerous voyage to an oasis might find it politic to add a petition to the local desert deity to his usual observances. But, as some towns became rich and powerful, their gods grew in status and ritual until, with Egypt united under one king ruling from Memphis, a loose hierarchy of gods developed with nationally recognized state gods at the top, locally significant gods in the middle and an amorphous mass of demi-gods and supernatural beings revered by the ordinary people at the bottom. Every city now had a main god whose authority was recognized within that city so that, for example, at Memphis the principal god was the craftsman-creator Ptah, while at nearby Heliopolis the sun god Re was dominant.

Shrines and temples, increasingly prominent within the new cities, started to attract royal funding. Slowly but surely they were transformed from flimsy reed structures into substantial buildings – initially mud-brick, then stone, which allowed the carving of texts and illustrations – surrounded by high walls designed to prevent contamination by uncontrolled chaos. These urban cult temples were very different in purpose and design from the sacred enclosures and mortuary temples that were being built in the desert Red Land to protect the interests of the deceased and newly divine king. Within the cult temples, the earthly houses of the gods, the primary concern was the welfare of the living Egypt and her ruler. Here daily rituals – the washing and dressing of the cult statue and the regular offering of food, drink, incense and prayers – ensured that the temple god remained happy and Egypt prospered. Within the mortuary temples the primary concern was the survival of the king in life and death, and the priests made regular offerings to sustain the soul of the dead king. Most kings aspired to build cult temples, and an extensive and costly building programme was recognized as one of the hallmarks of a successful reign. But priority was always given to the mortuary temple that would ensure the king's own, vitally important immortality.

Already it was recognized that the king was the only mortal capable of communicating with the gods. In theory, this meant that only he could make the regular offerings that were necessary to please the gods and prevent Egypt from disintegrating into chaos. The king was therefore the head of every cult: to him fell the awesome responsibility of ensuring that all necessary rituals were performed properly and at the correct time. In recognition of this, temple walls show the king, and the king alone, making offerings and standing beside the gods. In practice, as the king quite clearly could not be present at every ceremony in every temple, it was accepted that he could be assisted or replaced by a non-vocational priesthood drawn from the educated elite.

Meanwhile, as the king and his priests placated the state gods via formal rituals, his subjects, almost entirely excluded from state religion, continued to revere and fear an eclectic mix of local gods, demi-gods and supernatural beings: the spirits, daemons and ghostly ancestors who never developed formal cults and who today have little if any preserved mythology, but who undoubtedly had an enormous influence on the lives of the ordinary people. The Egyptian word *netcher*, which is usually translated simply as 'god', encompasses all these divine entities and probably many more. Magic was, at all levels of society, a real and potent power that could be used to protect the innocent and ward off harm. It could not be separated in any meaningful way from formal religion, nor could it be separated from science. Physicians healed with medical prescriptions supplemented by tried and tested incantations, kings eliminated remote enemies by burning or smashing their names in temple rituals, and assassins attempted to kill kings using wax figures and magic spells. Stories about magicians who performed impressive tricks – bringing a wax crocodile to life, parting the waters of a lake or rejoining and reviving a decapitated animal – have survived in contemporary literature and it seems reasonable to assume that other, equally exciting magical stories have been lost.

The state gods created the world, controlled the cosmic forces and directed the great human experiences, yet they displayed distinctly human behaviour and their domestic lives were, when compared to the gods of other societies, positively dull. They were emotional, irrational and capable of love, lust, loneliness, jealousy and hatred. They ate, drank and got drunk, slept, forni- cated, grew old, suffered and, in some cases, died. Rejecting the polygamy practised by the mortal kings they married and pro- duced small families: the divine triad of god, goddess and divine (usually male) child was considered ideal. They rarely interacted with non-royal humans and seldom lusted after mortal women. Indeed, although they were capable of knowing and understand- ing everything, they were curiously shy, resting in their dark temple sanctuaries and communicating with the outside world via their chosen intermediary, the king.

Many of these deities had strong associations with particular aspects of life or the natural world, or were the personification of things, places or concepts: Osiris, for example, was the king of the dead; Isis was a powerful magician and healer; the goddess Maat represented harmony and world order. However, it would be a crude mistake to classify any of the beings by a single 'power', or attribute. Isis was a healer, yes, but she was one of many healers, and she had many other abilities and interests; to categorize her as 'the goddess of healing' would be a vast over-simplification of her role.

An individual deity might separate into several aspects of the same being. We find, for example, one of the earliest and longest-lasting gods, the falcon-headed Horus, being worshipped at different times and in different places as Horus-the-Child or Horus-the-Elder, as Horakhty (Horus of the two horizons) or Horemakhet (Horus in the horizon), and as local variants such as 'Horus of Hierakonpolis' (the original Horus) and 'Horus Behdety' (a god associated with kingship and the royal throne). This local concentration on specific aspects is, however, unique neither to Egypt nor to the ancient world and an easy parallel may be drawn with the Catholic Church's recognition of many aspects of Mary. More unusual is the gods' ability to unite to form composite or syncretized deities. Horus, for example, could join with Re to form the supreme solar being Re-Horakhty, a manifestation of Re as the strong rising sun, while the warrior god Amen combined with Re to create the powerful state deity Amen-Re. To describe these syncretized deities as fused or merged beings is almost certainly an over-simplification; without knowing precisely how the ancients viewed them, it is clear that the gods are neither permanently nor exclusively connected, and neither partner dominates the other. It is notable that the earth god Osiris and the sun god Re, the sources of Egypt's two opposing mythologies, who were physically united each night in the dark caverns of the underworld, never formally combined to form a syncretized deity.

While their behaviour may seem reassuringly human, the appearance of the gods – to modern, western eyes at least – is not. Naturally, they follow the rules of Egyptian artistic representation, so that in two-dimensional art they appear without perspective, their faces shown in profile and their bodies facing forwards. This we would expect. Their combination of what at first sight appear to be randomly selected body-parts is more surprising. While some deities always assume a conventional human form, many others are depicted with a pure animal form, a part-animal form or, more rarely, an inanimate object form. This combination of animal and human elements was not restricted to the gods, and mortal kings were happy to be depicted as part-human/part-lion sphinxes as a means of emphasizing their royal authority and solar connections (lions being strongly associated with the cult of the sun god). Back in the divine world we find the mother goddess Hathor appearing as a woman, as a woman with a cow's head, as a woman with a human face but a cow's ears, or as a complete cow who allows the king to suckle from her udders. She might also, in reference to other myths, appear as a snake, a lioness, or a tree who, as she has breasts, is also capable of feeding the king. Even more peculiar, to modern eyes, are the goddesses Taweret – who is given the body and head of a pregnant hippopotamus, the tail of a crocodile and the limbs of a lioness topped, occasionally, by a woman's face – and Meskhenet, who sometimes appears as conventional woman, and sometimes as a brick with a woman's head. As almost all these gods married and produced children, some visually surprising family groups developed. The family of the dead and mummiform Osiris, his human-form and occasionally winged wife Isis and their posthumous, falcon-headed son Horus, is an obvious biological impossibility at many levels.

In order to make sense of these images we have to abandon any thought that a 'portrait' should be a literal, photographic account of the original. This is true both of mortals, who all tend to look the same in Egyptian art, and of gods, who can look startlingly different from scene to scene. In neither case is there any need for the artist to attempt a close physical resemblance, as the addition of the written name will prove and reinforce the identity of the person being depicted. Young children today understand this concept well: their drawings of stick-people may look similar if not identical, but the addition of a title ('mummy', 'daddy', 'me') confirms the identity of the subject to the most casual of observers, and everyone, even the most sophisticated art critic, accepts this.

Language and writing were divine gifts. Words, written in the hieroglyphic script, were actually sequences of miniature pictures, some being fairly abstract symbols, some less so. Indeed, some of the hieroglyphic pictures were so lifelike that the artists who carved funerary texts into tomb walls occasionally felt it prudent to dismember or impale the more dangerous animal 'letters' (the symbols of the snake and scorpion, for example) lest they spring magically to life and harm the tomb owner. At the same time, paintings and statues could be read as groups of words or statements. All formal art was produced for a specific ritual or political purpose; none was purely decorative and no aspect of the composition was left to chance. Size, position, posture, even colour, had meaning: black and green, for example, conveyed fertility and rebirth, so the black or green face of Osiris, king of the dead, signified his ability to regenerate rather than his racial heritage or his state of putrefaction. Puns, allegories, alliterations, metaphors and colour schemes were clearly important to both artists and scribes. It would be naive to think that we recognize all their wordplay and foolish to think that any form of official art can be interpreted at just one, superficial or literal level. This is particularly true of the composite divine imagery used to convey an idea of divinity beyond normal experience. The appearance of the gods was intended to reflect an element of their personality or interests. Thus the human-headed brick – the personification of the birthing-brick used by women squatting in labour – became an effective means of conveying the essential nature of a goddess associated with childbirth, while the cow best represented Hathor's role as a nurturing mother. In all cases it is the head that indicates the essential nature of the divine being, while the body is simply a means of allowing the deity to function efficiently. To take one final example, Thoth could be depicted either as a baboon or as an ibis. But, as ibises and, to a lesser extent, baboons are incapable of writing on a papyrus scroll or sitting on a divine throne to receive offerings, he could also appear as an ibis-headed man with the functioning arms and legs that would allow him to perform his allotted tasks. Animal-form deities therefore indicate a respect for the animals that played such an important role in Egyptian daily life, but they by no means indicate an unthinking or unsophisticated zoolatry. Some of the Classical authors – authors whose work had a profound influence on the development of Egyptology before the 1822 decoding of hieroglyphs released original texts for study – failed to understand this point. Oblivious to the subtleties and complexities of a centuries-old theology, they regarded the Egyptians as primitive animal-worshippers and thought less of them for it. Their view is one end of a spectrum, the opposite end of which persists in seeing the ancient Egyptians as the possessors of a deep esoteric knowledge.

Where exactly did these divine beings live? There was no Egyptian equivalent of Mount Olympus – no one place where all the gods dwelt together away from mortals. Some gods lived in very specific places according to their nature. Meretseger, goddess of the Theban Peak, for example, was the Theban mountain, while the dead Osiris ruled an afterlife kingdom known as the Field of Reeds. Re, the sun god, lived in the sky; his son Shu was the atmosphere; his son Geb was the earth. Other gods could be found anywhere and everywhere, yet all might take up residence in their temple(s), where the cult statue was treated as if it was an actual, living god.

It is appropriate to add a brief note on the names of the gods, and names in general, at this point. The ancient Egyptians spoke a language which evolved over time so that modern linguists are able to use linguistic traits to date otherwise undatable texts. They wrote using either the elaborate and time-consuming hieroglyphic script or the more speedy hieratic and demotic scripts. None of these scripts included vowels; not because vowels did not exist, but because there was no perceived need to write them down. It was assumed that the reader would be able to insert vowels as required, an assumption that text-messagers often make today. As the Egyptian language is now extinct outside the Coptic Church, we cannot be certain how the words were originally pronounced – what and where were the missing vowels? – and this uncertainty is reflected in our diverse spellings of the same name. Amen and Amun are one and the same god, as are Re and Ra. The situation gets more confusing when Hellenized forms of the Egyptian names are added into the mix. To take just two examples, the god whom we today call Thoth was known to the Egyptians as Djehuty, while Isis was Iset or Aset. Throughout this book I have used the best-known, most widely accepted versions of proper names. This sometimes leads to a conflict in styles (for example, like many others I use Amenhotep rather than Amenophis, but Tuthmosis rather than Thutmose or Djehutymes; I refer to the cult centre of the sun god by its Hellenistic name of Heliopolis rather than its more ancient name of Iunu or its modern name Matariyeh, while the cult centre of Thoth becomes Hermopolis Magna rather than Khmun or Ashmunein), but it helps with the understanding of an already complex cast of characters and places. To change Isis to Aset and Osiris to Usir would simply add to the confusion.

THE EGYPTIAN WORLD

Without the River Nile, there could have been no Egypt. The Nile, known simply as *iteru*, 'the river', flowed northwards, broad and calm, from a mysterious, almost certainly magical, source. Passing over a cataract it entered Egypt at the southern border town of Aswan, bringing water to a thirsty land that, as the dynastic age progressed, would grow increasingly arid. For the next 400 miles the river was confined to its valley. Then, just beyond the northern city of Memphis (near modern Cairo), the Nile broke free, splitting into seven branches and creating a lush delta before emptying into the 'Great Green', the Mediterranean Sea. Egypt was orientated towards the source of the Nile, so that one word meant both 'east' and 'left', and one word meant 'west' and 'right'. The Euphrates, a mighty foreign river which, perversely, flowed from north to south so that, in the words of Tuthmosis I, it 'goes downstream in going upstream', was considered an affront to the natural order of things and a sign, perhaps, of the frightening chaos which existed beyond Egypt's borders.

Once a year, in late summer, the Nile swelled, burst its banks and spread water and a thick, fertile mud over the parched, low-lying fields. The towns and villages, built on higher ground and protected by dykes, were now small islands, linked together by raised paths; the desert cemeteries, far from the river, remained dry and safe. The peasants, unable to work in the waterlogged fields, were freed to work on state building projects. By late October the waters started to retreat, leaving behind a saturated land, water-filled irrigation basins, and fields covered with a layer of fresh, dying fish. The peasants returned to their agricultural duties, gathered the fish and sowed their crops. In late spring they would reap a plentiful harvest. The land would then bake in the sterilizing sun, before the water level rose and the whole cycle started again. The Classical authors, accustomed to expensive and time-consuming state-controlled irrigation systems, were mightily impressed. They could not imagine how a river could flood so dependably in the summer rather than in the winter, when one might reasonably expect a river to flood. Meanwhile the Egyptians, consummate bureaucrats, recorded the height of the flood using a 'Nilometer'. A rise in river-level of between 7 and 8 metres (23–26 feet) was considered ideal. If the inundation was too low the fields would be left high and dry; too high and the water would flood the settlements, destroying the mud-brick housing and damaging the crops stored in the warehouses.

The Nile brought many blessings: it provided a plentiful supply of mud that could be used to manufacture bricks and pottery; it supplied abundant fish and attracted wild animals and fowl, providing both food for the peasants and sport for the elite; it allowed the papyrus plant to flourish in the Delta; it was both a laundry and a sewer. In addition, it was a splendid highway which allowed the rapid transport of heavy goods direct, via a network of canals, from quarries and fields to building sites and warehouses. River travel was both cheap and efficient, as a boat travelling north could take advantage of the north-flowing current, while a boat travelling south simply had to raise a sail to take advantage of the prevailing wind. It is little wonder that the Egyptians found it impossible to imagine a world without a river, beneficial floods and boats. Unfortunately, due to their nature and the organic materials used in their construction, few actual boats survive. However, references to boats permeate art and literature, making it obvious that, from earliest times, boats and power were inextricably connected. In a land without a road network and without bridges, where the horse-drawn chariot was unknown before 1600 BC, boats allowed the enterprising to trade. The profits from that trade allowed the possibility of investing in more boats and this, naturally, led to increasing wealth and increasing political power. Soon, boats became linked with kingship.

Long, thin Egypt was a difficult land to rule. It has been estimated that it would take a fortnight for a message to pass from northern Egypt to the southern border, and a reply could not reasonably be expected in less than a month. Mortal kings, recognizing the dangers of isolation, were constantly on the move, sailing up and down the Nile to remind their distant subjects of their existence. The god-king Re, too, was always on the move; shunning the flaming chariot favoured by the sun gods of other mythologies, he sailed across the watery blue sky in a solar boat.

As Re's boat vanished over the western horizon each night, boats became closely associated with the rituals of death. Large boats play a prominent role in the scenes painted on pottery recovered from Predynastic graves, and they featured on the walls of Egypt's earliest known painted tomb.[18] From the 1st Dynasty onwards this link between boats and death becomes more obvious as boats are now included in both royal mortuary complexes and private tombs. A dismantled cedarwood boat, one of two buried alongside the 4th Dynasty pyramid of Khufu at Giza, has been reassembled by the Egyptian Department of Antiquities and is currently displayed in a purpose-built museum beside the Great Pyramid. Made out of cedar planks sewn together with fibre ropes, the 43-metre boat is a wooden copy of a papyrus reed boat, complete with curved prow and stern, a central cabin and five oars on either side. Citing signs of use, some experts have suggested that this may well be the same boat that was used to carry Khufu to his funeral. Others believe that the boat was built for immediate dismantling and burial so that the dead and resurrected Khufu might use it to sail to his afterlife.

The contrast between life in the Nile Valley (Upper or southern Egypt) and the Nile Delta (Lower or northern Egypt) was very obvious. Protected by deserts and mountains to the east and west, the narrow Valley offered a hot, insular, traditional way of life centred on the river. Here, the junction between the fertile strip of soil bordering the Nile, the 'Black Land', and the infertile desert, the 'Red Land', was so pronounced that it was possible to straddle the boundary and stand with one foot on soil, the other on sand. It was natural that the Black Land should become the land of the living while the Red Land, the uncultivatable desert, became the land of the dead – home to cemeteries, ghosts and wild animals. Even the desert, however, had something to offer, and missions regularly departed the Black Land to exploit the hard stone which could be incorporated into buildings, semi-precious stones which could be used to make jewellery, and gold. Life in the Delta was very different: cooler, moister, flatter and, with the Sinai land-bridge to the east, the Libyan border to the west and the extensive Mediterranean coastline, more open to outside influences. The Egyptians would always consider their long, thin country to be two balanced but very different lands united under a double crown: the white crown of southern Egypt and the red crown of northern Egypt, worn together.

This ideal of a balanced tension between two matched, op-posing forces (Upper and Lower Egypt; the Red Land and the Black; the west and the east banks; night and day; men and women; life and death) was a constantly repeated theme in all of Egypt's myths. In particular, the conflict between chaos (*isfet*) and order (*maat*) was fundamental to Egyptian thought. Chaos is simple for us to understand; in ancient Egypt the concept included such 'non-right' things as illness, injustice, crime and the unusual (i.e. non-Egyptian) behaviour of foreigners. *Maat* is a more difficult concept; the opposite of *isfet* with no equivalent English name, it may be defined as a powerful combination of rightness, the status quo, control and justice. At all times the waters of chaos lapped around the edges of the well-ordered Egyptian world, threatening the existence of *maat*. To the king alone fell the awesome responsibility of holding back that chaos. For, without firm control, deprived of *maat*, the gods would flee and Egypt would surely fail. This overwhelming need to preserve *maat* encouraged a slow, conservative approach to life. Experimentation was both dangerous and unnecessary and it was safer and more comforting to stick to tried and tested ways.

The concept of *maat* was personified in the form of the goddess Maat, the eternally young daughter of the sun god who can be identified by the tall feather of truth worn on her head. Scenes from many dynasties show various rulers standing with Maat beside them, or offering a miniature image of Maat to the gods, while Maat herself crosses the sky every day, standing in the prow of her father's sun boat.[19]

DATING DYNASTIC EGYPT

The dynastic or pharaonic age, the time when a king, or pharaoh, ruled Egypt and the time covered by this book, lasted for approximately 3,000 years, or 150 generations. It started with the unification of the country by the southern warrior Narmer in *c.*3100 BC, and ended with the suicide of Cleopatra VII in 30 BC. Before the dynastic age came the Predynastic Period, a time without writing and therefore without history but not, or so art and archaeology would suggest, without myths and legends. After the dynastic age came a time of Roman rule, which falls outside the scope of this book. However, it needs to be remembered that under Roman rule and far beyond, Egypt's myths and legends continued to evolve. Indeed, some of Egypt's traditional deities, equipped with evolved mythologies, are still being worshipped today.

Traditionally, Egyptologists divide the dynastic period into 'dynasties'; lines of rulers who are in some way connected, but who are not necessarily blood relatives. The dynasties are conventionally grouped into times of strong, centralized rule (the Old Kingdom, Middle Kingdom, New Kingdom and Late Period), separated by times of decentralized or foreign control (the three Intermediate Periods). While it was usual for a son to inherit his father's throne this did not always happen, and a significant number of kings were adopted into the royal family. At the same time, a dynastic break may cut across a known family line: the kings of the late 17th and early 18th Dynasties, for example, belonged to the same birth family. Occasionally, at times of weak control, two or more competing dynasties ruled Egypt simultaneously.

The Egyptians, lacking our idea of a linear history, never developed a continuous calendar. Instead they dated events by reference to the current king's reign: Year 1, Year 2, etc. When the old king died and a new king took his place, the dating system started all over again with Year 1. Although this is by no means a perfect system it is the most accurate means of dating Egypt's past; it is the system used by Egyptologists today, and it is the system used throughout this book. To take just one example, Egyptologists conventionally date the death of the female King Hatshepsut to her regnal Year 22; her reign belongs to the early 18th Dynasty, which is itself a part of the New Kingdom. This is done not to confuse but to ensure the greatest possible accuracy. We know that Hatshepsut ruled for twenty-two years but her precise calendar dates are less certain: did she reign from 1504 to 1482 BC?; from 1490 to 1468 BC?; or from 1479 to 1457 BC? All are possible, although of course only one (or perhaps none) can be correct. By using her own regnal years we can establish a small island of chronological stability in the chaotic sea of dates.

The major divisions of Egyptian chronology are as follows:

Predynastic Period (c.5300–3100 BC)

Prehistoric 'Egypt' sees the evolution of independent city-states surrounded by satellite villages and hamlets. Each has its own, locally important deity and its own priesthood. Painted pottery recovered from graves shows scenes of water, boats, armed men and curious female figures who may, or may not, be goddesses. Well-organized desert cemeteries and tombs equipped with grave-goods suggest a well-stratified society with an expectation of a life beyond death but, without any written records, archaeologists cannot confirm this.

Early Dynastic Period (Dynasties 0–2, c.3100–2686 BC)

Unified by King Narmer, Egypt stretches from Aswan in the south to the Mediterranean Sea in the north. The kings of this united land rule from the northern city of Memphis, and build large mud-brick tombs in the cemeteries of Abydos and Sakkara. They associate themselves with the god Horus, just one of the gods in the already complex nationally recognized pantheon. As an efficient state bureaucracy develops, hieroglyphic writing is born and art and mud-brick architecture flourish.

Old Kingdom (Dynasties 3–6, c.2686–2181 BC)

The sun god Re is now the principal state god. Semi-divine kings, the sons of Re, build the great stone pyramids of northern Egypt; their courtiers are buried in state-controlled cemeteries surrounding the pyramids. Grave-goods, *Pyramid Texts* and tomb auto-biographies are provided for the deceased, but only the king has a spirit strong enough to leave the tomb. His people are destined to spend eternity trapped on earth.

First Intermediate Period
(Dynasties 7–early 11, c.2181–2055 BC)

With no centralized monarchy, fragmented Egypt is governed by local rulers. Although later writers will describe this as a dangerous, uncontrolled age, archaeology confirms that life continues as normal for most people.

Middle Kingdom
(Dynasties late 11–13, c.2055–1650 BC)

A centralized monarchy is restored and an empire is quickly established. Pyramid building continues and arts, crafts and literature flourish. Egypt is ruled from the now-vanished city of Idj-Tawy, situated close by the entrance to the Faiyum, and the warrior Montu is an important state god. This is the age of the first recorded fictional stories. An afterlife ruled by the god Osiris has opened to all, and *Coffin Texts* are now painted or carved on the coffins of the elite to help the deceased attain their goal of eternal life.

Second Intermediate Period
(Dynasties 14–17, c.1650–1550 BC)

Northern Egypt is ruled by 'Hyksos' kings of Canaanite origin; southern Egypt is ruled from Thebes by an ever more aggressive line of native kings. To the south of Egypt, the increasingly powerful Nubians are allies of the Hyksos. Despite the political tensions, most Egyptians continue to lead normal lives.

New Kingdom (Dynasties 18–20, c.1550–1069 BC)

A time of unification, empire and unprecedented wealth when the warrior Amen-Re of Thebes rules as king of the gods from his Karnak temple complex. Kings now build vast stone cult temples linked by processional avenues in the major cities, magnificent stone mortuary temples on the edge of the west bank desert, and rock-cut tombs in the Valley of the Kings. Funerary texts, written on tomb walls and on papyrus scrolls, help the deceased to negotiate the perils of the afterlife. The workmen who labour in the royal tombs live in the purpose-built, state-run village of Deir el-Medina where, highly literate, they record the minutiae of their daily life on papyrus and flakes of limestone.

Third Intermediate Period (Dynasties 21–24, c.1069–715 BC)

Egypt is ruled in the north by simultaneous lines of local rulers. With the Valley of the Kings abandoned and unsafe, the high priests of Amen open all the known royal tombs, collect the mummies, strip them of their valuables and store them in a series of caches dotted around the necropolis.

Late Period (Dynasties 25–31, c.715–332 BC)

A dynasty of strong Nubian kings is followed by alternating phases of native and Persian rule. With the traditional way of life under threat there is a renewed interest in Egyptian culture, and many of the ancient myths are developed into longer, more elaborate tales. It is at this time that Herodotus visits Egypt, recording his impressions in his *Histories*, Book 2.

Macedonian and Ptolemaic Periods (332–30 BC)

Greek-speaking kings of Macedonian heritage rule from Alexandria, worshipping a mixture of native Egyptian, imported Greek and hybrid Egyptian-Greek gods. The Ptolemies are happy to court the support of the native priesthood, and an extensive programme of restoration sees the rebuilding of many temples, which are frequently inscribed with details of rituals and performances. Following the suicide of Cleopatra VII in 30 BC Egypt becomes part of the personal estate of the Emperor Augustus and the dynastic age ends.

I

CREATION

I am the one that made me.

The Memphite creation myth

I

SUNRISE: THE NINE GODS
OF HELIOPOLIS

In the beginning nothing existed but the deep, dark waters of Nun. There was no land and no sky. No gods, no people, no light and no time. Only the endless, motionless waters. But deep within the still waters of Nun there floated a perfect egg. And trapped within that perfect egg was a solitary spark of life. Suddenly, inexplicably, the egg cracked open. Life broke free of its confining shell and, with a surge of energy, a mound rose out of the waters. Seated on that mound was the god Atum. Atum had created himself. He now shone as the sun, bringing light to his new-born world.

Lonely on his mound, Atum set about creating the living. He grasped his penis, and from the fluids of his body sprang twin children: Shu the god of the dry air and Tefnut the goddess of moisture. Atum and Shu and Tefnut lived together, happy and safe on their mound in the midst of the waters of Nun until, one dreadful day, Shu and Tefnut fell into the waters. Shrieking, they disappeared from view.

Blinded by his tears, Atum called upon his Eye to search for the lost twins. The Eye of Atum found Shu and Tefnut in the deep depths of the waters of Nun. As she restored them to their father, Atum's tears of grief turned to tears of joy. Copious, they fell to the ground. And from these tears sprang men and women. And so began a glorious age when humans and gods lived in harmony on the mound in the midst of the waters of Nun.

Shu and Tefnut loved each other as husband and wife, and Tefnut bore her brother's children: Geb the handsome god of the earth and Nut the beautiful goddess of the sky. Geb lay down and became the fertile land. He bore the fields and the marshes and the great River Nile. Grain sprouted from his ribs, and plants grew from his back. His laughter brought earthquakes, and his anger brought famine. Nut loved her brother and happily bore his children, the glittering stars that decorate the dark night sky. But one terrible day, just as a hungry mother pig might sometimes eat her young, Nut swallowed her starchildren. Geb flew into a furious rage and the land trembled and shook with his anger. To escape Geb's wrath Nut stretched herself above her brother, her fingers and toes resting on the horizons of the north, east, south and west. And Shu knelt with arms outstretched between his beloved children, holding them apart lest they should continue their quarrel.

Now Nut's arched body separated the world from chaotic waters of Nun. Her laughter rumbled as thunder and her tears fell as rain. Along her body the stars and moon twinkled at night, and the sun blazed by day. And every evening she swallowed the sun so that it passed through her body to be reborn from her womb at dawn.

THE MOUND OF CREATION

The priests who served the sun god in the temple of Heliopolis knew how their world had begun. Their myth of Atum and his mound of creation is not preserved in one single, straightforward account, but can be reconstructed from myriad references in art, solar hymns and funerary writings, where the birth of the world is equated with the rebirth of the deceased in the tomb. The principal written sources for this tale are, in chronological order, the Old Kingdom *Pyramid Texts*, the Middle Kingdom *Coffin Texts*, the various New Kingdom Funerary Texts and the Ptolemaic *Papyrus Bremner-Rhind*,[20] but it seems likely that these writings conserve a far older, prehistoric mythology.

The Heliopolitan myth reveals the spherical organization of the Egyptian cosmos. Geb, the male earth, was covered by Nut, the female sky, with Shu, the atmosphere, separating the two. Surrounding this bubble of life were the endless still waters of Nun (or Nu); a dark and unknown danger. Somewhere within the bubble, unmentioned in this tale, was the *Duat*, the land of the dead, the daytime stars and the night-time sun. Egypt was, naturally, the ordered centre of the world within the bubble. The life-giving River Nile rose from the waters of Nun somewhere to the south of the southern border town of Aswan and flowed northwards to empty into the sea. Lining both sides of the river was the fertile Black Land. Beyond this came the desert Red Land, then the mountains and the uncontrolled foreign lands where chaos ruled. The king of Egypt was, naturally, king of this entire world, although his foreign 'subjects' frequently had to be reminded of his god-given right to rule.

This cosmic plan was reflected in formal temple architecture, which allowed each temple to become the original mound of creation. A tall, undulating, wave-like perimeter wall surrounded the temple complex, holding back the forces, or waters, of chaos. The massive entrance gate, or pylon, suggested the mountains of the eastern horizon. Inside the main temple building the columns, often decorated to resemble papyrus stalks or lotus blossoms, represented the marsh plants that thrived on the island of creation. As the priests progressed from the light, public entrance to the dim and private inner sanctuary, the floor rose gradually so that it recreated the first mound. High above the priests, the dark ceiling was decorated with five-pointed stars or with astronomical scenes so that it became the night sky; meanwhile, the scenes of rituals and nature that decorated the inner walls between the mound (floor) and the sky (ceiling) represented life and activity within the harmonious temple-world. Outside the main building the sacred lakes offered a controlled form of the waters of Nun for use in temple rituals, while lesser temples or shrines housed gods connected with the main temple god. Simultaneously, at its most prosaic level, the temple was quite literally the home of the god who, in the form of a statue, inhabited the sanctuary, the innermost and most secret part. This arrangement of public or semi-public outer areas and private inner chambers reserved for the priesthood and the deity reflected the spatial distribution of all Egyptian houses and palaces.

Atum's story recognized the fact that there must have been a time before time: a time of pre-existence when Nun, who was neither created nor self-created, existed alone. Then, suddenly and inexplicably, the primeval mound emerged from the chaotic waters, just as Egypt's fields re-emerged each year from the life-giving waters of the Nile floods. However, while the beginning of time was marked by an abrupt surging of life and the rising of a mound (the sexual significance of which would not have been lost on the Egyptians), Egypt experienced a more gradual re-emergence; here the deep red waters retreated slowly, leaving behind a thick blanket of mud and a useful crop of stranded fish. As the Egyptians well knew, this 'new' land would be moist and fertile; with careful tending it would yield a crop that would be the envy of the ancient world. This idea of the life-giving mound found echo in the desert cemeteries, where raised mounds covered the most basic of graves: with its mound in place the grave became not only a symbol of death, but a promise of resurrection for the deceased. Eventually, the mound would be formalized in the form of the mastaba tomb – a subterranean tomb topped by a rectangular stone or brick superstructure – which would itself evolve into the royal pyramid.

Nun, the genderless, boundless waters carrying the potential for life, could be personified in the form of the god Nun: a human-form deity with a curled beard and a heavy wig, who was often shown holding the solar boat of the sun god in his raised arms. By the Middle Kingdom, Nun, who 'came into being by himself', had claimed the title 'Father of the Gods', although technically he was not related to Atum and his progeny. By the New Kingdom he was revered as the 'Lord of Eternity'. However, during the Late Period he developed into a more chaotic, threatening entity, while in the post-dynastic Christian era he became the void of hell. Nun's female element – the element that allowed him to become a creator god – could be independently personified as Mehet-Weret, the 'Great Swimmer' or 'Great Flood', a cow who, born from the first waters, gave birth to the sun god Re in the primeval marsh and raised him into the sky on her horns. Although both were respected throughout Egypt, neither Nun nor Mehet-Weret had specific cult centres or priesthoods.

ATUM: LORD OF TOTALITY

Atum, lord of totality, is an immensely powerful being with a dangerous dual nature. He has the ability to create everything but, as he completes his work, he simultaneously finalizes or ends it. In acknowledgement of the fact that he both creates and rules Upper and Lower Egypt, Atum is usually depicted in human form wearing the double crown; his curled beard confirms that he is a god rather than a human king. He may also be represented as a snake, a scarab beetle, a ram-headed man and, more rarely, as an ichneumon, lion, bull, lizard or ape, or as the mound of creation itself. Already, by the start of the Old Kingdom, Atum is a god of great importance, and the *Pyramid Texts* detail the deceased king's struggle to become one with the sun god. Although the *Pyramid Texts* will be eventually abandoned, and his cult and mythology will be absorbed by the cult and mythology of Re, Atum will remain a potent being until the end of the dynastic age.

Atum had no need to create a sun for his new world: as a solar deity, he brought his own light with him. Later versions of the myth clarify this, and it is Re, 'the sun', or the composite solar god Re-Atum, who now emerges on the mound of creation. While Re was celebrated as the powerful midday sun, Atum became associated with the old and dying evening sun, an association that linked him firmly with the dead and the afterlife. Meanwhile the beetle Khepri, 'the one who comes into being', was revered as the new-born morning sun. Thus the three aspects of the sun, the vigorous Khepri, the powerful Re and the tired Atum, came to symbolize morning, noon and evening – the three divisions of the Egyptian day.

Khepri is usually depicted as a beetle, although he might also be a beetle-headed man, or a beetle-headed falcon. He is a divine version of the humble scarab beetle whose habit of pushing around an unwieldy ball of dung suggested the image of a gigantic celestial beetle rolling the ball of the sun across the sky. Hidden within the dung-ball were beetle eggs that eventually hatched, crawled out of the ball and flew away, leaving observers to conclude that beetles, like Atum, were male beings capable of self-creation. Plutarch, writing about Egypt's animal gods, reflects this widely held belief:[21]

The race of beetles has no female, but all the males eject their sperm into a round pellet of material which they roll up by pushing it from the opposite side, just as the sun seems to turn the heavens in the direction opposite to its own course, which is from west to east.

Every night Khepri died, was dismembered and buried; every morning he was reborn good as new. This enviable ability to regenerate made the scarab one of Egypt's most popular amulets, used from the First Intermediate Period onwards by both the dead and the living. The living also used flat-bottomed scarabs as seal stamps, while Amenhotep III employed large-scale scarabs as 'newspapers': with brief propaganda texts carved on the base, they spread good news throughout his empire. Although Khepri had no cult temple, gigantic stone scarabs were included in the temple complexes of other gods. The best-known example of this is the huge, and to modern eyes curiously appealing, stone beetle which stands beside the sacred lake in the Karnak temple complex of Amen-Re. This statue has developed its own mythology and is today credited with granting wishes and causing the barren to conceive.

THE DIVINE TWINS

Having brought order to chaos, the solitary Atum determines to populate his world. His loneliness and need for companionship would have been understandable to a people who lived for protection and comfort in close-knit family groups, and who had no idea of the modern concept of 'personal space'. Egypt's deities are never too lofty to indulge in the most basic of human practices and, as the one and only self-created being, Atum has to mate with himself if he wants to reproduce. *Pyramid Texts* spell 527 makes the mechanism clear:[22]

> *Atum is he who [once] came into being, who masturbated in On (Heliopolis). He took his phallus in his grasp that he might create orgasm by means of it, and so were born the twins Shu and Tefnut.*

Single-handedly, the hitherto androgynous Atum has become the father of the gods. Meanwhile the hand that he used to masturbate now personifies his own feminine element (the hand, *djeret*, being feminine in the Egyptian language), so that Atum and his hand effectively become a divine couple just as Nun and Mehet-Weret may be considered a couple. At the same time, however, Atum's hand has been created by Atum himself, and is therefore his daughter. The goddess Iusaas, worshipped in the temple of Re at Heliopolis, is the personification of that same hand. By the Middle Kingdom she has split into two components: Iusaas, 'She Grows Great as She Comes', who represents growth, and Nebethetepet, 'Lady of the Field of Offerings', who represents abundance. The sexual stimulation of the gods will always be considered an important matter, and some of the uncompromising titles borne by human queens ('God's Wife'; 'God's Hand') hint at a duty to provide the necessary feminine element in rituals designed to physically stimulate male gods.

A more abstract account of this first birth, preserved in *Pyramid Texts* spell 600, tells us that Atum's children sprang from other bodily fluids: 'you spat out Shu, you expectorated Tefnut, and you wrapped your arms around them . . .' *Coffin Texts* spell 76 provides more detail:[23]

> *I am indeed Shu whom Atum created, whereby Re came into being; I was not built up in the womb, I was not knit together in the egg, I was not conceived, but Atum spat me out in the spittle of his mouth together with my sister Tefnut. She went up after me and I was covered with the breath of the throat . . . I am Shu, father of the gods, and Atum once sent his Sole Eye seeking me and my sister Tefnut. I made light of the darkness for it, and it found me as an immortal.*

This asexual birth fits well with the twins' names. 'Shu', derived from the Egyptian word meaning 'emptiness' or 'void', sounds like the word for sneeze, while the element 'Tef' in Tefnut's otherwise obscure name translates as 'spit'.

The Late Period Memphite Theology and the Ptolemaic *Papyrus Bremner-Rhind* offer further explanation, linking the two traditions neatly. Now Atum manually stimulates his penis before ejaculating into his own mouth, which effectively becomes a womb. This physically demanding technique – Atum performing a shoulder stand as he sucks his own penis – was illustrated in a straightforward manner by artists who saw nothing wrong with decorating sacred spaces and artefacts (temples, tombs and their contents) with blatantly sexual images. The Egyptians were first and foremost farmers who understood the role of intercourse and semen in reproduction. They recognized the potency of sexual creation and attempted to harness this power on relevant occasions: the creation of the gods, for example, or the rebirth of the mummy after death. But, thousands of years later, scenes of Atum impregnating himself caused many Victorian Egyptologists to blink, while images of the unashamedly ithyphallic gods Geb, Min and occasionally Amen led to such absurdities as strategically placed museum labels designed to conceal the gods' true nature from the eyes of delicate lady visitors.

More seriously, these overtly sexual images contributed to a general misinterpretation – fuelled by the apparently damning evidence of incest, polygamy, transparent dresses, sensual poetry and erotic papyri, and the complete absence of any wedding ceremony – of the Egyptians as a louche, even lewd, people. Yet there is no evidence to suggest that the Egyptians led promiscuous lives and, indeed, personal writings recovered from the New Kingdom workmen's village of Deir el-Medina confirm that society expected individuals to adhere to a firm moral code. In one such text we may read the cautionary true-life tale of a married man, Nesamenemope, who for eight months has been maintaining a mistress.[24] Unsurprisingly, the wronged wife's family do not approve of this arrangement, and one night they determine to do something about it. Raising a rabble of villagers, they march to the mistress's house with violence in mind: 'We are going to beat her, together with her people.' Fortunately, a steward is able to hold back the crowd before sending a message to the frightened couple. If they are to continue their affair, Nesamenemope must regularize the situation by divorcing his wife, thus providing for her and setting her free to marry another.

At Heliopolis, men and women are created at the same time and in the same somewhat careless way, as the accidental by-products of Atum's tearful joy. This is another deliberate play on words, as the Egyptian word for 'tear' (*remut*) sounds like the word for 'people' (*remetj*). As always, there are several variations on this theme. In some accounts the tears are shed by the Eye before the world is created. In the cosmogony of the goddess Neith, the new-born Re weeps sorrowful tears because he is separated from his mother; his despairing tears then become humanity. When Neith returns to her son his tears of joy become the gods.

Atum is both father and mother of the gods: from this time on, however, he will be considered to be a male god. His children, Shu and Tefnut, are Egypt's first sexually differentiated beings; they will reproduce in conventional, albeit incestuous, union, as will their children and their grandchildren. They have little choice in the matter of their incestuous match: there is an obvious shortage of eligible partners at the beginning of time. But in so doing they set a royal fashion. Incestuous royal marriages would never be compulsory, but brother–sister or brother–half-sister marriages were favoured as they linked the royal family to the gods, while setting them apart from their people, who would not practise sibling marriage until the very end of the dynastic age.

At a more practical level, incestuous marriages restricted the number of potential claimants to the throne, while ensuring that the queen could be trained in her duties from an early age.

Together, the twins form a void or bubble in the waters of Nun. Shu, son of Atum, is a life-force associated with dry air, mist and sunlight; the 'bones of Shu', mentioned in the *Pyramid Texts*, are probably clouds. As a creator, Shu is present at all births, and he has a great capacity to heal. *Coffin Texts* spells 75–80, occasionally described as the *Litany of Shu*, identify Shu with *ankh*, or life, while expressing the hope that he will be able to breathe that life into the dead. As Shu is capable of preserving the dead he is equated with the endlessly repeating cycle of time that sees the birth, death and rebirth of successive kings. As the son of Atum he is also heir to the throne, and it seems that Shu spent some time ruling Egypt before becoming weary and retiring to live with the sun god. Shu was usually depicted as a man with a feather headdress.

Shu's sister-wife Tefnut is his complement: a shadowy life-force associated with moisture who may, given the Egyptian love of symmetry, have physically supported her son Geb, serving as the atmosphere of the underworld just as Shu, supporting Nut, served as the atmosphere of the land of the living. We have little understanding of her nature and little, if any, associated mythology, but it is clear that she has links with the afterlife. *Pyramid Texts* spell 685 tells us that she, like her brother, was able to supply clean water for the reborn king.

Shu and Tefnut were together presented as Ruty, the twin or opposing lions who guarded the eastern and western horizons. By the New Kingdom Ruty had evolved into a pair of lions over whose back the sun rose every day. Tefnut herself might appear as a woman, a lioness or a lion-headed woman often wearing a long, mane-like wig and a solar disk. As the daughter of the sun god she could be equated with Maat, the personification of the concept of 'rightness' or non-chaos. At the same time, she was identified with the independent divine female being known as the Eye of Atum or the Eye of Re. As every eye needed light to see by, eyes and the sun would always be closely linked. Like the word for 'hand', the Egyptian word for 'eye' (*irt*: a word which sounds like the verb 'to do') was feminine, and so the eyes of male gods were considered female. The Eye of Atum was both a feminine aspect of the male sun god and, because he created her, the daughter who protected him. This role could be assigned to other solar goddesses, including Bastet, Sekhmet, Wadjet and Hathor. We will meet these ladies again.

Somehow, and this is never fully explained, Shu and Tefnut became physically separated from their father. Despairing, Atum plucked the Eye from his head and sent his daughter to recover his children from the waters of Nun. *Papyrus Bremner-Rhind* extends this tale, telling us how, when the Eye returned triumphant with the twins, she was disconcerted and angry to find that her father had replaced her with a new Eye. To placate his irascible daughter, the creator transformed her into a cobra and placed her as the rearing uraeus snake on his brow.[25]

Solar goddesses were intensely loyal, yet prone to fits of uncontrollable fiery temper and liable to act without thought for the consequences of their actions. This made them very suitable bodyguards for their father, Re. The tale of the angry Eye who abandons Egypt was popular during the Graeco-Roman Period. The basic myth, set in the peaceful time just after creation, tells how the Eye, having quarrelled with Re, ran away to a faraway land, which is usually identified as Nubia but may occasionally be Libya. Here the Eye took the form of a fiery lion to stalk the desert, killing her enemies and eating their flesh. Recovered by her brother Shu and/or the wise god Thoth, she was immersed in the Nile at Philae to cool her passion, then forced to marry either Shu or Thoth. In some versions of this tale the lioness is tracked down and returned by the hunter god Onuris of This, who then marries her. The best-preserved version of the myth is recorded on the demotic *Papyrus Leiden I 384*. This tells how Tefnut, who has assumed the form of a Nubian cat, is confronted by Thoth in the form of a baboon. Perhaps because they were known to chatter among themselves, baboons were regarded as good raconteurs: some Classical authors even believed that Egypt's priests could speak the language of the baboons, and that 'baboon-speak' was Egypt's true religious language. Thoth, a master of words rather than hunting skills, describes the warm welcome that awaits the goddess back in Egypt, then tempts her home with a series of stories. His most complete tale for Tefnut is *The Lion in Search of Man*.

Once upon a time there was a mighty mountain lion; a lion so strong and skilled in hunting that all the other animals were afraid of him and he feared no one. One day the mighty lion came across a semi-conscious panther whose fur had been stripped and whose skin had been cruelly torn.

'Who did this to you?' the lion purred.

'It was Man,' the panther replied.

'What is Man?'

'Man is the most cunning beast in all the world. I pray that you never fall into the hands of Man.'

The lion was filled with rage. Abandoning the dying panther, he set off on a mission to find Man and teach him a lesson. Soon he came across a team of animals yoked together uncomfortably.

'Who has done this to you?' he asked.

'Man, our master, did this,' was the reply.

'Is Man stronger than the pair of you, then?'

'There is no beast more cunning than Man. We pray that you never fall into the hands of Man.'

His rage intensified, the lion ran off in search of Man. In the course of his quest he encountered an ox and cow whose noses had been pierced, a bear whose claws had been removed and whose teeth had been pulled, and a lion whose paw had been trapped in a tree. In all three cases, the suffering animals blamed Man for their plight. The lion was angry as he had never been before:

'Man, you had better pray that I never catch up with you. For I will inflict on you the pain that you have inflicted on my fellow animals.'

Then, one day as he walked along, a tiny mouse ran between his paws. Instinctively, the lion prepared to crush the mouse and eat it. But the brave mouse squeaked at him:

'Please sir, do not crush me. I am too small to satisfy your hunger so there is no point in your eating me. But if you save my life, I will be free to help you when you most need help.'

Hearing this, the lion laughed out loud:

'How could you ever help a mighty hunter like me, little mouse? No one would dare to attack me!'

Nevertheless, the lion allowed the mouse to run free.

Not long after this, a cunning huntsman trapped the lion in a large pit. The lion found himself entangled in a net and bound with leather straps. Struggle as he might, he could not break free. Suddenly he became aware that the mouse was standing beside him.

'Do you recognize me? I am the little mouse whose life you spared. Now I have come to fulfil my oath and save your life.'

And the mouse set to work, gnawing away at the ties which bound the lion. Soon the lion was free. Then the mouse settled himself in the lion's mane, and the two ran away to the safety of the mountains.

Eventually, after much discussion and some rage – at one point Tefnut terrifies Thoth by transforming into a fire-breathing lion – Thoth persuades Tefnut to return home with him. After yet more adventures the pair reach Memphis and Tefnut assumes the gentle form of Hathor of the Sycamore for her reunion with her father. From this moment on she will dedicate herself to protecting Re against his enemies.

GEB AND NUT: EARTH AND SKY

The birth and subsequent quarrel of the visible gods Geb and Nut from the invisible Shu and Tefnut caused the world as we know it to come into being with a sky and an earth separated by the atmosphere. An alternative version of the Heliopolitan myth tells us that Shu, disapproving of his children's love for each other, forcibly separated the two, causing Geb to weep great tears which became the oceans. A third version tells us that Geb and Nut initially lay so close together that their children could not be born. Only when Shu forced them apart could Nut give birth.

Geb is an ancient and important earth god frequently referenced in the *Pyramid Texts*, where he represents both the fertile land and the graves dug into that land. For this combination of attributes, and for his prowess as a healer, he was both respected and feared. He usually appears as a man reclining, supported by his elbow, beneath the female sky. His naked green body often displays the erection which denotes his impressive fertility, and he may have grain growing from his back. Alternatively, as the son and heir of Shu and grandson of Atum, he might appear as a king wearing the crown of Lower Egypt. In animal form he might be a goose (or a man wearing a goose on his head) or a hare, or he might form part of the crew of the solar boat which sails across the sky each day. Like his father Shu before him, Geb rules Egypt during the time when people and gods lived togetherr. Much later Greek tradition would equate Geb with the Titan Chronos, who overthrew his father Uranos at the urging of his mother, Gaia.

Nut, Geb's sister-wife, is both a woman and the celestial cow or sow who arches herself above Geb, touching the earth with her feet and hands, so forming the firmament that separates the world from the waters of chaos and the darkness of the undefined place. She is a boundary or edge rather than a solid barrier, so that the sun is able to sail along her watery body during the daylight hours. She may even be the Milky Way. Every morning Nut swallows and so conceives the stars that are reborn each night. Every evening she conceives the sun on the western horizon and it sails through her body to be reborn at dawn, with the red staining of the morning sky bearing witness to her labour (or, perhaps, bearing witness to the death of the stars).[26] As a long-horned cow, Nut suckles the king and, after death, raises him into the sky where she protects him. As a goddess of rebirth she appears on tomb ceilings and on the under-surface of countless coffin lids, so that the dead lie directly beneath her outstretched body and, if the coffin is understood to represent Nut, are themselves reborn directly from her dark womb. As Osiris, god of the dead, is known to have been the son of Nut, the dead who are reborn from Nut's coffin-womb automatically become one with Osiris. At the same time, as she is known to give birth to the sun god, they also become one with Re.

Reconciled with Geb, Nut bore her brother two sons, Osiris and Seth, and two daughters, Isis and Nephthys. These children, together with Atum, Shu, Tefnut, Geb and Nut, form the Ennead, or the 'nine' of Heliopolis. Nine, being three times three (the number which signified plurality), was a significant number, representing 'everything'. Our first reference to the Ennead comes from the shattered remains of a shrine donated to the Heliopolis

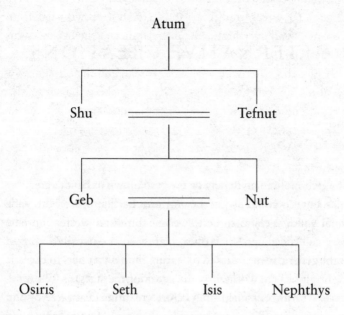

Family tree of the gods

temple by the 3rd Dynasty King Djoser; however, it seems likely that the nine gods had been grouped together before the Old Kingdom. While the first five of the nine, the gods of light, air, moisture, land and sky, play an important role in the creation of the world, the final four belong to the world after creation.

2

ALTERNATIVE CREATIONS

The Heliopolitan myth may be the best known of Egypt's creation tales, but it is certainly not the only one. Each temple might, with equal validity, claim to be the original mound of creation and most cults developed their own creation story – usually a version of the generic myth adapted to feature their own god – to explain the origins of the world. Broadly speaking these myths follow set stages: the uncontrolled time before creation is followed by the emergence of a divine creator who then makes light, time, gods and men and, in so doing, imposes *maat* on chaos. However, the means by which creation is achieved varies from cult to cult.

THE EIGHT GODS OF HERMOPOLIS

At the Middle Egyptian site of Hermopolis Magna (modern Ashmunein) the priests of the temple of Thoth told a well-developed tale which they claimed as Egypt's original creation myth. Unfortunately, their tale is not at all well preserved and, although it has been possible to reconstruct some contemporary elements from inscriptions on coffins recovered from nearby Middle Kingdom cemeteries and from scraps of Theban texts, it is primarily found in fragments of Ptolemaic Period writings which, as they date to the very end of the dynastic age, contain many late additions and distortions. However, the Egyptian name for Hermopolis is Khemnu or 'Eight Town', a clear reference to the Ogdoad, the eight gods of the Hermopolitan creation, and this suggests that theirs is indeed an ancient story. The more frequently used Greek name Hermopolis (Magna), literally 'City of Hermes', reflects the fact that the Greeks equated Thoth with their god Hermes, messenger of the Olympian deities.

The Hermopolitan myth shares many elements with the Heliopolitan myth. There are several known versions:

In the unknowable time before time there existed four pairs of gods. Nun and Naunet, Heh and Hauhet, Kek and Kauket, and Amen and Amaunet lived together in the primeval waters. Suddenly, with a burst of creative energy . . .

. . . the Mound of Flame rose out of the waters. The 'Great Honker', a celestial goose, laid an egg on the mound and, cackling, made the first sound in the newly created world. The egg cracked open, and the sun god was born. The sun god then created all living things.

or

. . . the Mound of Flame rose out of the waters. The sun god in the form of a falcon landed on the mound which was the first land.

or

. . . the Mound of Flame rose out of the waters. A lotus bud pushed through the mound. Opening, the blossom revealed the sun god in the form of a child . . .

or

> . . . a lotus bud appeared on the surface of the waters. Opening,
> the blossom revealed the sun god in the form of a child. The
> sun god brought with him time and creation.

Here, at the beginning of all things, there exist four inert couples;
four being a good, well-balanced number signifying totality, which
is reflected in the four cardinal points and, later, the four corners
of the sarcophagus and the four canopic jars that will be used to
house the viscera of the deceased.[27] Recognizing that creation
requires male and female elements these original deities are gender-
specific, the four frog-headed gods and the four snake-headed
goddesses representing male and female versions of the principal,
negative attributes of the primeval waters: chaos (Nun and Naunet),
infinity (Heh and Hauhet), darkness (Kek and Kauket) and hid-
denness (Amen and Amaunet). Although inert, together they have
the potential to spark life. They will become the fathers and the
mothers of the sun god, then, their role complete, they will die and
retire to the afterlife where they will control the rising and setting
of the sun and the rising and falling of the Nile waters. Later
tradition will recognize these deities as the children, or perhaps
the souls, of Thoth, Shu or Amen, and they will be represented as
the eight baboons who squat to greet the rising sun with loud
shrieks and upraised paws. Meanwhile, at the small temple of
Medinet Habu, on the west bank of the Nile at Thebes, they will
receive cult offerings in their 'sacred place'.

Once again a mound, sometimes described as the 'Mound of
Flame' or the 'Isle of Fire', suddenly rises, emerging either from
boundless dark waters or from a primeval slime. This emerging
mound is personified by the god Tatenen (literally the 'land that
becomes more distinct'), who also represents Egypt emerging
from the annual inundation and so is associated with the earth
god Geb. The *Book of the Mounds of the First Time*, recorded

on the walls of the Edfu temple, suggests that the mound offers a desolate, watery vista of islands, pools and reeds. This bleak landscape then bears a lotus bud whose petals open to reveal the blazing sun god in the form of a child or, in different versions, a ram or a scarab beetle whose tears become mankind. Or maybe the lotus blossom emerges directly from the waters of Nun, or the sun god in the form of a falcon (or perhaps a phoenix) alights on the mound which now becomes the first land. Or a cosmic egg – the perfect seed or womb – is laid by either the celestial goose Gengen (equated with the earth god Geb, and later with Amen of Thebes) or an ibis (the symbol of the god Thoth and, presumably, an attempt by his priests to integrate their patron deity into a pre-existing mythology) or, more unusually, a crocodile or snake. Alternatively, the world is created by a god with the power to force back the primal waters. It may be that the original egg, or even the original gods, was/were fertilized by the primeval serpent Amen-Kematef.

Whatever the precise sequence of events, it is clear that the lotus flower played an important role in the creation of the world. The heavily scented blue lotus (*Nymphaea caerulea*) is a form of water lily which flourishes in still water. By day it rises above the water and spreads its petals wide; by night, its bud tightly closed, it sinks out of sight beneath the surface of the water. This, combined with its beauty, made the lotus an obvious symbol of rebirth and resurrection and a suitable decoration for tomb walls. The ubiquity of the blue-lotus motif has, in turn, led to suggestions that the flower may have played a more direct role in religious rituals by serving as a mind-altering narcotic which might have been either inhaled, or added to wine and drunk. Scientific investigation has shown that this is unlikely; the blue lotus has no alkaloids that could produce a narcotic effect. However, the blue lotus flower is a good source of flavinoids, the health-giving colouring agents found in many fruits and vegetables. Today flavinoids are taken in concentrated form in herbal health preparations such as ginkgo biloba, a plant used in Chinese medicine to ward off the effects of old age and improve short-term memory.

In 332 BC, the year that Alexander the Great conquered Egypt, Petosiris, high priest of Thoth and controller of the Hermopolis Magna temple, started to build an elaborately decorated family tomb in the nearby desert cemetery of Tuna el-Gebel. Here, in a lengthy autobiographical inscription, we may read how Petosiris had been called upon to restore the temple of Thoth, which had been damaged during the second, turbulent period of Persian rule. He details his administrative improvements – restoring the rituals, maintaining the offerings, controlling the priests and filling the temple warehouses with grain, and its treasury 'with every good thing' – before telling how he founded a new temple for Re, 'the nursling in the Isle of Fire', and shrines for the goddesses Nehemtawy (consort of Thoth) and Hathor. Finally, he turned his attention to the badly neglected temple park:[28]

> I made an enclosure around the park,
> Lest it be trampled by the rabble,
> For it is the birthplace of every god
> Who came into being in the beginning.
> This spot, wretches had damaged it,
> Intruders had traversed it;
> The fruit of its trees had been eaten,
> Its shrubs taken to intruders' homes;
> The whole land was in uproar about it,
> And Egypt was distressed by it,
> For the half of the egg is buried in it . . .

It appears that the remains of the first egg to have hatched on the mound of creation were actually buried in the temple park at Hermopolis Magna. No wonder Petosiris was concerned that this area be made secure once again. Clearly Thoth approved of his high priest's actions, as Petosiris himself tells us that he died 'distinguished above all my peers, as my reward for enriching him [Thoth]'.

Six of the eight gods of the Hermopolitan Ogdoad sank into relative obscurity. But Amen and his consort Amaunet continued to be revered over 200 miles upstream of Hermopolis Magna, in the southern city of Thebes. Four kings of the 12th Dynasty, Thebans by birth, referenced Amen in their name Amenemhat, or 'Amen is pre-eminent'. During the New Kingdom Amen of Thebes united with Re of Heliopolis. Together they formed the potent god-king Amen-Re, who was worshipped alongside his new wife Mut (a more user-friendly replacement for Amaunet) and their son Khonsu in the extensive Karnak temple complex on the east bank of the Nile at Thebes. Despite this marital setback, Amaunet's cult survived in the Theban region until the Macedonian Period, and she was featured on the wall of the Karnak temple nursing and extending her protection to the pharaoh Philip Arrhidaeos: in this instance her protection failed, as Arrhidaeos, half-brother of Alexander the Great, was murdered without ever setting foot in Egypt.

Meanwhile, his increased status had caused a revision of Amen's back-story. Absorbing some of the mythology of the god Montu, he became a mighty warrior credited with the expulsion of the hated 'Hyksos' rulers from northern Egypt at the start of the New Kingdom. As successive pharaohs made increasingly generous donations to his temples, Amen grew in wealth and power until his priesthood controlled valuable assets – extensive tracts of land, mines, ships and peasant labour – throughout Egypt. In appearance a fit young man sporting a short kilt, a curled beard and a crown topped with two tall feathers, Amen was not dissimilar to the king whom he protected. This similarity is no doubt deliberate; no right-thinking king would have been averse to being mistaken for the great god himself. When the 19th Dynasty King Ramesses II found himself in dire straits, abandoned by his cowardly troops at the height of the battle of Kadesh, it was natural that he should turn in his despair to Amen. Although he was many miles away, safe in the dark sanctuary of his Theban temple, the god did not disappoint the king, and the dramatic story of Ramesses' legendary triumph was carved in prose, poetry and pictures on his stone temple walls for all to enjoy:

There was no officer with me, no charioteer, no soldier and no shield bearer. My infantry and my chariotry had fled before the enemy and not one soldier stood firm to fight with me. Desperate, I prayed aloud:

'O my father Amen, what is happening? Is it right that a father should turn his back on his son? Are you determined to ignore my plight? Do I not obey your every command? I have followed every order that you have given me. Amen, Lord of Egypt, is surely too great to allow foreigners to impede his way. What do these wretched, godless Asiatics mean to you, Amen? I have built you many monuments, and filled your temples with war booty. I dedicated my mortuary temple to you, and endowed it with all my wealth. I gave you the lands that you needed to support your altars. I sacrificed ten thousand cattle and burned many kinds of sweet herbs before you. I built magnificent gateways to you, and erected their flagpoles myself. I brought you seaworthy ships, and obelisks from Yebu. Will people now say, "There is little to be gained by trusting Amen"? I am counting on you. Do the right thing by me, and I will serve you with a loving heart. I call upon you, my father Amen. I am in the midst of a host of hostile strangers and all the countries are allied against me. I am entirely alone; there is no one with me. My troops have run away, and not one of my charioteers is prepared to defend me. I shout for help, but they do not hear my call and they do not come. Yet I know that Amen will help me more than a million troops, more than a hundred thousand charioteers, more than ten thousand brothers and sons. The deeds of mortals are as nothing – Amen is a far greater help than they could ever be.'

Although I prayed in a distant land my prayer was heard in faraway Thebes. Amen listened when I called to him; he gave me his hand and I rejoiced. He spoke to me as clearly as if he was nearby.

'Go forward, for I am with you. Your father is with you and is guiding your hand. I will triumph over a hundred thousand men, for I am the lord of victory and I will reward your valour.'

Suddenly my heart grew strong and my breast swelled with joy. I knew that I was invincible and unstoppable. I had become the great god Montu. I appeared before the enemy like Seth in his moment. The enemy chariots scattered before my horses. Not one of them stood to fight. Their hearts quaked with fear when they saw me and their arms went limp so they could not shoot. They simply did not have the heart to hold their spears. I made them plunge into the river just as crocodiles plunge into the water. They fell on their faces, one on top of another, and I slaughtered them at my will. They did not look back and they did not turn around. Those who fell down did not get up again.

But Amen was not simply the larger-than-life warrior that this 'true' story suggests. He was also 'the hidden one' whose real name would never be revealed; an ancient and powerful yet invisible creator with a strong affinity to the highly visible sun. The 19th Dynasty *Papyrus Leiden* is one of many texts to document this, recognizing Amen as the 'one who crafted himself, whose appearance is unknown', and the forerunner of all the gods.

As befits a hidden one, Amen keeps a low profile: his deeds

are, for the most part, hidden from us. However, we do know that he could be identified with both the Great Honker, the goose who created the first sound and laid the first egg, and with Amen-Kematef, 'Amen who has completed his moment', the potent snake who fertilized that first egg in the Medinet Habu temple. Amen's sexual potency was an important aspect of his persona. New Kingdom rituals (unspecified) required that he be stimulated by the royal priestess known as the God's Wife or the God's Hand; he even occasionally made love to the human queen to father a semi-divine king. During the Middle Kingdom Amen had become associated with the fertility god Min in the form of the ithyphallic Amen-Min and the self-engendered Min-Amen-Kamutef, 'bull of his mother'. By the end of the New Kingdom he was also recognized as a sexually potent ram.

PTAH OF MEMPHIS

The Old Kingdom capital city of Memphis lay about 20 miles across the river from Heliopolis. Here Ptah, an ancient earth god with a particular interest in masons, builders and sculptors, was worshipped by a priesthood led by the 'Greatest of Those who Supervise the Craftsmen'. Ptah's temple, the royal palaces and administrative quarters and the nearby pyramid complexes would have created a constant demand for high-quality artefacts, which may in turn have contributed to the importance of the craftsman god in the city. In its heyday, the Memphite temple complex of Ptah must have rivalled or even surpassed the Karnak temple complex of Amen in both size and complexity, with major and minor temples, lesser shrines, monumental gateways, processional avenues and sacred lakes. Unfortunately, Ptah's complex is today almost entirely destroyed, its stone re-used in later buildings.

The human-form Ptah invariably wore a long, tight-wrapped

cloak or shroud which left his hands free to hold a sceptre combining the symbols of the *djed* pillar (the backbone of Osiris which signified stability), the *was* (symbol of dominion) and the *ankh* (the looped cross which signified life). He wore a tight-fitting artisan's skullcap and a broad collar with a prominent tassel-tie hanging down his back. His face was blue, the colour of the sky, while his beard, initially curved like the beards of the other male gods, was, by the Middle Kingdom, straight. At Memphis Ptah was associated both with the god Tatenen, the emerging mound of creation, and with Sokar, another ancient craftsman deity who is associated with metalwork, the cemetery and the afterlife. The triple deity Ptah-Sokar-Osiris came to symbolize the cycle of life – creation (Ptah), death (Sokar) and rebirth (Osiris) – and so made a suitable judge in the afterlife. Ptah's wife, Sekhmet, was the fierce lion-headed alter ego of the gentle goddess Hathor, while their son, Nefertem, was the personification of the blue lotus and so was associated both with Re and with the first flower that blossomed on the Isle of Flame. Other parents laid claim to Nefertem, however, and he might also be recognized as the son of the goddesses Wadjet or Bastet.

Egypt's gods seldom had direct contact with ordinary mortals. Ptah, however, listened and responded to the prayers of the people. In recognition of this, stelae dedicated to Ptah are often ornamented with large carved ears to help the god to hear, while Ptah himself is sometimes associated with the divine personification of hearing, Sedjem. Ptah's ever-listening ears were not always a good thing. When the New Kingdom draughtsman Neferabu offended Ptah by swearing a false oath, the god responded by striking him blind:[29]

> I am a man who swore falsely by Ptah, Lord of Maat.
> And he made me see darkness by day.
> I will declare his might to the fool and the wise,

To the small and the great.
Beware Ptah, Lord of Maat!
For he does not overlook anyone's deed!
Refrain from uttering Ptah's name falsely,
Lo, he who utters it falsely, Lo, he falls.

Ptah's better-known role as the creator who brings agricultural fertility to Egypt is mentioned in the *Coffin Texts*, and is explored again in hymns dating to the Ramesside age where he is described as 'Ptah, father of the gods, Tatenen, eldest of the originals ... who begot himself, by himself'. It seems that Ptah the metalworker designed and smelted the whole land, forging a body for the deceased and newly divine king from electrum (a precious mixture of gold and silver), copper and iron. Metals were reserved for the gods, whose gold flesh covered silver bones, and this was reflected in the golden cult statues found in most temple sanctuaries, although Re and his fellow solar deities had no need of a golden cult statue as their temples were open to the skies, allowing the officiating priest direct communication with the god himself. The Ptolemaic *Papyrus Jumilhac*[30] offers an explanation for the unusual, and extremely expensive, silver cult statue of the falcon-headed god Anti. Having committed an awful crime (possibly the decapitation of a cow deity), Anti was stripped of his skin, and his golden pelt was hung on a pole, leaving his silver bones exposed. Eventually the wronged goddess forgave him and restored his flesh with her milk, but his cult statue was henceforth made of silver. The rather disjointed *Coffin Texts* spell 942 adds to the tale by telling us that Anti was either flayed alive or had his side-whiskers shaved because he 'turned the land upside down'.

Ptah's creation myth is primarily preserved in sixty-two columns of hieroglyphic text carved on a dark green breccia slab known today as the Shabaqo Stone.[31] The Shabaqo Stone has no known provenance, although its text suggests that it is likely to have come from the temple of Ptah at Memphis. During Roman times, when some of the temple blocks were re-used, it was employed as a millstone, and this has caused considerable damage to the middle of the text. The Stone tells how the 25th Dynasty Nubian King Shabaqo, an ardent antiquarian with a strong interest in traditional Egyptian religion and an equally strong wish to align himself with the pharaohs of old, was horrified to discover that an ancient papyrus scroll housed in the library of the temple of Ptah had been partially eaten by worms. Shabaqo immediately ordered that the undamaged part of the scroll be copied on to a stone slab (the Shabaqo Stone) and exhibited in the temple.

The archaic language of the text initially persuaded scholars that Shabaqo had indeed copied an ancient papyrus, dating, most probably, to the Old Kingdom. However, it is now realized that the text is, in fact, a much later composition couched in deliberately archaic terms to give it a patina of old age and wisdom. It seems unlikely that the text was composed much earlier than Shabaqo's own reign, and certainly not before the New Kingdom; it would therefore appear that it was a deliberate attempt to ingratiate Egypt's new royal family, who now ruled from Memphis, with the ancient priesthood of Ptah. Although Ptah is an ancient god worshipped during the Early Dynastic Period, his early mythology is lost and he is barely mentioned in the *Pyramid Texts*. And so, the unanswerable question is whether Shabaqo preserved an already existing myth, or invented his own tale.

Shabaqo's myth is today known as the Memphite Theology. Eleven columns of text on the right side of the stone reconcile the mythology of Ptah to the Heliopolitan creation story. They confirm that Ptah-Tatenen came into existence before Atum, and that he was able to create all things 'through his heart and through his tongue'. It is through this heart and tongue that Atum and the Ennead themselves are born. Ptah, the supreme creator, has no need of a partner and does not need to resort to masturbation. Shunning the physical, he is able to reproduce using intelligence (the heart rather than the brain being assumed to be the centre of the intellect) and the spoken word (command). [32] The actual order of creation is obviously important to Shabaqo, and is listed in some detail: [33]

> Thus it is said of Ptah: 'He who made all and created the gods.' And he is Tatenen, who gave birth to the gods, and from whom every thing came forth, foods, provisions, divine offerings, all good things. Thus it is recognized and understood that he is the mightiest of the gods. Thus Ptah was satisfied after he had made all things and all divine words.
> He gave birth to the gods,
> He made the towns,
> He established the nomes,
> He placed the gods in their shrines,
> He settled their offerings,
> He established their shrines,
> He made their bodies according to their wishes,
> Thus the gods entered into their bodies,
> Of every wood, every stone, every clay,
> Every thing that grows upon him
> In which they came to be.
> Thus were gathered to him all the gods and their kas (souls),
> Content, united with the Lord of the Two Lands.

This seemingly simple story, when deconstructed, becomes amazingly complex. Born from the heart and tongue of Ptah, Atum is both a child of, and manifestation of, Ptah, who houses either or both Nun and Naunet. Alternatively, in a later tradition, Tefnut might be considered to be the tongue of Ptah; Tefnut thus becomes a creator goddess. The *Coffin Texts* personify the creative attributes of the sun god as the deities Sia (perception), Hu (authoritative speech) and Heka (magic, or creative energy); combined, these three beings serve as a catalyst which helps the sun god, either Atum or Re, to create. Later tradition maintains that Sia and Hu grew from blood which dripped from Re's slashed penis on the mound of creation, and so both could be classed as children of the sun god. During the New Kingdom they were also recognized as the heart and tongue of Ptah. With Sia and Hu by his side, Ptah was first able to plan creation, then articulate it. Later writings would link Ptah more firmly with the Hermopolitan theology, recognizing him as the father of the Ogdoad.

Within the precincts of his Memphite temple lived the physical manifestation of the soul of Ptah. The Apis bull was not Ptah himself, and Ptah never appeared as a bull. Rather, the Apis was the avatar of the god. He may, however, have started life as a deity in his own right, as festivals linking the Apis with royalty were celebrated from the 1st Dynasty onwards. There could only ever be one living Apis. Following the death of the old bull, his successor was identified by his distinctive markings, which were, according to Herodotus, 'black, with a white diamond on its forehead and, the image of an eagle on its back, the hairs on its tail double, and a scarab under its tongue'.[34] Once recognized by the priests, the new Apis was taken to Memphis where he lived the pampered life of a king, with his own palace and a harem of nubile young cows. His mother, who was identified with Isis, enjoyed a similarly luxurious life. Following his death, mummification and burial in the Sakkara Serapeum (the bull cemetery), the Apis was transfigured into Osirapis, a form of Osiris who was himself known as the 'Bull of Abydos'. Meanwhile, as the old Apis underwent the rituals of the embalming house, an Egyptwide search began to find his successor.

As time went by the Apis developed his own birth story. It was generally accepted that he was born to a virgin cow who had been impregnated by Ptah. Plutarch, however, tells us that the Apis was born from the pale light of the moon, while Herodotus was convinced that he was conceived in a flash of lightning. The priests of Re even claimed that their own sacred bull, the Mnevis bull of Heliopolis, was the father of the Apis. The Mnevis (or Mer-Wer) served as an avatar for Re-Atum. The son of the previous Mnevis and one of his sacred cow wives, the Mnevis was black all over. When illustrated he, like the Apis, wears a solar disk and uraeus between his horns.

From the very beginning of the dynastic age, wild bulls had been accepted as symbols of male dominance and fertility. As such, they quickly became equated with political power. The Nagada III/Dynasty 0 Narmer Palette is a large ceremonial cosmetic palette recovered from the ruins of the ancient temple of Horus at Hierakonpolis (modern Kom el-Ahmar). Too large to have had any practical use, the Palette is presumed to have been a part of the original temple paraphernalia, and may perhaps have been displayed in a frame designed to show the elaborate scenes carved on both faces. Here we may see Egypt's first king taking the form of a bull to gore an enemy outside a walled town. The two principal scenes show Narmer in human form, with a bull's tail attached to his belt and dangling down below the level of his kilt. The bull's tail would remain a part of the royal regalia, and part of the costume of some gods (including Atum, Re, Shu, Amen and Thoth) throughout the dynastic age.

The first bull-hunting scene dates to the 1st Dynasty reign of Narmer's son Aha. Bull-fighting (bulls fighting each other rather than men fighting bulls) features in several Upper Egyptian Old Kingdom tombs, with the southern cemetery of Akhmim providing the best representations. Here the black-and-white Buchis Bull, a fighter of national renown who specialized in curing eye

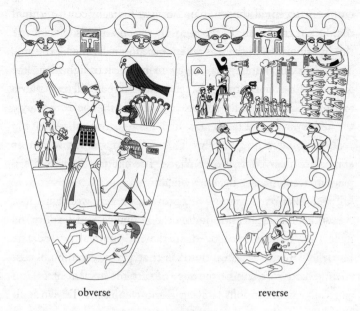

obverse   reverse

The Narmer Palette

diseases, was associated with the local warrior god Montu of
Armant.

There is no writing to explain the Narmer Palette and the other,
similarly decorated Predynastic palettes, but the link between
strong leadership and powerful animals – bulls and lions in
particular – is obvious. It seems that the hunter who kills a wild
animal may absorb part of the essence of that animal, while the
warrior who takes the form of an animal to kill possesses the
characteristics and strength of his chosen animal. Royal hunting
scenes will always be an important part of the artistic repertoire
as successive kings use real or imaginary adventures in the hunting
field to confirm their superiority over the chaotic natural world.
So, when Amenhotep III boasts of slaughtering 96 wild bulls and
102 (or 110) lions he is both confirming his own fitness, and

emphasizing his ability to maintain *maat* which, in turn, shows that he has the favour of the gods. By the end of the dynastic age this hunting symbolism was taken to almost ridiculous extremes. The Ptolemaic kings were happy to be depicted 'spearing the tortoise of Re', not because they actually left their palaces to hunt tortoises, but because the tortoise, along with the snake, the onyx, the Seth animal and foreigners, had come to symbolize chaos.

In a similar vein, all of Egypt's kings used 'smiting scenes' to emphasize their control over chaos. The smiting scene is a set-piece image depicting the king wielding a club, mace or sword to kill a smaller-scale enemy who grovels, unresisting, at his feet. Again this image is first found on the Narmer Palette, and again it persists, almost unchanged, to the end of the dynastic age. Battlefield images of kings riding in chariots to crush small-scale enemies convey a similar message of ruthless royal control. It is generally assumed that smiting scenes represent the symbolic bringing of justice (*maat*) to a defeated (and chaotic) enemy. But, given the acceptance of animal sacrifice plus the contempt felt for prisoners of war, it may be that such scenes should be read as a literal representation of an occasional ritual.

KHNUM OF ELEPHANTINE

Khnum dwelt at Egypt's southern border, on the Island of Elephantine (opposite the modern town of Aswan). Here he controlled the waters of the inundation which poured into Egypt from Nun via secret underground caverns. The so-called *Famine Stela*, a Ptolemaic inscription carved on a rock face at Sehel Island, near Aswan, celebrates his prowess. It tells how King Djoser, worried by seven years of famine caused by drought, consulted a priest of Imhotep. The priest retired to study the problem in the temple library, then returned to tell the king about Khnum's role as director of the floodwaters. That night, before retiring, Djoser performed a series of tasks set by the priest. He was rewarded with a dream visit from the great god himself. Khnum promised to end the famine: 'I shall allow your people to fill up ... the hungry years will end.' With his problem solved, the grateful king granted a generous endowment to the Elephantine temple.

The River Nile was not only the centre of Egypt, it was central to Egyptian thought. It was quite simply impossible to conceive of a land without a river, and every imagining of the afterlife included some form of waterway. So, it is very difficult to understand why Egypt never developed a powerful river deity to stand alongside the gods of sun, atmosphere, earth and sky created at the beginning of time. Instead, Egypt had Hapy, the god of the inundation who might also, on occasion, represent the river itself.

Hapy, 'lord of the fishes and the birds', is a plump, blue- or green-skinned man whose swollen belly and drooping breasts give him an androgynous look. In a land where elite women were invariably depicted as svelte, their husbands and fathers often chose to appear with the rounded stomach and stylized rolls of fat which testified to an enviable, food-rich life, and so we can assume that Hapy is well-rounded because he has eaten often and well. He wears a headdress of papyrus and lotus stems and a long wig, dresses in a brief loincloth, and often carries an offering tray piled high with produce. Other, anonymous, river deities who appear in temple scenes to bring their own copious offerings to the king, celebrate Egypt's abundance but have no known mythology.

Hapy was believed to live in the underground caverns near Aswan (although in some accounts the inundation began further north, at Gebel Silsila); here he was supported, most appropriately, by crocodile gods and frog goddesses. His potency was undeniable:

the *Famine Stela* tells how 'he brings the floodwaters; jumping up he copulates as a man copulates with a woman'. Of course, this being Egypt, there were alternative interpretations of the annual floods, which might be the gift of Sothis, or the tears that Isis wept for her dead husband, or even the liquids that seeped from the decaying body of Osiris.

As controller of the inundation Khnum was associated both with rebirth and with Nile mud; a freely available resource of immense economic importance which not only served as a fertile soil, but also provided pottery and the mud-bricks used to build domestic architecture that was appropriately warm in the chill of winter and cool in the fierce summer heat. Mud, or clay, was a mysterious, magical substance capable of taking and retaining shape. While children formed small mud animals as toys and their parents made bricks and pots, Khnum fashioned human beings and their souls from clay that he shaped on his potter's wheel. His use of the potter's wheel must, however, have been a relatively late development in his mythology as, while Khnum was worshipped at Elephantine during the Early Dynastic Period, the potter's wheel is not known in Egypt before the 5th Dynasty. This career progression is confirmed by the *Pyramid Texts*, which tell us that Khnum started life as a craftsman-builder making inanimate objects – boats and ladders – rather than living things. By the Middle Kingdom Khnum had progressed to the creation of the living, but was not yet recognized as a universal creator god. *Coffin Texts* spell 882, a spell to be spoken by the sun god, mentions that either 'the potter's wheels are broken' (Raymond Faulkner's translation) or 'the flame of the potter's wheel when the disk is spun' (Peter Dorman's translation):[35] the spinning potter's wheel which emits light while giving life to the inanimate clay is therefore linked to the solar disk, as it will be again in New Kingdom funerary literature, where it serves as a symbol of regeneration.

The New Kingdom Khnum was credited with the creation of gods, people (both Egyptians and foreigners who spoke other languages) and animals, a role that he retained to the end of the dynastic age. The predominantly Roman-period temple of Khnum at Esna preserves the details of his work, and of the cult festivals that celebrated that work, on the walls and columns of its hypostyle hall. The *Great Hymn to Khnum* was recited at the annual 'festival of installing the potter's wheel'. The hymn provides an almost anatomical breakdown of the construction process, making it clear that the creation of mankind is here a deliberate, well-thought-out act:[36]

> *He knotted the flow of blood to the bones,*
> *Formed in his [workshop] as his handiwork,*
> *So the breath of life is within everything.*
> *Blood bound with semen in the bones,*
> *To knit the bones from the start . . .*
>
> *He made hair sprout and tresses grow,*
> *Fastened the skin over the limbs;*
> *He built the skull, formed the cheeks,*
> *To furnish shape to the image.*
> *He opened the eyes, hollowed the ears,*
> *He made the body inhale air;*
> *He formed the mouth for eating,*
> *Made the [gorge] for swallowing . . .*

With the body complete, Khnum supervises conception and, at the appropriate time, initiates the contractions that herald the onset of labour. The *Great Hymn* concludes by detailing the various aspects of Khnum, who is identified with the other creator gods.

Khnum does not have a particularly rich mythology, but he

does have a complicated family life. Originally he was associated with the divine midwife and frog goddess Heket, but later mythology links him with the goddesses Satis and Anukis. Satis, the original deity of Elephantine and the guardian of Egypt's southern border, wears the white crown of southern Egypt. When Khnum is identified with Re, she may be identified with the Eye of Re; in other mythologies she is the consort of Montu of Thebes. Anukis the huntress wears an unusual, tall, feathered headdress. Both Satis and Anukis, who may or may not be mother and daughter, are daughters of Re, while Anukis may also be the daughter of Khnum. As a mother goddess associated with Hathor, Anukis was sometimes shown nursing the king. Meanwhile, at Esna, Khnum was associated with the obscure lioness goddess Menhyt (another uraeus goddess) and with the creator goddess Neith; his role as 'lord of the crocodiles' suggests that he may have fathered Neith's otherwise fatherless crocodile son, Sobek.

Khnum was a ram-headed god. Originally he sported the long, rippling horns of *Ovis longipes*, the first sheep to be reared in Egypt. Later he acquired a second, additional set of horns, the curled horns of *Ovis platyra* occasionally worn by the god Amen. The Egyptians appreciated the consistent fertility of the ram, and this fertility, naturally, was transferred to Khnum. The Egyptian word for ram, '*ba*', sounded like the word '*ba*' meaning spirit or personality and, because of this, Khnum was variously recognized as the *ba* or spirit of the sun god Re, the earth god Geb and the king of the underworld, Osiris. Re, on his nightly journey through the underworld, was often shown with a ram's head and occasionally identified as Khnum-Re.

But Khnum was not the only creator ram. Heryshef (literally 'he who is upon his lake') of Herakleopolis Magna (ancient Hnes; close by the mouth of the Faiyum) emerged from the waters of Nun at the beginning of time to serve as the 'lord of blood and butchery', who protected the weak against evil. The *Book of the*

Dead tells how, when the syncretized deity Osiris-Heryshef was crowned king, all other gods bowed before him; even the discontented Seth bowed, although his suppressed rage made his nose bleed. However, Osiris-Heryshef soon overreached himself. When he placed the uraeus of Re on his brow his head swelled alarmingly, causing him unbearable pain. Re was able to cure him by cutting into the swelling, releasing a lake of blood and pus, which became the sacred lake at Herakleopolis. A similar, Ptolemaic tale is told about the time Geb rashly attempted to don the uraeus of his father Shu. At the very end of the dynastic age, Heryshef, now identified with the deified Hellenistic hero Heracles, was credited with helping Alexander the Great to expel Egypt's hated Persian overlords.

MIN OF KOPTOS

While Hapy's plump physique hinted at his fecundity and his access to rich food, some gods displayed a more obvious sexuality. At the southern city of Koptos (modern Qift) the god Min was worshipped from late predynastic times until the end of the dynastic age. Min was a fertility god blessed with the ability to create: to celebrate his prowess he was consistently depicted as a mummy wearing a tall plumed crown, carrying a flail in his raised right arm and displaying an erect penis. His black face emphasized his rejuvenative powers, and he was often shown standing in front of a garden of lettuce plants. Lettuce, which grew long and tall and emitted a milky substance when squeezed, was considered a potent aphrodisiac. Min's Early Dynastic temple boasted a series of colossal limestone figures, Egypt's earliest anthropomorphic cult statues, measuring over 4 metres high, each with a left hand supporting a now vanished (perhaps made of wood?) erection and each bearing the curious symbol of Min, which has been variously identified as a lightning bolt, a meteoric rock, a door bolt, an arrow or a shellfish.[37]

The mythology of Min developed as the dynastic age progressed. Initially a relatively insignificant local god, during the Middle Kingdom he was absorbed into the extended Heliopolitan mythology, becoming 'Min-Horus the victorious', either the son of Isis and Osiris, or the husband of Isis and the father of Horus. By the New Kingdom Min was associated with the creator god Amen of Thebes and both now wore a headdress of two tall plumes. Min-Amen was recognized as Kamutef, the 'bull of his mother', a god who secretly, at night, fornicated with his mother and so incestuously fathered himself. Mother–son incest was not considered acceptable in the human world, yet Kamutef, a means of emphasizing the continuous nature of kingship, was acceptable within the semi-divine royal family. During the Festival of Min, celebrated at Karnak, the queen consort played the role of the mother of Min: as first the wife and then the mother of a king (albeit different kings) she effectively continued the tradition of the king fathering himself.

The Greeks associated Min with their own deity Pan; a half-man, half-goat god of shepherds, fields and fertility, Pan was the seducer of many innocent maidens and was frequently depicted with an erect penis. The fact that Min, in two-dimensional art, is always shown from the side with his two legs bandaged together, has inspired the development of a entirely modern myth told to tourists today; the tale of the one-legged god who travelled, or hopped, around Egypt impregnating all the women.

3

SUNSET

Like Atum before him, Re was a self-generated solar being with the power to create all living things. His personal story differs little from the original Heliopolitan myth. Emerging from the waters of chaos, Re slashed his penis to release two divine children, Hu and Sia, from his own blood. With the help of these children Re created the world, which he then ruled until, growing old and tired, he retreated to the heavens to sail his sun boat across the sky.

ASPECTS OF RE

Re could take many forms, although he is usually shown as a winged sun disk, as a falcon or as a man with the head of a falcon, a ram or a beetle. The sun shining in the sky might be either Re himself or his independently functioning daughter, the Eye of Re. The New Kingdom *Litany of Re*, one of the *Books of the Underworld*, provides us with seventy-four different nocturnal versions of Re: here, while Re might take the form of an instantly recognizable god or goddess (Hathor, for example), the majority of his manifestations are mummiform, so that Re superficially becomes the bandaged Osiris. Written more than 1,000 years earlier, *Pyramid Texts* spell 600 preserves the myth that the creator assumed the form of the *benu* bird to perch on top of the *benben* stone and utter the shriek that represented the world's first noise. As his cry shattered the timeless silence, the world was born.

The *benu* was a shining solar bird with a phoenix-like ability to regenerate. While it would be unwise to try to identify this obviously mythological creature with a real bird, contemporary images have led ornithologists to suggest that it resembled either a yellow wagtail, or a grey heron with long feathers on its head and breast and, more often than not, blue plumage. The *benu* could be identified with both Re and Osiris: as Osiris, it guided the spirits of the deceased through the underworld. Herodotus, like many of his time, believed that the phoenix was a real bird with a red-gold plumage, which visited Egypt once every 500 years. The *benben* stone was a greatly revered cult object housed in a special temple known as the *hwt benben* (the house of the *benben*) within the precincts of the Heliopolis temple. Later, other solar temples would acquire their own *benben* stones. As the word *benben* is derived from the verb *weben*, meaning 'to shine', the *benben* stone has been interpreted as a representation of the first land, or the first ray of sunlight or, perhaps, the seed of the sun god in solid form. There is no surviving illustration of the original *benben* stone, but Egyptologists assume that it was a naturally shaped round-topped rock, perhaps even a meteorite. By the 5th Dynasty artists had formalized the *benben* into a squat obelisk, while Middle Kingdom scenes feature a long, thin obelisk. In the New Kingdom Amarna tomb of Panehesy we can see the Amarna Age *benben*, which takes the form of a large, round-topped stela standing on a raised platform.

Benben-like, the pyramids rose out of the desert sands of northern Egypt, close to the solar temple at Heliopolis. It does not take a huge leap of the imagination to see them as stairways or ramps leading the deceased to the sun. Indeed, glimpsed through half-closed eyes, they resemble the sun's rays slanting earthwards through clouds and dust. The New Kingdom monarchs abandoned the highly conspicuous pyramid form in favour of burial in less obvious rock-cut tombs in the Valley of the Kings, but they did not abandon the solar cults. In place of pyramids they raised obelisks: tall, tapering stones, inscribed with royal and religious texts and often entirely or partially covered with gold foil. The obelisk, a fossilized ray of sunlight, was a man-made *benben* and, as such, was strongly associated with Re. To erect a large-scale obelisk was a magnificent technical achievement; an unmistakable mark of powerful kingship and a sure and certain sign that *maat* was flourishing in Egypt.

THE VOYAGES OF RE

Every day the young and vigorous Re sailed his boat *Mandjet* (its name derived from the verb 'to grow fat') on a fairly uneventful voyage across the sky. The twelve hours of the day were personified as twelve solar deities (Maat, Hu, Sia, Asbet, Igaret, Seth, Horus, Khonsu, Isis, Heka, the god who is given the tow-rope in the solar boat and the god who gives protection in the twilight) but, as there were always twelve hours allocated to the time between sunrise and sunset, and always twelve hours between sunset and sunrise, these 'hours' varied somewhat in length, depending on the time of year.

The priests of Heliopolis, led by their high priest, the 'Great Seer', observed and encouraged the progress of Re's day boat. After sunset, with their god now lost from view, they performed the hourly recitations and rituals that would allow his night boat to complete its endless cycle. This imperative to monitor the sun's journey had led to the development of the northern calendar. By observing the position of the sun as it rose at dawn, the astronomer-priests calculated that it took 365 days for Re to return to his birth place on the south-eastern horizon at the winter solstice. From this knowledge, and from observations of the lunar cycle, they developed a highly complex calendar with a year of twelve months of varying lengths, with an occasional thirteenth month added. Meanwhile, the priests of southern Egypt developed their own calendar, based on their observation of the moon. When Egypt became one land in *c*.3100 BC the two calendars merged to form one civil calendar. The year was now divided into three seasons (inundation or *akhet*, planting and growth or *peret*, and summer and harvest or *shomu*), each with four months of thirty days. An extra five days – days which came to be regarded as the birthdays of the gods – were added between the old and new year to give a total of 365, but there was no leap year, so the civil calendar slowly shifted out of alignment with the natural agricultural calendar by one day every fourth year.

The 'five days over and above the year' were considered hazardous, chaotic days: they were days of plague and destruction when anything might happen. Precautions, therefore, had to be taken, and the Ptolemaic *Papyrus Brooklyn 47.218.50* details fourteen days of complex New Year rituals to be performed by the king in order to safeguard himself and his country at this most dangerous of times. The more ordinary days of the civil calendar might be classified as either lucky or unlucky, with the anniversaries of 'good' mythological events being considered particularly propitious. By the end of the dynastic age every day had a significance, and calendars served as horoscopes with 'good' days marked in black ink, 'bad' days in red. Brief instructions, such as 'do not burn incense today', helped the superstitious to avoid bad luck. Unfortunately, as with modern horoscopes, these calendars did not always agree with each other.

The night sky, too, was closely monitored, although only the more significant stars and constellations were regarded as deities. The *Pyramid Texts* admitted the possibility that the king might twinkle as one of the 'imperishable ones', the undying stars that shone around the Pole Star, which, during the Old Kingdom, was Thuban in Draco, the Dragon. It was around Thuban that the dead kings expected to shine, and so it was towards Thuban that they angled the entrances to their pyramids. The bright Sothis (Soped; Sirius the Dog Star) had a unique importance, and her own cult. The heliacal rising of Sothis on the eastern horizon at dawn, after an absence of seventy days, heralded the start of the annual inundation and the start of the agricultural year. Sothis had started life as a celestial cow, but the authors of the *Pyramid Texts* associated her, and her husband Sah (the constellation of Orion), with Isis and Osiris. Meanwhile, the visible planets were considered to be manifestations of Horus, and the other, anonymous, stars represented the souls of the dead.

The moon – the pale reflection of the sun – was personified by the rather colourless god Iah, a deity named in the *Pyramid Texts*, who later became absorbed into the mythology of the lunar deity Khonsu. Generally speaking, the moon gods lacked the defined mythology of the solar gods, and were best known for their skills as administrators, scribes and accountants; a reflection, perhaps, of the role of the lunar temples in maintaining the monthly calendar. So, the baboon- or ibis-headed lunar intellectual Thoth was, by the New Kingdom, first and foremost the scribe who invented writing. He was associated with knowledge, secrets and magic and, as he was known to be an exceptionally just god, he acted as the record-keeper at the judgement of the dead. He was also a skilled healer.

While his private life is barely mentioned – it seems that he was either self-created, that he was the motherless son of Re, or that he was, perhaps, the 'son of two fathers', born to Horus and Seth; he was married either to the obscure goddess Nehmettawy or to Seshat, the patroness of mathematics, architecture and astronomy, who might also be either his sister or his daughter – Thoth continually appears as a peripheral character in other people's tales where, invariably, he acts as a calming influence and displays great wisdom. However, even the most mild-mannered of accountants may be capable of violence. The original Thoth, the Thoth who appears in the *Pyramid Texts*, is an altogether more aggressive, knife-wielding being, prone to decapitate the enemies of the deceased.

Khonsu, too, enjoys a colourful early life as the angry deity who helps the dead king to catch, strangle and eat the minor gods whose flesh will increase his powers. While real-life cannibalism might be considered a classic example of *maat*-less chaos, this cannibalism is simply a means of demonstrating the strength of the dead king. We will find other instances of gods mutilating and, perhaps, consuming each other in the next section of this book. Meanwhile, Shu, who, despite his very obvious solar connections, may also be classed as a moon god, conforms to the tradition of *Pyramid Texts* violence by serving as an executioner in the underworld.

By the New Kingdom the bloodthirsty Khonsu has mutated into the innocuous child of Amen and Mut in Thebes and the equally blameless son of Sobek and Hathor at Kom Ombo. Like Thoth, Khonsu is a judge, accountant and record-keeper; his *Books of the End of the Year* list those who are fated to die within that year. Both Thoth, and to a lesser extent Khonsu, could be represented as a *Cynocephalus* baboon with a lunar crescent headdress. *Cynocephalus* baboons were, however, primarily associated with solar cults, and baboons were often depicted standing with their paws upraised, singing a greeting to the rising sun. Khonsu might also appear as a falcon-headed man, but his most regular appearance is as a child wearing the sidelock-of-youth hairstyle and a somewhat incongruous beard. He is wrapped in a tight cloak or bandages but his arms are left free so that he may hold the crook and flail and the *was*-sceptre.

Around his neck he wears a heavy necklace with a crescent-shaped pectoral.

The Late Period priests of the Theban Khonsu-the-Provider rewrote their god's mythology to incorporate a link with the long-dead but still charismatic King Ramesses II.[38] An engraved stela, erected in their temple, told how 800 years previously Ramesses had despatched a healing statue of Khonsu to cure his sister-in-law Bentresh, the youngest daughter of the king of 'Bakhtan', who was possessed by an evil spirit. After a seventeen-month journey the statue arrived in Bakhtan and cured Bentresh by driving out the evil spirit; a series of offerings ensured that the spirit would not return. Unfortunately, the king of Bakhtan, highly impressed by the god's performance, decided to keep the statue and it was only after several years, when the statue appeared in a dream to the king and demanded to be sent home, that Khonsu returned to Thebes in triumph.

By the Ptolemaic Period, Khonsu had developed his own creation myth. The Khonsu cosmogony of Karnak mixes the creation story of Amen and Khonsu of Thebes with the myths of Hermopolis and Memphis:[39]

> *Earth came into existence, the sky spat forth an egg, like the egg of a falcon . . . Amen in that name of his called Ptah created the egg that came forth from Nun . . . he ejaculated and made [it] at this place in the lake . . . He fertilized the egg and the eight came into existence . . . He languished there in Nun, in the Great Flood . . . He travelled to Thebes in his form of Khonsu. He cleared his throat from the water in the flood. Thus came into existence his name of Khonsu the Great in Thebes, the august being in the seed.*

The story continues with Khonsu lying on Hathor and 'opening' her to create the Ogdoad: four male gods and a wife for each one.

Re had enjoyed one glorious moment of self-creation. Yet, perversely, he was fated to experience his birth over and over again. Each evening the aged and frail Re transferred to his night boat *Mesketet* (its name ominously derived from the word 'to perish'), prior to passing through the underworld. He entered the *Duat*, the hidden world of the night-time sun, when his boat was swallowed by Nut in the west; he left the *Duat* when he was reborn from Nut in the east each morning. So, as light precedes sunrise and continues beyond sunset, we can pinpoint the entrance to the *Duat* as lying just beyond the western horizon and its exit just beyond the eastern horizon. But the *Duat* might also be found beneath the earth, where it was associated with Geb and with the primeval earth god Aker. While the whole of the underground realm might be described as the *Duat*, the second part might also be described as the *Akhet*, or the 'place of becoming effective', as it is here that Re, having united with Osiris, prepares to be born.

He might sail solo in his day boat, but Re never journeyed alone at night. Depictions of his night boat vary, but his loyal crew might include his children Hu and Sia, the deities Shu, Tefnut, Geb, Isis, Horus, Maat, Thoth and Hathor, the divine entity Heka, and beings with particular attributes such as the 'Guide of the Boat'. Other boats, packed with divine helpers, might sail alongside. These were not mere passengers; it was the crew and their specialist skills, rather than Re himself, who fought off the many enemies that threatened to extinguish his light.

We can follow Re's night voyage by studying the walls of the New Kingdom royal tombs in the Valley of the Kings. The various *Books of the Underworld* provide us with maps and written descriptions of Re's nocturnal adventures. As we might expect from compositions written over a time span of several centuries, the books differ slightly in content and detail; the earlier books, the 18th Dynasty *Amduat* and the *Book of Gates* for example, break the journey down into its twelve-hourly sections, each of which features the ram-headed Re in his solar boat, while the later books represent Re as a sun disk. This natural evolution is complicated by areas of text where the ancient draftsmen, unable to make sense of their notes (and, perhaps, in some cases unable to read fluently), either inserted the comment 'source defective' into their narrative, or simply used nonsensical words to fill in the gaps. Nevertheless, read together, the funerary texts allow us to make a fair reconstruction, hour by dangerous hour, of the perilous night journey of Re. Our account of this journey is chiefly based on the information supplied by the *Amduat*, where each well-defined hour of the journey signifies a particular region of the underworld and is personified with a female name.

Hour 1 'Smiter of the Heads of the Enemies of Re': At sunset the solar boat is welcomed into the underworld by the singing baboons of the horizon and the twelve snake goddesses who will light the dark path ahead. Maat is present as a reminder that, even in the underworld, justice must prevail. Re, now an old, ram-headed king known as 'Flesh', distributes fields among his crew, so that they may be sustained by their crops. A second solar boat holds out the hope of rebirth by housing Re in the form of a scarab beetle.

Hour 2 'The Wise Protector of Her Lord': The solar boat, accompanied by at least four other boats carrying sacred symbols, spends some time in the watery region of Wernes. Again Re performs an administrative task, distributing fields to the blessed dead who dwell in Wernes.

Hour 3 'She Who Slices Souls': The solar boat moors in the field of the riverbank dwellers and Re revives the dead Osiris.

Hour 4   'Great in Her Powers': Leaving the watery regions, the solar boat starts to follow a complicated, diagonal passageway. This is the corridor used by the dead; it leads to the desert domain of Rosetau, the 'Cavern of Sokar who is on his sand', and to the tomb of Osiris who has been hidden in the underworld by Anubis. The passage is guarded by unnatural snakes equipped with wings, legs and human heads. Unable to sail, the solar boat has to be pulled by four tow-men; it now assumes the form of a fire-breathing snake whose breath lights its way through the darkness.

Hour 5   'She Who is in Her Boat': As the solar boat is dragged across the sandy 'Mound of Sokar' the tow-rope is pulled by seven males, seven females and the solar beetle who stretches down from the sky. The falcon-headed creator god Sokar emerges on the back of the ancient earth god Aker, whose two sphinx-like heads face away from each other at either end of his flat body.

Hour 6   (Midnight) 'Proficient Leader': In the middle of the night the solar boat spends some time in the 'watery depths', the home of Egypt's deceased kings and all the blessed dead. Re is reunited with his own corpse, which takes the form of a beetle rather than a mummy, and Thoth sits before the solar boat.

Hour 7   'She Who Repels the Forces of Chaos and Decapitates the Savage-Faced': The evil serpent Apophis calls to the solar boat in an attempt to halt its progress. He is defeated by Isis, Seth and Serket, and is cut to pieces. Re now rests in the cavern of Osiris, while the enemies of Osiris are bound and decapitated by a knife-wielding, cat-headed being. Twelve star gods and twelve star goddesses suggest the passage of time.

Hour 8   'The Coffer of Her Deities': A band of human-headed staffs, each armed with a knife, continues to slay the enemies of the sun boat. Re encounters the 'Cavern-Dwellers', Egypt's most secret and ancient gods. They sit on the hieroglyphic symbol for 'cloth', and cry out with joy as Re passes their crypts.

Hour 9 'The Wise Protector of Her Lord': Re meets the twelve fire-spitting cobras who protect Osiris and who feed off the blood of enemies.

Hour 10 'The Raging One, Who Boils the Rebel Alive': A last judgement, where the damned are punished by eight aspects of the lion goddess Sekhmet and their bodies are destroyed by Horus. Meanwhile, the bodies of the drowned, who have been claimed by the gods, float peacefully in the water. They will be granted life after death even though they have not been accorded a proper funeral. The solar Eye, or Eye of Horus, is healed by Thoth and Sekhmet.

Hour 11 'The Instructor, Lady of the Sacred Boat, at Whose Emergence the Rebels are Punished': The punishment of the damned continues. Isis and Nephthys take the form of serpents and prepare for the sunrise by carrying the crowns of the two lands to the goddess Neith of Sais.

Hour 12 'Who Sees the Beauty of Re': The divine crew, now twelve males and thirteen females, drag the sun boat and the weary Re through the body of the coiled snake Mehen, 'life of the gods'. They pass through a liminal region that is neither part of the underworld nor part of the ordered world. Emerging, Re is reborn as the youthful Khepri. He enters his day boat to sail over the eastern horizon and Shu seals the entrance to the underworld.

THE SUN AND THE SNAKES

Re found his greatest enemy, and one of his most loyal defenders, among the snakes of the underworld. The plethora of serpent deities, and the profusion of snakes and snake-like beings who writhed and slithered in the passageways of the *Duat* – some with human heads and limbs, some with human bodies and serpent heads, others with multiple heads or heads at each end of the body – reflect the love–hate relationship that the living Egyptians enjoyed with the snakes who shared their land. Long, thin Egypt incorporated diverse habitats and climates, ranging from hot, dry deserts, sand dunes and rocky mountains to oases, wetlands and the cool Mediterranean coast, and this diversity of habitat is reflected in the diversity of snakes represented, with great accuracy, in two-dimensional art.

Snakes were very much a mixed blessing. A resident snake would protect the granaries (which, in the absence of money, were effectively bank-vaults) against the rats and mice who would not only eat all the grain, but who might also spread disease. A relatively harmless snake might even ward off other, more dangerous serpents. However, no one wanted to share their home with a snake, and so, while the *Pyramid Texts* included spells specifically designed to ward off snakes, *Papyrus Ebers* suggested, quite sensibly, that those suffering an infestation should try blocking the snake hole with an onion bulb. A snake bite may have been a rare event, but it was always a serious wound; it has been estimated that one in ten bites from the relatively docile Egyptian cobra would have proved fatal, while the adder, or asp, inflicted a far more painful, and far more poisonous, venom. The author of the specialist medical document known today as the *Brooklyn Snake Papyrus* listed thirty-eight different types of snake, describing the appearance of each and giving instructions for the treatment of a bite.[40]

Ophidiophobia – the fear of snakes – is one of the most common phobias in our modern world, where even those who have no prospect of seeing live snakes in their natural habitat may find them both frightening and disgusting. As babies and young children generally do not share this fear, it seems that it may be, at least in part, a learned response. Certainly the Egyptians seem to have experienced respect rather than repulsion. The snake's unsegmented, limbless body and its habit of living underground suggested links with the afterlife, while its ability to slough its skin and so, apparently, regenerate after death, a link with the solar creators: both Atum and Amen could be represented as land or water snakes.

Snakes were recognized as very early beings. The Hermopolitan creation myth confirms that there were four female snakes at the very beginning of the world, while *Coffin Texts* spell 312 speaks of the 'serpents which the Sole Lord [the creator god] made before Isis came into being'; these early snakes helped with the work of creation before vanishing. While the *Pyramid Texts* provide vague references to the snakes who will hinder the progress of the dead king as he journeys towards his destiny, the First Intermediate Period tomb of the provincial ruler Ankhtifi at Moalla provides the first specific mention of the 'sandbank of Apophis', which threatens to obstruct the corridor through the *Duat*. The danger here is that the solar boat will founder on the coils of the giant snake, just as a real boat might become trapped on a sandbank in the Nile. From this time onwards, the awful serpent makes regular appearances in the funerary literature where, with his sandbank coils, his hypnotic powers and his impressive ability to drink and drain the waters of the *Duat*, he is a danger both to the solar boat and to the dead. *Coffin Texts* spell 414 offers some protection with its instructions for 'Driving Apophis from the Boat of Re':[41]

*I have fallen down and have crawled away, because I am he of
the was-sceptre, the Great Power at the neck of Geb. O you
entourage of Re, of the right-hand and the left-hand* (a reference
to the two crews who powered the larger Nile boats), *regard
me as one wholly unique, for Re has spoken to me, I have
driven off the rebel, I have made Apophis impotent . . .*

Apophis is an immense, aggressive serpent of obscure origins.
He might be the son of Mehet-Weret, or a snake who grew from
the saliva of the goddess Neith within the waters of Nun, or
simply an ancient, timeless being who came into existence in the
primeval waters long before the time of creation. His name, the
'great babbler', suggests that he is capable of making a loud noise,
but not necessarily of producing rational speech; the funerary
texts imply that he lives in water. He is a malevolent snake (or,
just occasionally, a crocodile or turtle) with no redeeming features,
who embodies the forces of chaos and non-being and who, since
the creation of the world, has been the sworn enemy of Re. When
he is illustrated in the funerary texts he is often shown restrained
or chopped into sections, so that the deceased may be protected
against him. Every night Apophis attacks the solar boat as it sails
through the dark and dangerous underworld; every night he is
defeated and destroyed; every day he regenerates so that he might
attack again, and again, and again. The *Coffin Texts* confirm that
the evil eye of Apophis is able to hypnotize everyone in the solar
boat; fortunately Seth is able to resist and to 'bend him with
his hand'. The *Book of the Dead* chapter 108 tells us that the
awesome serpent, thirty cubits long with gleaming teeth and
foreparts of flint, will swallow seven cubits of the great waters,
and thus halt the progress of the solar boat. Fortunately Seth is
once again on hand to threaten him with an iron lance, and cause
him to vomit up the waters.

Apophis can be captured and killed in many and various ways.

He might be slaughtered by the valiant Seth, by the protective goddesses Isis, Neith and Serket, by the loyal Eye of Re, or by Re-Atum himself taking the form of a mongoose. He might be speared by the deceased or hacked to pieces by the Great Tom Cat of Re, a knife-wielding, feline version of the sun god, who is known to have killed Apophis under the *ished* tree of Heliopolis before splitting the tree in two to create the twin trees of the horizon. He might be captured in a magical net thrown by monkeys, or be forced to ingest his victims, whose twelve heads will then emerge from his coils to consume his body.

Back in the living Egypt, Apophis was identified with all of Egypt's enemies. Even though they might be many miles away, these enemies could be thwarted by remote magic. Kings could, for example, employ the ritual of 'hitting the ball', first seen during the 18th Dynasty reign of Tuthmosis III, which required the king to literally strike a ball with a stick so that he might symbolically destroy the malignant eye of Apophis. A different ritual, the 'Overthrowing of Apophis', was performed at the Karnak temple of Mut, and involved destroying wax images of the enemies on a brazier. As a lioness or a cat, and a loyal daughter of Re, Mut was well-suited to dealing with a troublesome snake, while fire, with its obvious solar connections, was a sure and certain means of destruction. This ritual is detailed in *Papyrus Bremner-Rhind*, a collection of four ritual writings known today as the *Songs of Isis and Nephthys*, the *Ritual of Bringing in Sokar*, the *Book of Overthrowing Apophis* and the *Names of Apophis, Which Shall Not Be*. The lengthy section dedicated to the destruction of Apophis and the enemies of Re and the king details rituals to be 'performed daily in the temple of Amen-Re, Lord of the Thrones of the Two Lands, who dwells in Karnak'. The rituals involve spitting on Apophis, trampling him with the left foot, smiting him with a spear, binding him, slashing him with a knife and burning him while reciting potent spells:[42]

The magic spell to be uttered when putting Apophis on the fire. Recite: Be thou utterly spat upon, O Apophis, get thee back, thou foe of Re; fall, creep away, take thee off! I have turned thee back, I have cut thee up, and Re is triumphant over thee, O Apophis – FOUR TIMES. Be thou spat upon, O Apophis – FOUR TIMES. Get thee back, thou rebel; be thou annihilated! Verily I have burned thee, verily I have destroyed thee, I have condemned thee to all ill, that thou mayest be annihilated, that thou mayest be utterly spat upon, that thou may be utterly non-existent . . .

Both Re and the dead Osiris might be shielded from evil by the thick, heavy coils of Mehen, another huge underworld snake, but this time the benign possessor of a great and mysterious knowledge. Mehen is the very opposite of Apophis: with the help of the deceased, he guards the captured enemies of Re. The first, unequivocal, written references to him are found in the *Coffin Texts*. In spells 758–60 he appears as the Coiled One whose boat navigates nine concentric roads, four being roads of fire, for all eternity. Illustrations show Re sitting on a throne at the centre of this realm of Mehen, wearing a crown of snakes. By the New Kingdom Mehen has joined the crew of the night boat of Re to guide its passage through the underworld. Now his heavy coils are used both to protect Re and to trap his enemies.

A far earlier mention, in *Pyramid Texts* spell 332, 'I am this one who has escaped from the coiled serpent', is either a reference to the serpent Mehen (who here might be identified with the evil Apophis), or to the board game of the same name. *Mehen*, the snake game, was popular throughout the Predynastic Period and Old Kingdom, but disappeared at the end of the First Intermediate Period when the god Mehen started to play a more prominent role in the *Coffin Texts*.[43] Whether or not this is a coincidence is unclear – had the game been prohibited for religious reasons, or had it merely fallen out of fashion? Board games were considered an effective means of linking the living with alternative worlds, and so it comes as little surprise to find *mehen* featuring on tomb walls. Played on a circular board shaped like a long snake, coiled so that it resembled a tightly wound spring with scale-like slots carved along its back, the object of the game was to race a token or tokens around the snake, working inwards towards the centre from the tail to the head. Moves were determined either by throwing gaming sticks, or by guessing the number of marbles held in an opponent's hand.

While Mehen was a coiled snake, the Ouroboros, a personification of time who might also be considered an aspect of Mehen, was a long, uncoiled snake who swallowed his own tail (or swallowed the hours) to form an unbroken hoop or circle symbolizing eternity and the state of non-existence which always encloses the world. Although the concept of the Ouroboros is known from the Old Kingdom (*Pyramid Texts* spell 393 describes this curious being: 'your tail be on your mouth, O snake'), its first unequivocal illustration is found on the second gilded shrine recovered from the tomb of Tutankhamen where, named Mehen, it appears as a snake encircling the head and feet of the mummified king. The *Book of Gates* emphasizes this connection between snakes and time by showing the twelve hour-goddesses of night standing either side of a pit housing a long, twisted snake which represents infinite time.

THE SHIPWRECKED SAILOR

Just one lengthy, snake-based myth has survived. The Middle Kingdom story of *The Shipwrecked Sailor* is preserved on a single papyrus of unknown provenance.[44] The papyrus shows no sign of damage, but the way that the scribe, Amen-aa, son of Ameny, plunges straight into his story has led to speculation that he may have omitted the very beginning of his tale.

Even by Egyptian standards this is a fantastic, complex myth told mainly in the first person, with a tale (told by the anonymous snake) within a tale (told by the anonymous sailor) within a tale (told by the scribe Amen-aa). As we advance deeper into the story's coils we enter increasingly unreal worlds. Accepted interpretations of this myth range from a simple folk or fairy tale, through a fictionalized account of the sun's daily voyage across the sky or a coded manual for living the ideal life, to an allegory dealing with mankind's lonely journey through the cosmos to stand before a nameless creator god.

The island that will sink beneath the water as the sailor departs is the reverse of the mound of creation that emerges from the waters of Nun. The location of this unnamed, fictional, disappearing island is, naturally, hard to pinpoint although there is a clue in the snake's title, 'Lord of Punt'. Punt was a real, far-distant and now vanished trading post lying somewhere along the Eritrean/Ethiopian coast. Travel to Punt meant first dragging a dismantled ship overland from Thebes to the Red Sea coast, then a lengthy voyage on the dangerous, unfamiliar waters. Good river sailors though they were, the Egyptians were never very confident on the sea, so a successful expedition to Punt soon became the hallmark of a divinely inspired reign. The falling star that burns up the village of giant snakes is equally difficult to explain but, if the myth has to have some basis in reality, it might perhaps be a reference to a falling meteorite. The snake, sole survivor of this tragedy, promises the sailor, another sole survivor, that he will soon find his way home, and that he will eventually be buried with the proper ritual in his local cemetery. This would have been a promise of immense comfort as all Egyptians hoped to be buried in their homeland, where they knew that they would be accorded the funeral rites that would assure them eternal life.

[The great ship had at last reached its port. The sails were furled, the gangplank had been lowered, and the sailors were hurrying ashore in high good humour, eager to spend their wages. Their long voyage had made them hungry for beer, for fresh bread and meat and, of course, for women. But not everyone was happy, and not everyone was rushing to disembark. Huddled in his cabin, the high official sat silent and unmoving on his stool. He had failed in his mission, and was now very frightened indeed. How would the king react to his failure? What would be his fate?]

A royal attendant approached the high official, speaking with all the familiarity of a favoured servant:

'Cheer up, my lord. We have reached home safely, and our boat is now secure in its mooring. You should be thanking the gods for our good luck. We have survived a long and difficult journey, and have travelled all the way from Nubia without any loss of life among the crew. And that is a very good thing indeed.

'Now listen to me. You must pull yourself together, and snap out of your depression. Have a wash and a shave, put on clean clothes, and make yourself look decent. Prepare to face the king and be ready to answer when questioned. You will be able to explain to him exactly what happened, and your speech will save you.'

The high official, brooding over his shattered career, made no move. And the attendant, irritated by his silence, lost all patience with him:

'Do as you like then, it is up to you. Give in, and do nothing to save yourself. It is a waste of time talking to you. But remember, disaster can turn to unexpected triumph. Something similar happened to me once. Listen, while I tell you my story:

'A long time ago I too went to the land of mines in the service of my king. I sailed on the great green sea in a massive ship, one hundred and twenty cubits long and forty cubits wide, crewed by a hundred and twenty of Egypt's most experienced sailors. A fine, lion-hearted bunch they were, the bravest and the best in the whole land. They could predict a storm before it broke, and see a torrent of rain before it happened.

'For many days our voyage went well and we made good time with a strong wind behind us. Then, with little warning, a violent storm broke while we were in the middle of the great green sea, far away from land. The heavens grew dark and angry, and the sea threw up huge foam-flecked waves, each larger than the last. Our boat rocked dangerously, and there was nothing we could do. We clung to the ropes in fear until one enormous wave – it must have been at least eight cubits high – smashed down on us, snapping the mast and bringing it thundering down on the deck. That was the end. The ship sank, and the rest of the crew were drowned. I was the only survivor.

'The waves carried me to a sandy shore and I crawled up the beach to the shelter of a grove of trees. And there I lay semi-conscious for three days and three nights. On the fourth day, slowly regaining my strength and my senses, I staggered to my feet and looked around for something to eat, for I was famished. I was very lucky. I discovered that I was on an island stocked with the most tempting of foods. I found figs and grapes, and all kinds of fine vegetables including cucumbers as tasty as those picked from the best gardens. There were plump fish swimming in the sea, and fat fowl sitting in the trees. There was nothing that I wanted to eat that I could not find. I ate and ate until I was stuffed full and could eat no more. Then I cut myself a fire drill, lit a fire, and made a burnt offering to the gods who had saved me.

'Then I heard it. A low rumbling, thundering noise. The earth shook, the trees splintered, and I fell to the ground, squeezed my eyes shut and hid my face in fear. I thought that another enormous wave was about to carry me out to sea, and I clung to the ground in panic. When I plucked up the courage to open my eyes I found that I was facing something far worse than a mere wave. A gigantic golden snake was slithering towards me, his head raised up, as if about to strike. This was no ordinary snake. He was at least thirty cubits in length. His eyebrows were formed from precious lapis lazuli and his beard was long – at least two cubits – and impressive.

'The snake noticed me cowering on the ground, and hissed:

'"Who brought you here, sailor? If you do not tell me at once, I will destroy you utterly."

'Trembling with fear I tried to make a sensible reply, but could only stutter. The snake listened in silence, then lowered his magnificent head and picked me up in his mouth. He carried me to his den, and placed me gently on the ground. Then he spoke to me again, this time with greater kindness.

'"Who brought you here, sailor, to my island in the green sea?"

'And I answered him with a rush of words, telling him all about the king's mission, the magnificent ship, the terrible storm, the enormous wave and the death of my companions – the best of Egypt's men.

'He spoke again to me, hissing softly:

'"Do not be afraid, sailor. Do not tremble with fear now you have come to me. The gods have decided that you should live, and have brought you to this spirit island. It is an island that lacks for nothing that a man might desire. It is an island full of good things. You shall live here for four months. Then a ship will come from Egypt, crewed by your friends. You will go home with them and, eventually, after a long life, will die in your hometown."

'Then the snake grew thoughtful and sad.

'"How happy is the man who is able to tell of his adventures long after his suffering has ended. I have a similar story of disaster to tell, but my story can have no happy ending. Many years ago I lived on this blessed island with my wife and my brothers and their wives and children. All together we were seventy-five giant snakes plus my much-loved little daughter, who had been granted to me by the gods after many years of longing and prayer. We were one happy family, and life was good. But one day, while I was away hunting for food, a flaming star fell from the sky. It burned up our village, and when I returned to my home everyone had died. I myself wished to die when I saw the charred heap of corpses, but I was destined to live on, alone. And I tell you this. If you are brave, and strong in heart, you will see your home and hug your children and kiss your wife once again."

'Quaking on the ground before the magnificent snake I felt a wave of gratitude wash over me. I was not going to be eaten – I would see my home and family again. Impulsively, I spoke without thinking:

'"I will tell the king of Egypt of your kindness to me. I will send you precious oils, and fragrant perfumes, and ships full of treasure. Everyone in the world shall hear of your goodness. I will slaughter geese and oxen for you as a burnt offering. For this is how we treat the gods who befriend lost Egyptians far away from home."

'At this the snake hissed and spat with laughter, for my words must have seemed foolish to one so great.

'"Don't be foolish. I know that you are a poor sailor who could never afford such splendid gifts. Besides, I am the Lord of Punt, and I have all the oils and precious perfumes that I need right here on my island. Just make sure that my deeds are known in your land – that will be reward enough for me. Now,

I tell you this. This island will vanish when you leave it, and turn to water and waves and dissolve into the great sea. Once you have gone from me, you can never come back."

'And everything happened exactly as the giant snake had predicted. The ship came, crewed by people from my village. I sighted it from the top of a tall tree and went to tell the snake what I had seen. Of course, he already knew. I made my farewell, bowing low, and the snake gave me precious gifts: perfumes, oils, eye-paint, giraffes' tails, huge lumps of incense, elephant tusks, long-tailed monkeys and much, much more. I loaded these presents on to the ship, and we sailed north, to Egypt. Two months later we reached the royal palace. I disembarked, and I presented my goods to the king. He rewarded me by making me a royal attendant with servants of my own. And this is how my disaster was turned into triumph.'

As he finished his long story the attendant looked encouragingly at the high official. But the official was not brave enough to face up to his problems and make the best of a bad situation. He spoke for the first time, with great bitterness:

'Do not try to help me, my friend. My doom is come, and who would give water to a goose that is about to be slaughtered?'

[He refused to leave the ship and continued to sit huddled on his chair, quaking with fear.]

II

DESTRUCTION

You have gone, but you will return, you have slept but you will awake, you have died but you will live.

Pyramid Texts *spell 670*

4

THE DEATH OF OSIRIS

The crown of Egypt passed from divine father to divine son until Osiris, son of Geb, inherited the throne to rule with his beautiful sister-wife Isis by his side. Osiris proved a wise and just king, but his reign was marred by a fierce sibling rivalry that culminated in his murder at the hand of his brother Seth.

THE OSIRIS MYTH

Although the elaborate tale of the death and resurrection of Osiris is one of Egypt's most important myths, it is not preserved in its full form before the Ptolemaic Period. The earlier references – hymns and prayers, non-narrative fragments of texts, and illustrations – conform to the long-established Egyptian reluctance to commit anything bad to writing, lest that bad thing should bring its own bad luck. They therefore stress the good news – the resurrection of Osiris – while shying away from the awful detail of his betrayal and death. So we learn, in *Pyramid Texts* spell 532, that 'they have found Osiris, his brother Seth having laid him low in Nedyt'. Nedyt, literally 'the striking place', was a town in the Abydos province. Spell 477 tells us that Osiris has fallen 'on his side' (mummies routinely being laid to rest on their sides). Spell 364, in contrast, is one of three references which imply that

Osiris was drowned: 'Horus has mustered the gods for you, and they will never escape from you in the place where you drowned'; while spell 218 hints that Seth did not act alone: 'See what Seth and Thoth have done, your two brothers who do not know how to mourn you.' Equally vague references infer that Seth was subsequently tried before a tribunal of the gods, and that he was punished for his wickedness by being made to carry the dead Osiris. Finally, it seems, Seth and Horus joined forces to assist the dead king: together they provided the twin ladders that would allow him to ascend to the stars, and together they executed the malevolent snake spirit who threatened his safety. As a reward for his good behaviour, Seth was then married to either Nephthys or Neith.

With the crime itself obscured it is difficult to determine what sparks Seth's murderous assault. Cryptic references hint that Seth may have become enraged when kicked by his brother, or that he may simply have grown jealous of Osiris' marriage with the desirable Isis. The modus operandi, too, is obscure and there are apparently no witnesses to the killing, although again there are suggestions that Seth either drowned Osiris, or transformed into a wild animal to maul him. It may even be that Osiris, as a god, had to suffer a double death and was therefore killed twice by different methods.

The *Great Hymn to Osiris*, carved on the 18th Dynasty stela of Amenmose, is our most complete, purely Egyptian version of the myth, but even here Seth's role in the tragedy is not made explicit and the villain is given the soubriquet 'the disturber'. This brief extract tells most of the tale:[45]

> His sister was his guard,
> She who drives off the foes,
> Who stops the deeds of the disturber
> By the power of her utterance.

The clever-tongued whose speech fails not,
Effective in the word of command,
Mighty Isis who protected her brother,
Who sought him without wearying.
Who roamed the land lamenting,
Not resting till she found him,
Who made a shade with her plumage,
Created breath with her wings.
Who jubilated, joined her brother,
Raised the weary one's inertness,
Received the seed, bore the heir,
Raised the child in solitude,
His abode unknown.

A thousand years later, Diodorus Siculus preserved a full but regrettably short version of the myth; the pure Egyptian tale had by now been diluted by Hellenistic concepts and concerns, but his account is worth repeating in full:[46]

When Osiris was ruling over Egypt as its lawful king, he was murdered by his brother Typhon (Seth), a violent and impious man; Typhon then divided the body of the slain man into twenty-six pieces and gave one portion to each of the band of murderers, since he wanted all of them to share in the pollution and felt that in this way he would have in them steadfast supporters and defenders of his rule. But Isis, the sister and wife of Osiris, avenged his murder with the aid of her son Horus, and after slaying Typhon and his accomplices, became queen over Egypt.

The most detailed version of the Osiris myth survives in Plutarch's masterpiece *Isis and Osiris*, which, written in c.AD 120, adds Roman influences to the tale.[47] Some of the elements of

Plutarch's story – the details of the elaborate chest-coffin, for example – are likely to be late additions for the benefit of his non-Egyptian readers. Uncertain himself as to the accuracy of his tale, Plutarch occasionally gives different versions of events. His myth, adapted to fit with traditional Egyptian accounts, is as follows:

Nut bore her brother Geb two sons, Osiris and Seth, and two daughters, Isis and Nephthys. Osiris, her first-born son, was all that a mother could wish for, and the people rejoiced in his birth. But Seth, her second-born son, was troubled and angry, and his birth caused Nut great pain as he punched his way into the world through his mother's side. In the fullness of time Osiris became king of Egypt with his sister-wife Isis as his consort.

Seated on his golden throne, Osiris ruled as a caring and just king. He rescued the people from their savage state by teaching them how to plant crops, obey laws and worship the gods, while Isis, who was as wise as she was beautiful, taught the women the mysteries of weaving, baking and brewing. With Egypt civilized and at peace, Osiris travelled the whole world, beguiling the people with his poetry and songs. Back home, Isis ruled wisely on her husband's behalf and Egypt flourished. Isis, however, had recognized what Osiris had failed to see: Seth was deeply unhappy with his brother's rule. For the brilliant Seth, who so longed to be king, was being forced to stand by as his dull but worthy brother ruled in his place. While Osiris was away on his travels Seth managed to hide his discontent behind a smiling face, for he knew that the all-seeing Isis was watching him. But when Osiris returned home Seth started to plan his brother's death.

Having recruited seventy-two evil men as his co-conspirators, Seth planned a magnificent banquet. The guest of honour was his brother Osiris. The guests were served with delicious food, and with copious amounts of beer and wine. Finally, when Seth judged that enough had been consumed, he signalled to his servants, and a long, narrow chest was dragged into the centre of the chamber. The chest was a beautiful piece of work. Carved by a master-craftsman from the finest wood, it was inlaid with bands of gold and silver and decorated inside and out with ebony, ivory and semi-precious stones. The guests marvelled at the chest and each coveted it.

Seth spoke. The chest was a game: the climax of the evening's entertainment. Whoever could lie down inside the chest could keep it. There was a scramble as Seth's allies rushed forward and attempted to squeeze their bulky bodies into the narrow space. But none fitted. Then the slender Osiris, his perceptions blunted by the wine, stepped forward to take his turn. He lay down in the chest. It was a perfect fit, as Seth knew it would be – he had secretly measured his brother's body weeks before. Before Osiris could sit up to claim his prize Seth slammed the lid shut and bolted it. The elaborately decorated chest, tailored exactly to Osiris' measurements, had become his coffin.

The party was over. Seth coated the coffin in lead, then dragged it to the Nile and threw it in. Caught by the current, the coffin slowly sailed northwards into the great green sea. Seth laughed out loud. With Osiris dead and vanished, he could now claim his throne. And these events happened in the twenty-eighth year of Osiris' reign.

News of the tragedy soon reached Isis in her palace at Koptos. Distraught, the queen cut her hair and assumed mourning as a mark of respect for her vanished husband. Refusing to forget Osiris, the grieving Isis spent many years wandering the length and breadth of Egypt, asking everyone she encountered if they had seen an ornate, sealed chest. None had. But eventually she heard a rumour that a precious chest had washed ashore in the faraway land of Byblos. Here the chest had lain against a young cypress tree, and the tree had grown to envelop the chest so that it became completely hidden within its trunk. The tree had grown tall and beautiful, until eventually it was cut down and used as a pillar in the palace of the king of Byblos.

Isis made her way to the palace of Byblos, where she sat next to a splendid fountain and wept bitter tears. Here the queen's serving maids found her, and spoke kindly with her. And Isis, putting aside her grief, braided their hair and perfumed their skin. When the queen of Byblos saw her maids she wished to meet the woman who had effected such a transformation, and summoned Isis. The queen and the goddess became firm friends, and the goddess became nursemaid to the queen's younger son.

Isis allowed the baby prince to suckle her finger rather than her breast. At night, when no one could see, she burned away the mortal parts of his body so that he might gain eternal life. At the same time she transformed into a bird so that she might fly round and round the pillar that held Osiris. And as she flew around the pillar, she gave great cries of grief. But her cries woke the queen of Byblos who rushed to the hall. Seeing Isis in the form of a bird, and her baby son a ball of fire, she screamed in horror. This sudden noise broke the potent spell and denied her son his chance of immortality. Isis regained human form and demanded the pillar that supported the roof of the hall. Shocked by what she had seen, the queen at once agreed. Taking the pillar from beneath the roof Isis cut into its wood: the discarded splinters would be venerated forever in the temple of Isis at Byblos. When Osiris' coffin was revealed Isis let out an ear-piercing shriek – a shriek so loud that the baby prince died from shock. Isis took both the coffin and the elder son of the queen of Byblos, placed them in a boat and set sail for Egypt.

The boat came to rest in the bleak Egyptian desert. In a secluded place Isis opened the coffin and seeing the beloved face within, kissed it and wept. The young prince of Byblos approached silently from behind, for he wanted to see what great treasure might be held in the ornate chest. But when he caught sight of Isis' awful face, he died of fright. Isis hid Osiris in his coffin and went to visit the Nile Delta.

Seth, hunting wild boar alone in the moonlight, stumbled across the remains of his brother. Incredulous and furious, he hacked Osiris into fourteen pieces and flung them far and wide. Transforming themselves into birds, Isis and her sister Nephthys searched high and low, recovering the scattered parts one by one until only the penis was missing. This would never be found, for the greedy Nile fish had eaten it. Isis, a divine healer with awesome magical powers, was able to equip her husband with a replica organ. She then bandaged him, and sang the spell that would bring him back to a semblance of life. Transforming herself once again into a bird, she hovered over her husband's restored body. Her magic was very powerful; nine months later she bore Osiris a son.

Osiris was alive, but he was no longer a living king. He abandoned his family and retreated in sorrow to the underworld where he would henceforth rule as king of the dead. Isis was forced to flee with the baby Horus to the papyrus marshes. Here she protected her son with her potent magic until he was old enough to claim his inheritance.

With the appearance of Osiris, Isis, Seth and their shadowy sister Nephthys we meet the final four members of the Ennead who, in the Heliopolitan tradition, were the direct ancestors of Egypt's living kings.

CEMETERY DOGS

Osiris rose from obscure northern origins, perhaps starting life as a minor fertility or vegetation god. Initially linked to the dead king only – the king being the sole Egyptian with a spirit strong enough to escape the confines of the tomb – by the end of the Old Kingdom he was offering an afterlife to everyone. This promise of life beyond death, and his denial of the corruption of the flesh, made Osiris an intensely comforting figure to the masses. As his power and influence grew he was able to usurp the stories developed by other deities until he had accumulated a complete and complex mythology of his own. Unable to compete with his powerful appeal, the priests of Re absorbed the upstart into the Heliopolitan cycle.

Some of the elements 'borrowed' from other mythologies are obvious: the story of Osiris' resurrection, for example, comes from the obscure cult of Andjety of Busiris (ancient Djedu; modern Abusir), while his role as king of the dead was taken from Anubis, the jackal-headed guardian of the cemeteries, 'the dog who swallows millions'. One of his most frequently used titles, 'foremost of the westerners', was usurped from Khentamentiu, the original canine god of the Abydos cemetery and patron of its Old Kingdom temple. Later, Osiris would also be equated with a range of foreign resurrected earth gods including the Semitic Tammuz, the Phrygian Attis and, more specifically, the Greek Dionysos. Whereas Osiris had died and been reborn, Dionysos had been born twice: once when ripped from his mortal mother Semele, and again when he was delivered from the thigh of his divine father Zeus. Dionysos offered his faithful a lifetime of secret rituals and ecstatic experiences culminating in union with the god and salvation beyond death. This was a tempting prospect. As the austere cult of Osiris retained its popularity with the Egyptian people, the more flamboyant cult of Dionysos flourished among Greek settlers in Egypt.

The association between hungry feral dogs and ill-guarded cemeteries full of shallow pit graves would have been an obvious and terrifying one to a people determined that their bodies would survive for all eternity. It is little wonder that they wanted the jackal Anubis on their side. Following Osiris' rise to prominence, Anubis was re-branded as the first embalmer, the scientist who developed the rituals of mummification to preserve the dead Osiris. As the 'master of [embalming] secrets' he was now given the specific role of caring for the deceased during the mummification process. We know that Anubis took these duties very seriously. A Late Period tale tells how, when Seth disguised himself as a leopard in a failed attempt to snatch the body of Osiris, Anubis caught him, branded him all over his body, then flayed him alive. This, apparently, is how the hitherto monochrome leopard acquired its spots.

Anubis was originally considered to be the son of the cow goddess Hesat, 'the wild one', who might also be the mother of the dead king, and of the Apis and Mnevis bulls. An all-white cow, Hesat's milk had strong healing powers. In later mythologies Anubis became the legitimate son of Osiris and Isis. Alternatively, he might be the illegitimate son of Osiris, born when the amorous but apparently shortsighted god mistook his sister-in-law (and sister) Nephthys for his wife Isis. Nephthys slept with Osiris and became pregnant but, fearing the reaction of her brother-husband Seth, exposed her new-born infant son. When Isis learned about the child, she used dogs to track him down. Isis then raised Anubis to become her faithful attendant. As the exposure of unwanted infants was a Greek tradition, it is unlikely that this is an original Egyptian tale. It is, however, one of the few myths to feature Nephthys, 'mistress of the house' or 'mistress of the temple', who otherwise acts as a pale support to, and reflection of, her more forceful sister. Together, Isis and Nephthys may be identified with the two horizons, or with the east and west banks of the Nile; the east and west, in turn, may be associated with the life cycle of the sun and of the living.

Wepwawet, Lord of Abydos, is yet another ancient cemetery jackal. In some versions of the Osiris myth it is he, rather than Anubis, who helps Isis to restore Osiris to a semblance of life. His name, 'opener of the ways', refers to his role as a guide through the complex pathways of the underworld.

KING OF THE DEAD

Osiris invariably appears as an uncompromising mummy. He is a white, tightly bandaged being whose crossed arms hold the crook and flail symbolizing the principal royal duties of leadership and punishment, and whose unwrapped head is fitted with a curled beard and an *atef* crown: an elaborate, composite crown which, in Osiris' case, takes the form of the white crown worn with an ostrich feather on each side. He quickly came to represent, jointly and severally, all of Egypt's dead kings. They, mummified like their new sovereign, were eternal monarchs in the afterlife while their successors, the Horus kings, ruled the living Egypt. But Osiris did not only symbolize death, he was also a god of rejuvenation, agriculture and the inundation, whose occasionally erect penis harked back to his original role as a fertility god. Osiris beds – seeded and watered silhouettes of the god – were placed in New Kingdom tombs so that they might sprout and serve as a living symbol of resurrection. Later, corn mummies – miniature mummies moulded from seed and soil and shaped like the ithyphallic Osiris – were encased in falcon-headed coffins whose inscriptions linked them with Ptah-Sokar-Osiris.

In Osiris' heavily bandaged body we find a neat mythological explanation for the heavily bandaged mummies who lay in Egypt's elite tombs. It is difficult to state which came first, the myth or the mummy, but most experts are agreed that experiments in mummification preceded the fully formed Osirid tale. Artificial mummification was a combined art, science and religious rite; a practical response to a desperate desire to preserve the corpse in a lifelike state for ever. This desire for preservation was itself a direct response to the belief that only those with a lifelike body had any hope of living beyond death. The corpse served as the vital bridge between the spirit of the deceased and the sustaining offerings provided by the living.

When did this very particular belief develop? We cannot hope to understand the religious beliefs of the illiterate Predynastic Egyptians, but we do know that they maintained well-regulated cemeteries where they provided their dead with grave-goods, and this strongly suggests a hope of some form of existence beyond death. By the 5th Dynasty we have enough textual, artistic and archaeological material to confirm a sophisticated belief that, given the right circumstances, the dead could indeed live again. Those right circumstances included a well-preserved body. Even so, not everyone could look forward to an afterlife free of the grave. Only the king could hope to escape, for he was blessed with three distinctive and ineffably complex spirits or souls which, trapped in his body during his lifetime, would be released at his death, allowing him to sail in the solar boat of Re, dwell in the Field of Reeds or shine as an eternal star in the deep blue sky.

The Egyptians have not left anything resembling a detailed explanation of their three spiritual entities, and it is extremely difficult to translate their subtle ideas using our own words and concepts. However, evidence pieced together from art and religious texts allows us to attempt crude definitions:

The *ba*: an active spirit representing the soul or personality of the deceased. Often depicted as a human-headed bird, the *ba* lived in the tomb but was able to pay flying visits to the land of the living. Gods, too, might have *bas*. The wind was considered to be the *ba* of Shu, while the Apis Bull was the *ba* of Ptah.

The *ka*: a more passive spiritual essence, or life-force, which was created when the body was formed and which could only survive death if the corpse survived in a recognizably human form. The *ka* had to remain close to the body, could never leave the grave and needed constant, sustaining offerings of food and drink. While mere mortals had just one *ka*, gods and kings might have more than one. As everything in existence could be traced back to the original creator Atum, everything in existence could, in theory, be classed as a *ka* of Atum.

The *akh*: an ill-understood spirit representing the immortality of a deceased person which has become effective through the performance of the correct rituals and knowledge of the correct spells. The *akh* did not need to remain close to the corpse, and could survive elsewhere.

The Egyptians knew that all meat – human bodies included – rotted rapidly in their hot climate. But they also knew that the ancient desert pit graves, simple holes scooped out of the sand, held bodies which, while shrunken and tanned, were still recognizably human when exposed by animals or grave robbers. These naturally mummified corpses had skin, internal organs, hair and even finger- and toe-nails in place. They had been preserved by direct contact with the hot and sterile sand, which leached moisture away from the decomposing body and inhibited the growth of bacteria. As long as the Egyptians continued to bury their dead in simple desert pit graves, their bodies would defy death and survive. And, as long as their bodies survived, their *kas*, too, had a chance of survival. The problem was that wealthy Egyptians did not want to be buried in sandy pits. They wanted to provide for a comfortable afterlife, and this meant coffins and stone tombs offering plenty of space for grave-goods. And so a great deal of effort was put into developing a technology which would, as far as possible, replicate the natural drying effect of the desert.

Egypt's earliest mummies conserved the shape of the body, but not the actual tissue. Contracted into a foetal or sleeping position, layers of well-padded, plaster-soaked bandages allowed the undertakers to mould the facial features and the limbs before burial in a short wooden coffin. Beneath the bandages, however, the bodies continued to rot. By the end of the 3rd Dynasty, evisceration followed by a lengthy dehydration in natron salt was becoming routine and the hollow bodies, no longer contracted, were wrapped and buried in long coffins.[48] Centuries of experimentation would lead to the perfection of this technique during the Third Intermediate Period.

Properly mummified, and interred with the correct funerary rituals, the Old Kingdom elite expected to live for ever in their tombs: being an intensely practical people, they packed their eternal houses with everything, from food and drink to toiletries, and even toilets, that they might need to maintain an acceptable standard of living. Only the king would escape to live a new life: the king, therefore, had less need of grave-goods than his people. Eventually, as it was realized that not even the wealthiest of families could hope to take enough provisions to the grave, they started to rely on small-scale models, and on scenes carved and painted on the tomb walls, which could magically come alive to supply everything that was needed. Nevertheless, they did not quite lose the habit of taking valuable goods to the grave, and it was this habit that sparked the incessant robberies which in turn threatened the mummies and their eternal afterlife. It was not until the very end of the Old Kingdom that Osiris became king of all the dead and his afterlife kingdom was thrown open to everyone who could afford a mummified body and a proper funeral. The newly democratized Field of Reeds was a truly wonderful place – the mirror image of living Egypt complete with an unfailing river, fertile fields and a powerful king. It is this perfect land of the perpetually healthy and happy dead, rather than the flawed mortal world, which features on so many tomb walls.

Some versions of the Osiris myth maintain that Isis discovered her husband's intact corpse at Abydos. More usually, however, we are told that Seth dismembered his brother's body and scattered the parts far and wide in order to deny him a proper burial. This would have been a fate almost too horrible to contemplate for any right-thinking Egyptian. There are variations on this theme. Diodorus Siculus tells us that Osiris was hacked into twenty-six pieces, which were then distributed among the followers of Seth, so that all might be considered to have played a part in his demise and all would feel bound to Seth. While some traditions insist on a mere twelve body pieces, Graeco-Roman temple walls might mention forty-two, one for each nome or province. Plutarch records fourteen pieces dispersed throughout the world (which in this case probably means Egypt); he tells us that Isis recovered and restored all but one of these body-parts before burying them in their find-spots:[49]

> *The traditional result of Osiris' dismemberment is that there are many so-called tombs of Osiris in Egypt; for Isis held a funeral for each part when she had found it. Others deny this and assert that she caused effigies of him to be made and these*

> *she distributed among the several cities, pretending that she*
> *was giving them his body, in order that he might receive divine*
> *honours in a greater number of cities, and also that, if Typhon*
> (Seth) *should succeed in overpowering Horus, he might despair*
> *of ever finding the true tomb when so many were pointed out*
> *to him, all of them called the tomb of Osiris.*

The towns blessed with body-parts exploited their link with Osiris to the full, developing tombs for the recovered limbs and, as the willow tree or tamarisk had become associated with his cult, cultivating sacred willow groves. Athribis, for example, claimed to be the location of the god's heart, while at least four rival towns claimed a lost leg. One of these, the tomb of Osiris' left leg, situated on the Nile island of Bigah, was believed to be the source of the Nile inundation.

Just one body-part was missing. Plutarch tells us that no town was able to declare a link with the dead god's penis, as that most important member had been eaten by the rapacious oxyrhynchus fish. Henceforth, or so he believed, the Egyptians avoided eating fish, classifying them as unclean animals. Archaeology reveals a very different story, with vast quantities of Nile fish – an invaluable, free source of protein – consumed by rich and poor alike. The town built to house the workers on the Giza pyramid field even included a large fish-processing plant. Nevertheless, given the plethora of snake and bird deities, it is striking that Egypt recognized remarkably few fish gods. While Atum might take the form of an eel, and Hathor and Neith might appear as the two fish (a *lates* and a *tilapia*) who guided the solar boat across the Turquoise Lake, only the Delta deity Hatmehit, 'she who is before the fishes', was an entirely piscine (or, perhaps, dolphin) deity.

Tradition maintained that Osiris had been born at Rosetau, in the cemetery-desert just outside Memphis. This was a highly appropriate birthplace as Rosetau, 'mouth of the passageways', was one of the recognized entrances to the underworld. While he was worshipped informally in the temples and shrines of many local gods, the two main temples of Osiris were situated at the Delta city of Busiris and the southern city of Abydos. Today ancient Busiris has almost entirely vanished but Abydos, some 80 miles downstream of Thebes, survives as a vast archaeological site housing, among other things, Egypt's earliest royal burials and an important series of New Kingdom temples. Already, by the 12th Dynasty, Abydos had been identified as the last resting place of Osiris, and excavations had been conducted to try to identify his tomb. Eventually the 1st Dynasty mud-brick tomb of King Djer was re-roofed, refurbished and provided with a stairway so that it might serve as his cenotaph. This part of the cemetery now became Poker, the domain of Osiris. A basalt statue, added to the 'tomb' during the 13th Dynasty, showed the dead Osiris impregnating Isis in the form of a bird.

The Old Kingdom elite, believing that proximity in death to either a god or a king could bring an enhanced afterlife, had hoped to be buried in the state-run cemeteries surrounding the royal pyramids. Now, as the 12th Dynasty pharaoh Senwosret I dedicated a new temple to Osiris-Khentamentiu at Abydos, the Middle Kingdom middle classes longed for burial close to the tomb of Osiris. This was an impossible dream: despite the development of the new 'North Cemetery', there simply wasn't enough room for everyone. Instead, Abydos became a popular place of pilgrimage, with many Egyptians visiting to watch the ritual performances and dedicate either statues or *mahat* (mud-brick shrines of varying size and complexity, each holding a limestone stela, which could act as dummy burials). The statues were placed in the temple of Osiris-Khentamentiu, while the *mahat* were set up overlooking the processional way linking the temple to the tomb of Osiris. The pilgrims who flocked to Abydos left behind the millions of pottery offerings which have given this part of the site its modern name of Umm el Qa'ab or 'mother of pots'. Those who could not make the journey in life hoped to make it in death, and it became customary for tombs to include one or two miniature boats (one with the sail up, to sail south; one with the sail furled, to row north) which would allow the deceased to visit Abydos.

Middle Kingdom Abydos was a place of festival and public spectacle, all, naturally, centred on the mysteries of Osiris. These rituals, and their incidental snippets of mythology, are recorded on the stela of Ikhernofret, treasurer to Senwosret III, who travelled to Abydos charged with the triple task of adorning the cult statue of the god, refurbishing his portable boat shrine, and overseeing the annual Festival of Osiris, a scripted passion-play using actors to play the parts of the gods, which saw the statue of Osiris travel from his temple to his tomb and back again.[50] With tantalizing brevity, Ikhernofret outlines the four main elements of the dramatized story:

The procession of Wepwawet (during which Osiris is killed?).
The procession to the tomb.
A sojourn at the tomb (during which Osiris is restored).
The triumphant return to the temple, all enemies defeated.

Some kings established large-scale *mahat* at Abydos, with Senwosret III building a particularly splendid cenotaph-temple which may, perhaps, have replaced his Dahshur pyramid as his final burial place. The first king of the New Kingdom, Ahmose I, continued this tradition by building a cenotaph for his grandmother Tetisheri, and it seems that other kings followed suit, although the majority of their monuments are now lost. The most impressive surviving *mahat* are the temples built by the kings of the early 19th Dynasty. Seti I built a small temple for his father, Ramesses I, and an enormous temple for himself. His son, Ramesses II, subsequently completed his father's monument and built his own. Uniquely, Seti's temple has seven sanctuaries dedicated to Osiris, Isis, Horus, Amen-Re, Re-Horakhty, Ptah and the deified king himself. His temple walls preserve a sequence of scenes and images which have allowed Egyptologists to reconstruct the daily rituals performed by the priests. There are references to the Osiris myth and the conception of Horus is illustrated but, as we find elsewhere, there is no depiction of the murder at the heart of the tale. At Abydos, Seti's name – the same name as the murderous Seth – is occasionally written with the image of Osiris replacing that of Seth.

Immediately behind his Abydos temple Seti excavated a subterranean structure with a central hall whose granite roof was supported by giant pillars. This structure is a dummy tomb today known as the Osireion. Although, as far as we know, the Osireion housed neither the king's body nor anything believed to be the body of Osiris, a room opening from the central hall was given the shape and decoration of an enormous sarcophagus, while a channel surrounding the hall effectively provided a ground-water moat, allowing the hall to become the mound of creation.

The struggle between Osiris and Seth has been variously interpreted as the tension between the fertile, controlled Egypt (Osiris) and her chaotic deserts (Seth); as the contrast between the Nile inundation (Osiris) and the storm (Seth); as the struggle between two brothers for their father's crown at the start of the dynastic age; or as a reflection of the ancient (and unproven) tradition of slaying old and infirm kings during the *heb-sed*, the jubilee celebration held after thirty years of rule. However, this was not the first time that the authority of a divine king had been challenged by a close family member. The relationship between Shu and his son Geb was never a good one and Geb, angry that

Shu had forcibly separated him from his beloved sister-wife Nut, eventually rebelled against his father, forcing Shu to retire to the sky. The late dating el-Arish *naos* preserves the damaged tale of this dysfunctional family, a tale which bears a striking resemblance to the tale of Osiris-Heryshef and the uraeus of Re. The *naos* is an inscribed stone temple shrine which, cupboard-like, once held the cult statue of the god but which, when discovered in the late nineteenth century, was being used, tipped on its back, as a water trough for cattle.[51] Reading the *naos* we learn how, following Shu's retreat to the heavens, Geb seized his mother, Tefnut, by force (the implication is that he raped her), effectively separating Shu from his own beloved sister-wife just as Shu had separated Geb from his. After nine dark days of tempest, Geb left the palace wearing his father's crown. However, when he attempted to place the uraeus on his brow the snake's fiery breath killed his companions and burned Geb, who was only saved by placing the sacred hair or wig of Re on his head.

Just as Geb had challenged his father Shu, so there are hints that the good son Osiris may have challenged his father Geb. Quarrels, it seems, were an accepted part of divine family life at a time when there was no accepted mechanism for the crown to pass from undying father to eager son. Nevertheless, the assassination of a king, a grievous offence against *maat* which threatened the safety of the whole nation, was a particularly difficult subject, and so while the Classical authors were happy to spread dramatic tales of intrigue and violence at the Egyptian court – Herodotus, for example, tells of the attempted murder of the fictional King Sesostris who narrowly escaped death by fire – the Egyptians themselves record just two assassinations in over 3,000 years of royal rule. These two cases, the murders of the 12th Dynasty King Amenemhat I and the 20th Dynasty King Ramesses III, are remarkably similar. In both the plot is hatched in the royal harem, and in both the aim is not to abolish the system of kingship, but to divert the succession away from an already appointed heir.

While the murder of Ramesses III is recorded in a straightforward manner in a series of legal papyri detailing the trial of the assassins and their accomplices, the death of Amenemhat I is preserved in the more opaque *Instruction of King Amenemhat*, a document which purports to be a letter addressed by the dead king to his son Senwosret I but which was actually written by the scribe Khety, soon after the king's death. In his letter Amenemhat warns his son of the potential treachery of his subjects and explains how he met his own untimely death: murdered, while sleeping in his palace, by his own bodyguard.

THE STORY OF SINUHE

Confirmation of Khety's account of dark deeds at court may be drawn from the contemporary *Story of Sinuhe*, an epic tale of adventure and misadventure which details the experiences of a courtier who flees Egypt only to discover that there is no place like home. His story takes the form of a tomb autobiography written in the first person, but the portrayal of Sinuhe in a less than heroic light (something that a genuine tomb autobiography would never do) indicates that it is fiction. The fact that several copies of the tale survive as papyri and ostraca, dating from the Middle Kingdom to the New and preserving extracts of varying length, bears testament to its popularity.

This tale is told by the courtier Sinuhe, count, commander and governor of Pharaoh's eastern territories, and the most loyal and beloved friend of the king. I was an attendant who served his lord, a servant in the royal harem who was assigned to Nefru, wife of King Senwosret and daughter of King Amenemhat.

Day 7 of the third month of the inundation, Year 30.

On this dreadful day the King of Upper and Lower Egypt, Amenemhat, died suddenly. His spirit ascended to heaven. It flew into the blue sky to become one with the golden sun disk. The divine king and his creator were merged into one being. Egypt was stunned, and fell silent in her grief. The great palace doors were shut, the nobles mourned without restraint and the common people wept in the streets.

Now, a short time before his death, King Amenemhat had sent a military expedition to the western deserts under the command of his eldest son, the good Prince Senwosret. Their brief had been to smite the foreign lands and punish the disrespectful Libyan nomads. This campaign had proved a great success and Senwosret, ignorant of his father's death, was already on his way home bringing with him many Libyan prisoners and a vast herd of captive cattle. I, too, had a place on that mission.

The palace officials sent their swiftest messengers to intercept Senwosret on the western border. The messengers travelled hard, and that night they found the prince and his companions camped by the road. Senwosret did not hesitate. He sped off to the palace, swift as a falcon, taking his most loyal attendants with him but leaving his army, and me, behind.

Before he rushed away, Senwosret told the royal sons of the tragedy at the palace. One of the princes received the dreadful news while I was standing on duty close by, and I happened to overhear the conversation. The words had a terrible effect on me. My mind went blank, my heart pounded in my chest and I trembled from head to foot. At once I knew that I was not safe in Egypt. I had to flee; I had to find somewhere to hide.

To think was to act. I hid myself behind two bushes, then I started my long and lonely journey southwards. Imagining scenes of riot and bloodshed, I steered clear of the palace. I was scared that I might die there, just as the king had died. Instead I travelled along the edge of the western desert, reaching the Isle-of-Snefru. Here I spent the daylight hours hiding on the edge of the cultivated land. At daybreak I set off again. I met a man who greeted me politely, but I was too scared to respond to his courtesy. At suppertime I reached the jetty and, with the help of the west wind, was able to cross the water in a rudderless boat. I then passed to the east of the quarries of the Red Mountain, and walked northwards until I reached Walls-of-the-Ruler, a mighty fortress built to repel the Asiatics and crush the desert nomads. Here I squatted behind another bush, hiding from the guards high up on the fortress walls.

At night I left the security of my bush and made for Peten, stopping at the Isle-of-Kem-Wer. But here I collapsed. Desperate with thirst, I could go no further. My lips were blistered and my throat so parched from lack of water that I thought my end had come. Just as I resigned myself to death I heard the welcome sound of lowing cattle and, raising my eyes from the sand, saw a caravan of Bedouin. With the greatest of good fortune their leader, who had once visited Egypt, recognized me. He gave me water and boiled milk and took me to live with his tribe. These were very good people.

I travelled to Byblos and returned via Qedem, spending many happy months there. Then Ammunenshi, chief of Upper Retenu, summoned me. He had heard of my integrity, intelligence and high position, and he wanted to interrogate me about recent events in Egypt. Exactly why had I left my beloved homeland in such a hurry? Had something untoward happened at the palace? I told him what I knew of the tragedy, but I spoke guardedly, because the news of the king's death had not officially been broken to me. I was, however, able to reassure him that, although I had been filled with such fear that I had run away, I had never been accused of any wrongdoing. I was not guilty of any crime, and I was not a wanted man. As to what had brought me to Retenu I was not sure – it was as if the gods themselves had directed my footsteps.

The chief asked me how Egypt would fare, deprived of her great king Amenemhat. And I responded with a lengthy poem in praise of my former master Senwosret, who would now rule in his father's place. Senwosret was a much-loved and mighty prince; a fearless warrior who had already proved himself on the battlefield, yet a gentle and cultured man who was not afraid to show mercy to the innocent and weak. I urged Ammunenshi to write and introduce himself to Egypt's new king. For Senwosret would surely look kindly upon such a loyal ally.

Ammunenshi then turned his attention to me.

'Well, it seems that Egypt is now happy under her new king. And you shall stay here and be happy with me. I will take care of you.'

The chief was as good as his word. He married me to the most beautiful of his daughters and allocated me a prime tract of land. This was a wonderful, fertile region named Yaa. There were fat figs on the trees, plump grapes on the vines, and wine was more plentiful than water. There was no shortage of sweet honey, and olives by the basketful; the trees were loaded with fruits, the fields were ripe with golden grain, and there were many kinds of cattle. Ammunenshi made me a tribal chief. Generously, he ensured that I received a rich supply of foods. Every day, bread was baked for me, wine was brought to me, and meats were cooked for me: beef, and fowl and desert game caught especially for me. For pudding I had my choice of sweet and milky confections.

Here I spent many happy and prosperous years watching my sons grow into strong men. Each of my sons eventually became chief of his own tribe. My tent was famed for its hospitality, and every passing envoy and traveller stayed with me. I gave water to the thirsty, directions to the lost and help to those who had been robbed. When my father-in-law's territories were threatened I fought bravely on his behalf, carrying out numerous successful missions. I vanquished the hill tribes, plundered their cattle, seized their families and killed their menfolk. For this service the chief of Retenu loved me very much.

Then, one day, a man came to my tent to challenge me. He was a huge man, a man of unparalleled strength, and the champion of his people. He meant to defeat me in combat and steal my goods and cattle. He had no personal grudge against me beyond the fact that I was an Egyptian living in the land of the desert dwellers, yet he wanted to ruin me. I knew that I had to prove myself. Frightened though I was, I had no choice but to accept his challenge. That night I made my preparations. I strung my bow, checked my arrows, honed my dagger and polished my weapons.

When morning came I left the safety of my tent and saw that many people had gathered to watch our fight. I stood, inwardly quaking, in my allotted place. I knew that the crowds were on my side, and that gave me the courage that I so badly needed. The champion raised his battleaxe and shield, shot his arrows into the air and threw his javelins towards me. I stood firm, and by some miracle his weapons all missed their mark. Then, as the champion charged forward, I shot him just once in the neck. He screamed and fell forward on to his face, breaking his nose with a loud crunch. Seizing his axe, I cut off his head. And as the people shouted their appreciation, I gave a cry of triumph and offered thanks to the great god Montu.

Ammunenshi hugged me in his arms, weak with relief. Now

I was able to plunder the champion just as he had planned to plunder me. I took all his cattle, and everything in his tent. In so doing I became wealthy beyond my wildest dreams. And I knew that at last the gods were pleased with me – my folly in fleeing Egypt had been forgiven. But just at the moment when I should have been at my happiest I felt a pang of longing for my homeland.

Many years passed. I grew older and feeble; death was looming ever nearer. I sent up a prayer to whichever god had directed my footsteps eastward. For I now yearned to return home so that I might be mummified and buried in the traditions of my fathers. I did not want my body to be wrapped in the sheepskin of my adopted people. But having fled Egypt, I was too scared to return. I did not know what reception might await me.

My plight came to the attention of the King of Upper and Lower Egypt, Senwosret. And the great king's heart was softened towards me. He sent me messages and gifts, and the royal children also sent me gifts. The king did not oppose my return for, as he graciously admitted, I might have acted foolishly in the grip of my fear, but I had done no actual wrong. On the contrary, he begged me to return so that I might look forward to a proper Egyptian funeral, with all its attendant rituals and promise of eternal life. 'Sinuhe, think of your dead body, and come home.'

This message reached me while I was standing in the midst of my tribe. So kind were the words of the great king to his servant that I threw myself to the ground and covered myself in dirt to demonstrate my humility. Then with great delight I replied to my lord, assuring him of my loyalty and accepting his generous invitation to return.

I spent one more day in Yaa, ordering my affairs. My eldest son was to take over my position, and I left him all my goods and chattels: my servants, my herds and my fruit trees. Then I started my journey homewards, accompanied by my faithful Bedouin kinsmen. When I reached the Ways-of-Horus fort the commander of the garrison sent a message to the palace. An escort came to meet me, and there were ships full of precious gifts for the Bedouin who had cared for me for so many years. I embarked, and set sail for Egypt, leaving my desert life behind me. And at daybreak I reached the capital city Itj-Tawy.

Ten men came to escort me to the king. At last I saw the mighty sphinxes at the palace entrance and I bowed low so that my head touched my native ground. And here were the young royal children standing beside the doorway to greet me. I was taken to the great audience hall and stood at last before my king. He sat splendid on a carved throne beneath a golden canopy. I flung myself on the ground before his feet, and once again my wits left me. I could not look up, I could not hear properly. I could not speak. As the great lord spoke gentle words of welcome I could only quake with fear. His majesty had to order a courtier to pick me up and support me while he spoke:

'Welcome home, Sinuhe. You have returned at last, after many years of roaming the foreign lands. You fled a young man, but old age has arrived and you are now looking forward to death. It is good that your body will eventually receive a proper Egyptian burial. But in the meantime, do not be frightened. Do not fear that you will be punished for your folly.'

In a quiet voice, but with growing confidence, I somehow found the words to reply: 'I am not being disrespectful in my silence, my lord, but I am still very frightened. I am here now, and you must do with me as you wish. I place myself entirely in your hands.'

The king summoned the queen and the royal princesses, and they rushed in to greet me as a long-lost friend – hesitating only slightly at my unkempt appearance for my beard and layers of desert dirt made me almost unrecognizable. They danced, and sang and shook their rattles, offering praise to Hathor for my return. Then they took me by the hand and led me from the audience chamber into the house of a prince. This seemed a house of great luxury to my weary, travel-worn eyes; it had a cool bathroom and mirrors, linen clothing, ointments, perfumes and servants to attend to my needs. I was washed, and the years fell from my body. I was shaved and my hair was cut so that I once again appeared as a true Egyptian gentleman. I was dressed in the finest linen and perfumed with the sweetest unguents. That night, I slept in a bed for the first time in years.

Through the mercy of the king I was given a house, a garden and a regular ration of food. Best of all, I was allocated a small stone pyramid in the middle of the royal cemetery. The royal masons built my pyramid, a master architect designed it and a master sculptor carved it. Inside there was a burial shaft, and all the goods necessary for the afterlife. I was given mortuary estates, and mortuary priests to maintain my cult forever. And my statue was covered with gold and with electrum. Truly, no other commoner had been so blessed by his king. I remained in the king's favour until the day that I died.

It is finished, as has been found in writing . . .

Why does Sinuhe feel the need to flee Egypt in such a precipitous fashion? He is far from the palace when the news of the king's death is announced, and so can have had no direct involvement in it. Yet, in the few seconds that it takes to eavesdrop on a private conversation, the whole course of his life is irredeemably changed for the worse. Of course, Sinuhe is a fictional character. He acts in this irrational way because his author makes him do so. But, if we go along with the pretence that he is real, we must ask why he is so very frightened when, as far as we know, there has been no mention of murder. Amenemhat was an elderly man already in his thirtieth regnal year; in a land where 40 was considered a good age, his natural death was more or less imminent and should not have provoked such extreme terror. Does Sinuhe know that the king had been assassinated? And is he somehow – perhaps in his role as servant of the royal harem – implicated in the conspiracy?

Meanwhile Senwosret, already acknowledged as co-regent to Amenemhat I, is absent from the palace; he is off subduing the Libyan nomads who are a constant irritation along the western border. On hearing the sad news he abandons his army and rushes to the palace to claim his inheritance. This is a very sensible move. The proverb 'he who buries, inherits' may not have had the force of law, but it was widely respected and is even quoted in a private Deir el-Medina document: 'Let the possession be given to him who buries, says the law of the pharaoh.'[52] The royal harem could surely have provided many brothers eager to step into Senwosret's sandals.

Like the Shipwrecked Sailor, Sinuhe is forced to travel out of his normal environment. His declared intention is to flee south but his chaotic journey actually takes him north-east, from the Libyan Desert, across the Nile, past Memphis (the location of the Isle-of-Snefru, which is not actually an island but a funerary estate), and over the Sinai land bridge. Here he follows the inhospitable 140-mile desert road, the Way-of-Horus, into southern Canaan. On his journey, and again on his return, he passes the impressive mud-brick fortresses built to serve as combined garrisons and customs posts. Walls-of-the-Ruler is one of these fortresses, built by Amenemhat I to provide protection, water and provisions for those passing on legitimate business, while discouraging the uncontrolled migration of Asiatics (a general, derogatory term for Easterners). After a quick trip to

1. The Red Land, the Black Land and the River Nile.

2. The Red (Northern) Pyramid of Snefru at Dahshur emulates the Mound of Creation as it rises out of the desert.

3. Funerary texts carved within the pyramid of the 6th Dynasty king Teti, at Sakkara, will help the dead king to reach his afterlife.

4. Atum and the God's Wife of Amen Shepenwepet,
in her Late Period tomb-chapel at Medinet Habu.

5. Nut depicted on the painted inside of a coffin lid, where she stretches over, and protects, the deceased.

6. The earth god Geb, displaying his goose emblem, in the Valley of the Kings.

7. The Middle Kingdom monarch Senwosret I offers to the
ithyphallic form of Amen on the White Chapel at Karnak.

8. Nectanebo I offers Maat to Thoth in his ape form.

9. The creator Ptah, depicted on a Ramesside stela from Deir el-Medina.

10. A post-Ramesside depiction of the solar deity
Re-Horakhty on a wooden, private, stela.

11. The solar boat of Re on its journey.
From the sarcophagus of Nectanebo II.

12. The Souls of Pe and Dep pull the solar boat of Re.
From the cenotaph temple of Ramesses II at Abydos.

the Syrian port of Byblos he travels through Qedem, which is most probably a forested area to the east of the Lebanese mountain range. Then he is summoned, or captured, by Ammunenshi, chief of Upper Retenu, a region on the River Litani in Palestine. Finally he settles in the fertile and possibly fictional land of Yaa.

Sinuhe's new life in Canaan is one of totally un-Egyptian luxury. He lives in a tent rather than a house; he has no bathroom, no fresh linen and no barber to shave his beard; the meats in his new land are cooked in milk. His courage fully restored, Sinuhe gains wealth as a pastoralist and respect as a warrior. His life is as happy as any life away from Egypt can ever be. Only when the mighty challenger attempts to rob him is he reminded that he is a stranger in a strange land. At this point we see the fleeting return of the old, frightened Sinuhe. But this time Sinuhe is determined to meet his fate face to face. In a battle strongly reminiscent of the Biblical tale of David and Goliath, which at the same time brings to mind the timeless scenes found on Egypt's temple walls of pharaohs smiting unfortunate foreigners, he defeats his enemy with a single well-placed shot. In so doing, he gains both riches and respect. His story then proceeds, with a startling abruptness, to a second Biblical theme. It becomes the parable of the prodigal son.

At the very moment of his triumph, Sinuhe realizes that he must return to Egypt. Leaving Egypt is neither a good nor a desirable thing and the gods do not make it easy. Sinuhe had been forced to escape using a rudderless boat that he could not steer, and a perverse western wind. His homeward journey is far more controlled; it is a journey in the right direction, from chaos to *maat*. He has an escort and a boat, complete with rudder, which sails swiftly to the (now lost) palace at Itj-Tawy. Here the queen and the curiously un-aged royal children are shocked by Sinuhe's appearance. Not only is he old, he has become a bearded desert dweller, and it takes a lengthy session in the bathroom to restore him to the well-groomed ideal of Egyptian manhood. Sinuhe is reborn. Clean, scented and appropriately dressed in white linen, he is given both a house and a tomb in the royal cemetery of Lisht. His story has come full circle, and he now looks forward to the time when he will join Osiris in his Field of Reeds.

5

THE CONTENDINGS OF HORUS AND SETH

With Osiris dead and vanished, Seth ruled Egypt in his brother's place and life continued much as it had done before Osiris' untimely disappearance.

A DYSFUNCTIONAL FAMILY

Protected by his devoted mother Isis, and nourished by the divine cow Hathor, Horus-the-Child was raised in the papyrus marshes of the Delta. His childhood was marred by an unfortunate series of accidents and illnesses but, thanks to his mother's potent magic, Horus survived unscathed. When the time came for him to claim his inheritance, Horus travelled with Isis to testify before the council of the gods. Here, things did not go quite as Isis and Horus had planned. Seth was not prepared to surrender his crown to his nephew, and many of the gods were on his side, favouring age and experience over youth and birthright. The legal quarrel between Horus and Seth was to last for eighty years.[53]

Seated before the great throne of the Universal Lord, Horus formally requested the crown of his dead father Osiris. Shu, son of Re, spoke in favour of the fatherless boy. Surely it was right that Horus, son of Osiris, should be king of Egypt? Thoth, scribe of the gods, agreed: 'It is a million times right that Horus should be king.'

On hearing this, Isis let out a great shriek of relief. Running forward to stand before the Universal Lord, she ordered the north wind to fly westwards and carry the glad tidings to Osiris, isolated and sorrowing in the land of the dead.

But Isis had acted in haste, and the Universal Lord was not amused. The gods had taken it upon themselves to pronounce judgement without waiting to hear his opinion, and he had been inclined to award the crown to Seth, son of Nut. For Seth was infinitely strong and cunning while Horus was an untried and untested boy. Uncertain how to proceed, the Universal Lord sat in silence. Eventually, he reached a decision. He would send for Banebdjedet, the great living god, so that he might judge between Horus and Seth and stop them quarrelling. For their dispute had already lasted for many years and everyone was weary of it.

Banebdjedet duly presented himself before the council of the gods, but declined to offer an opinion. The matter should not be decided in ignorant haste. A letter must be written to Neith, mother of the gods, asking her advice. She alone should decide between the rival kings. And so Thoth wrote an elaborate, diplomatic letter explaining matters to Neith: 'What shall we do with these two claimants who for eighty years now have been asking the council for a decision? No one wants to judge between the two. Write quickly, and tell us how to act.'

Neith, the great mother, replied in writing, and Thoth read out her judgement before the Universal Lord and all the gods in the great hall. Horus was the rightful king of Egypt, and any attempt to trick him out of his birthright would make Neith so angry that she would bring the sky crashing down. Horus should receive his father's throne, but Seth should receive suitable compensation, including Anath and Astarte, the beautiful daughters of the Universal Lord, as wives.

The gods at once agreed, calling out that of course the wise Neith was right. But the Universal Lord was angry again, as the judgement had not gone the way he intended. Turning on Horus he hurled a childish insult at him: 'You are too feeble to be a strong king, and what's more, your breath stinks.'

This so incensed the other gods that they, too, started to insult each other. As the opinionated god Babi abused the Universal Lord, 'No one cares what you think – you are a worthless god with no followers and your shrine is empty!', the council meeting degenerated into chaos and confusion and the Universal Lord stormed out.

The Universal Lord was so upset by the behaviour of the council that he retired to his tent where he lay sulking on his bed. After a long time his daughter Hathor, Lady of the Sycamore, came to find him. Sensing his gloom, and wishing to cheer him up, she stripped off her clothes and stood naked before him. This made the Universal Lord laugh out loud. His humour and his strength restored, he left the tent and returned to the council of the gods. He had decided that Horus and Seth should each be allowed to plead his case.

Seth spoke first: 'I am Seth, son of Nut and greatest in strength of all the gods. Every day I sail in the solar boat of Re, and every night I slay Apophis, the great serpent who threatens the life of the sun. No other god is able to do this. Therefore I should receive the crown of Osiris.'

The gods were impressed by Seth's powerful speech, and divided among themselves. Some argued that Seth should indeed be king, but Thoth repeated the pertinent question: 'Is it ever right that a brother should inherit when a dead father has left a living son?'

Banebdjedet, no longer a neutral observer, argued in turn

that it was wrong to overlook Seth in favour of his young nephew. Then the Universal Lord spoke. But his words were not fit to be heard, and were not written down. All we know is that they outraged his fellow gods, who made a great outcry.

Next it was the turn of Horus, son of Isis, to speak. His message was simple and direct. 'It is very bad indeed that you are defrauding me, and denying me the crown of my father Osiris.'

Hearing this, the passionate Isis could remain silent no longer. She swore an impressive oath: 'By my mother, the wise goddess Neith, and by Ptah-Tatenen, this matter should be brought before Atum of Heliopolis, and also before Khepri in his boat.'

And the gods agreed with her that it should be so.

In a towering rage, Seth in turn swore an oath: 'Upon my word, I will take my heavy sceptre and kill one of you each and every day. But I will not go to court if Isis is allowed to be there.'

The Universal Lord agreed that the over-emotional Isis should be kept out of the case. He ordered that the gods should sail over the water to the Isle-in-the-Midst, and there decide the matter. To ensure that they reached their decision undisturbed, he forbade the ferryman to transport any woman to the Isle, and in particular he banned any woman who looked even remotely like Isis. And so it was done. The gods crossed to the Isle, and there they sat down in the cool shade of the green trees to eat bread.

Isis, great in magic, would not be thwarted. Turning herself into a bent old woman she hobbled up to the ferryman Nemty and pleaded for passage to the Isle: 'For I have brought a bowl of gruel for a hungry young lad who has been tending cattle on the Isle for five long days.'

Nemty was worried. This aged crone looked nothing like a beautiful goddess, but how could he be sure? He had been specifically told not to ferry any woman across the river. Finally he managed to stifle his doubts, and accepted Isis' valuable gold signet ring as payment for her passage.

Walking under the green trees of the Isle-in-the-Midst, Isis saw her fellow gods enjoying their meal in front of the splendid tent of the Universal Lord. And Seth looked up from his meal and saw Isis, but he did not recognize her, for she had transformed into a nubile maiden, the most desirable girl in the whole land. Seth left his food, and walked quickly to intercept her, before the other gods could see her. Hiding behind a sycamore tree, he called out to Isis in what he considered to be an irresistibly seductive manner.

'Well hello, most beautiful girl in the world. Here am I, waiting for you. Let us walk and talk together in the shade of the tall green trees.'

Isis replied in a whisper: 'First let me tell you my story, stranger. I was once the wife of a herdsman. I loved him, and I bore him a son. We were a very happy family. Then my husband died, and my young son began to look after his cattle. But a stranger came and took over my stable. The stranger threatened to beat my son, to confiscate his cattle, and to evict him from his rightful home. Now, please sir, I would like you to give me your opinion on this matter.'

Seth, moved by the beautiful woman's plight, replied without thought: 'It can never be right to give a family's cattle to a stranger when the son of the dead father lives. The intruder must be beaten with a stick and thrown out, and your son must claim his rightful place.'

On hearing Seth's words Isis became a giant bird and flew to perch in the topmost branches of an acacia tree. She shrieked down to Seth in triumph:

'Weep for yourself, Seth, not for me. For you have condemned yourself with your own words.'

Then Seth indeed began to weep, and he ran to the Universal Lord and cried before him, explaining all that had happened. The Lord listened with a grave face. Seth had condemned himself with his own mouth – what more was there to be said? But Seth demanded that the ferryman Nemty be summoned before the gods, and that he be punished severely, for he had ignored the orders of the Universal Lord and had brought Isis to the Isle. And so Nemty was dragged before the council, and his toes were cut off in punishment. And from that day forward the ferryman hated the sight of gold.

The gods left the peace of the Isle-in-the-Midst and crossed the water to the western mountain. Here, Atum and Re-Horakhty decided that the crown should be given to Horus. Furious, and not prepared to admit defeat, Seth immediately challenged his nephew to a duel. They would each transform into a hippopotamus, and plunge to the deepest depths of the sea. They would stay underwater for three whole months. If one of them should emerge before the appointed time, he would forfeit his right to the crown. Horus agreed, and into the swirling waters they plunged, side by side. But Isis, hearing of the challenge, sat on the shore and wept. For she feared that Seth would kill her son. Isis decided to help Horus. She took a length of flax and twisted it into a rope. Next she fetched an ingot of copper, melted it, and cast it in the form of a harpoon. She tied the rope to the harpoon, and threw it into the water at the point where Horus and Seth had vanished. Under the water the harpoon bit into the flank of Horus, who gave a loud shriek. 'Help me, mother, tell your barb to let me go, for I am your son, Horus.'

Isis ordered her harpoon to release Horus, and threw it again into the water. This time it bit into the flesh of her brother, and it was Seth's turn to give a loud wail: 'What harm have I ever done to you, Isis? I am your brother, yet you hate me more than you would hate a complete stranger.'

Hearing his words Isis was greatly moved and once again she commanded her harpoon to release its victim.

Horus interpreted his mother's mercy as a betrayal, and was enraged. He left the water carrying a huge cleaver, his face fierce like the face of a leopard. With one mighty blow he struck off his mother's head. As Isis transformed herself into a headless flint statue, Horus picked up her head and carried it up the mountain. The other gods watched in horror. Horus had to be punished, but first he had to be caught. So the entire council, including Seth, went into the mountains in search of Horus, son, and now murderer, of Isis.

Seth found Horus lying on his back in the shade of a tree. Seth was the stronger of the two, and he easily overpowered his young adversary. Plucking out Horus's eyes, he buried them in the ground. Then Seth returned to the other gods and, without revealing that he had already found and fought Horus, helped them in their fruitless search. Meanwhile the two eyes became bulbs that grew into beautiful lotus blossoms on the mountainside.

Eventually, gentle Hathor found the blind Horus weeping from pain and self-pity. She knew exactly what to do. She caught a wild gazelle and milked it. Then she forced Horus to open his empty eyes. Milk was dribbled into the left eye socket, and milk was dribbled into the right eye socket, and Horus was made whole again.

Once again the council summoned Horus and Seth. Weary of their quarrelling, the Universal Lord told the pair to try to resolve their differences amicably over a jug of wine, or perhaps a meal. And so Seth invited Horus to dine at his house. Uncle and nephew ate and drank until it grew dark, when a bed was prepared for them. And they lay down together on the bed and fell asleep. During the night Seth became aroused, and he slipped his erect penis between the sleeping Horus' thighs. But

Horus was not asleep. He caught Seth's semen in his hands and went crying to his mother. He told her what had happened, and showed her the semen. Isis let out a great shriek, cut off Horus's contaminated hands and threw them into the water. By magic she fashioned her son a new pair of hands. Then she thought long and hard, for she suspected Seth of trickery rather than simple lust. Fetching an exotic oil Isis massaged it into Horus's penis until it grew stiff. She used a pot to collect his semen. Then, early next morning, she visited Seth's garden and interviewed his head gardener. Learning that lettuce was Seth's favourite food, she sprinkled Horus's semen on to the lettuce patch. And when, later that day, Seth ate the lettuce from his garden he became pregnant with the seed of Horus.

Seth went to Horus and asked him to appear with him once again before the council of the gods. Following his mother's advice, Horus agreed. Immediately, Seth condemned Horus before his fellow deities: 'Let me be the king of Egypt, for Horus has allowed me to use him exactly as a man uses a woman.'

The gods were horrified, and spat at Horus. But Horus merely laughed. Taking an oath, he spoke in turn: 'All that Seth says is untrue: quite the opposite happened. Call forth our semen, and see whence it answers.'

And so Thoth laid his hand on Horus's arm, and called to the semen of Seth. The semen answered not, as Seth had expected, from inside the body of Horus, but from the depths of the waters. Then Thoth laid his hand on Seth's arm, and called to the semen of Horus. The semen answered from inside Seth and, as Thoth demanded that the semen reveal itself, emerged as the sun's disk on top of his head. Thoth took the golden disk from Seth's head and placed it as a crown on his own head. On the basis of this evidence the gods gave their judgement: 'Horus is right and Seth is wrong.'

With an angry shout, Seth issued a further, desperate challenge to his nephew. They would both build boats of stone and race each other. Whoever won the race would win the crown of Egypt. But, while Seth cut the top off a mountain, and carved a true stone boat, Horus cheated by building a wooden boat which he covered in plaster and paint so that it looked like a ship carved from stone. Of course, when the race started, Seth's boat sank while Horus's boat floated. Furious, Seth transformed himself into a hippopotamus and holed Horus's boat. In retaliation Horus seized a copper harpoon and attempted to spear Seth, until the council of the gods ordered that Seth should not be injured.

Horus sailed downriver to Sais, home of the mother goddess Neith. He intended to plead with her to intervene on his behalf, for he had been in dispute with his uncle for eighty years and, although he had been victorious in the law courts, he still did not have his throne. Realizing this, the gods decided to write to Osiris and ask his advice. And so Thoth put paintbrush to papyrus, and a letter was duly despatched to the land of the dead. As they might perhaps have expected, Osiris was intensely displeased and replied by return: 'Why is my only son being dispossessed, when you owe everything to me? I alone made you strong. I made barley and wheat to sustain both the gods and mankind. No other god could do this.'

The Universal Lord was not impressed with this argument, and he sent a brief, but cruelly accurate, note back. 'Barley and wheat would have existed even if you had never been born.'

Osiris, stung to the core, sent a longer and more considered reply in defence of his son's claim. 'You must give this matter your full attention, or something bad will surely happen. The land where I now dwell is full of daemons who fear none of you, neither god nor goddess. If I release these daemons they will rip out the heart of every wrongdoer, and bring it to me.

For I am the mightiest of all of you. You, who are still blessed with life, have allowed injustice to come into being.'

The gods listened to Osiris' scarcely veiled threat and hastily declared him to be right. Horus should inherit the throne. But Seth once again asked that he and Horus be taken to the Isle-in-the-Midst where they could compete for the crown. This was done, and Horus was once again victorious. Then, at last, the Universal Lord ordered Isis to bring Seth before him, bound in chains. And so, publicly humiliated, Seth was brought before his peers. And finally Seth agreed that Horus should be king of Egypt. Horus son of Isis was brought in triumph before his fellow gods. He was crowned with the white crown, and placed on the throne of his father Osiris. Isis, happy at last, sang a hymn of triumph for her son.

As for Seth, he was not punished but sent to live with Re, where even today he thunders in the sky and brings fear to the hearts of mankind.

The gods that we meet in this tale are not the awesome, omnipotent beings of our earlier encounters, and the struggle for the throne is not a straightforward contest fought fair and square. Each bout is won by trickery and cheating, and the all-divine cast is weak, indecisive and, occasionally, ridiculous. We have already met, or will meet, most of the main characters in this drama. Joining the company is Banebdjedet, a ram god of such awesome sexual prowess that he is known as the 'lord of carnal pleasure'. The northern equivalent of Khnum, Banebdjedet was believed to represent the souls of Osiris, Re-Atum, Shu and Geb, and all four were worshipped in his Mendes (ancient Djedet) temple. On the face of it he is an unlikely judge in a matter of such importance. The rude baboon god Babi is another divine being famed for his sexual potency. Babi is rather a mixed blessing – a guardian of the sky and friend of Seth, who both feasts off the entrails of the dead and helps the deceased to regain their sexual powers. Nemty the naive ferryman may be the ill-fated falcon god Nemty. In this myth Nemty loses his toes: a healing spell tells us that he was poisoned while sailing with Horus, and was only cured when he revealed his true name. Nemty, in turn, may be equated with the falcon Anti, who may be considered to be either an aspect of Seth, or a personification of the less admirable traits of Horus.

For modern readers this lengthy myth is short on pace and action. But we should not be too quick to criticize the author; the original audience would have been all too well accustomed to the slow-moving Egyptian bureaucracy, and may well have relished the constant repetition and fruitless debates as an ironic comment on their own legal system, which allowed too many lengthy civil cases to end with no judgement at all. The best illustration of the time-consuming complexities of the bureaucracy is provided by a true case recorded on an ostracon recovered from Deir el-Medina.[54] This tells how Mentmose, the chief of the village police, bought a valuable pot of fat from the villager Menna. Mentmose asked for credit, claiming: 'I will pay you with barley obtained from my brother; he will guarantee the deal.' When the promised payment failed to materialize, Menna took the police chief to court – on four separate occasions. The court was happy to find in Menna's favour, but unable to enforce judgement. Eventually Mentmose swore an oath: 'If I do not pay Menna for the pot before the last day of the third month of summer of Year 3, may I receive a hundred blows with the stick, and be made to pay double.' By now the case was already some eighteen years old. Mentmose eventually paid Menna some two and a half months after the agreed payment date when Menna, clearly not one to learn by experience, agreed to accept an ox in settlement of his debt. However, as the ox was worth far more than the original pot of fat, he then had to provide Mentmose with a coffin, and still ended up owing him 65 *deben* of copper, more than twice the value of the initial loan.

Another, this time fictional, example of the tediously lengthy and frequently fruitless legal process is found in the *Tale of the Eloquent Peasant*, which is told in Chapter 11. It is perhaps little wonder that many Egyptians preferred to refer their legal disputes to the local oracle who was, if nothing else, likely to give an instant judgement.

The divine council is the worst sort of committee, capable of generating a great deal of hot air but incapable of reaching a firm decision. Throughout his eighty-year struggle to claim his father's crown, Horus never wavers in his belief that he has right on his side. He is the only son of the previous king and so is clearly the heir to the Egyptian throne. And yet he does not get the automatic support of his fellow gods, and the influential Universal Lord, a combination of all the manifestations of the sun god whom we may name Re-Atum-Horakhty-Khepri, is a firm supporter of Seth. It seems that the principle of father–son inheritance is not yet firmly established in Egypt and that Seth has an equally valid case to argue. He, like Horus, is the son of a king. Furthermore he is older, wiser and far stronger than Horus; he alone has the physical strength to fight off the malevolent serpent Apophis each night. In this version of the tale it is Seth who emerges as the more cunning and experienced political campaigner and, in some ways, as the better developed and therefore more sympathetic character.

HORUS OF HIERAKONPOLIS

Our hero (in so far as *The Contendings* can be said to have a hero) is a version of the ancient falcon-headed deity Horus of Hierakonpolis, the 'city of the falcon'. From the very beginning of the dynastic age Horus exhibits strong links with the living king-ship; this suggests that *Contendings* may represent a romanticized version of the struggles that eventually saw the lengthy land of independent Predynastic towns and city-states united under one king. The time of transition between the un-unified Predynastic and the unified Early Dynastic Periods is obscure and, of course, there are no contemporary writings to help our understanding. But the Egyptians themselves believed that their first kings were gods (in order, Ptah, Re, Shu, Geb, Osiris, Seth, Horus, Thoth and Maat; or perhaps the Ennead ruling together), and that these divine rulers were succeeded by a line of semi-mortal kings known as the 'Followers of Horus'. When the first fully mortal, historically authenticated kings started to rule at the beginning of the 1st Dynasty they confirmed their continuing allegiance to Horus by placing a falcon on top of the *serekh*, the schematic representation of the royal palace that outlined and defined their names. These first kings were buried in extensive mud-brick tombs in southern Egypt, in the already ancient Abydos cemetery.

With the change from the 1st to the 2nd Dynasty came a change of royal cemetery; the first five kings of the 2nd Dynasty built their tombs in the north, in the Sakkara cemetery. This suggests that these kings were northerners who, having displaced the ruling family, wished to be buried in their homeland. Peribsen, the sixth king of the 2nd Dynasty, returned to the Abydos cemetery but, uniquely, placed a Seth animal rather than a Horus falcon on top of his *serekh*, so that he could be said to have a Seth-name rather than a Horus-name. Peribsen's successor used two Horus names. His original name, Khasekhem or 'The Power [Horus] Rises', is found on vessels discovered inside the Hierakonpolis temple and dated to 'the year of fighting the northern enemy'. Here Horus, restored to the top of the *serekh*, wears the white crown of Upper Egypt. His second name, Khasekhemwy or 'The Two Powers [Horus and Seth] Rise', is topped with both Horus and Seth, and is accompanied by the phrase 'the two lords are at rest in him'. It seems that Khasekhemwy, king of southern Egypt, had managed to reunite a temporarily divided land, and in so doing had united the estranged Horus and Seth.

With Egypt reunified at the end of the 2nd Dynasty we might have expected to see increased devotion to the cult of Horus. Instead, we see the emergence of a stronger, northern-based, pyramid-building kingship which allowed both Horus and Seth to be overshadowed by the rising solar deity Re of Heliopolis. This was by no means a religious revolution, however, and Horus would remain one of Egypt's most effective deities, while the living pharaoh, now a 'son of Re', would always be equated with Horus. This allegiance to Horus is made most obvious in the official royal titulary. By the end of the Old Kingdom the *serekh* had been abandoned and each king used a series of five names or titles, four of which were brief sentences chosen at the time of his coronation to convey the essence of his reign. The first of these names was the Horus name, the third was the Golden Horus name. The final two names, the pre-nomen and the nomen, were each written inside an oval loop known today as a cartouche. So, to take just one example, the 19th Dynasty monarch Ramesses II was officially known as:

The Horus King: Strong Bull, Beloved of Maat
He of the Two Ladies: Protector of Egypt who Curbs the Foreign Lands
The Golden Horus: Rich in Years, Great in Victories
King of Upper and Lower Egypt: Usermaatre Setepenre
Son of Re: Ramesses, Beloved of Amen.

Today we call Egypt's kings by their last name, the nomen or personal name. Ramesses' subjects, however, would have known him by his pre-nomen, Usermaatre Setepenre.

Mythology reveals two very different forms of Horus. In his earliest incarnations Horus, the 'distant one', is both lord of the sky (his strong, green, right eye the sun; his weaker, white, left eye the moon) and a sun god who, as Horakhty, 'Horus of the Two Horizons', is specifically linked to the vigorous rising sun. The earliest *Pyramid Texts* references recognize this Horus as a young yet fully mature man who first helps Isis and Nephthys to gather together the scattered pieces of Osiris' body, and then avenges him. This version of Horus is known as Horus-the-Elder (Harwer; Haroeris to the Greeks). He is variously considered to be the child of Re or Geb by either Hathor or Nut, and the Ptolemaic *Legend of the Winged Disk*, preserved on the walls of the Edfu temple, confirms that it is this Horus who defends Re against his enemies. Plutarch, however, accords Horus-the-Elder a more complicated family history. He tells us that Nut, whom Plutarch knew by her Greek name Rhea, bore not four but five children. Cursed by the sun, and unable to give birth on any day of any month of the year, she delivered these five children in the five days which did not belong to any official month. Osiris was born on the first day and Seth was born on the unlucky third day, followed by Isis on the fourth and Nephthys on the fifth. 'Arueris whom they call Apollo, and some call him Horus-the-Elder' was born on the second day, but he was probably not the child of Nut and Geb, but the fruit of the *in-utero* union of Osiris and Isis. Thus Osiris, Seth, Isis, Nephthys and Horus-the-Elder may be classed as siblings. In order to preserve the tale of Isis conceiving a son by the dead Osiris, Plutarch adds that: 'Osiris consorted with Isis after his death, and she became the mother of Harpocrates, untimely born and weak in his lower limbs.'

The myth of Horus-the-Child (Har-pa-khered; Harpocrates to the Greeks), weak and in need of his mother's protection, had been added to the *Pyramid Texts* by the 6th Dynasty. Absorbed into the Heliopolitan mythology, this version of Horus was the child of Isis and the dead Osiris, and the nephew of Seth, although in local temples he might be the child of local gods; at Medamud, for example, he became the child of Montu and Rat-tawi (a version of Hathor). An aspect of Horus-the-Child, Shed or 'saviour', might appear armed with a bow or sword to ward off wild animals.

Although the tone of the *Contendings* is deliberately light, the levity is interrupted by some disturbing episodes of violence. Seth plucks out or otherwise injures either one or both of Horus's eyes;[55] in some versions of the myth Horus retaliates by castrating Seth. Isis harpoons both Horus and Seth, causing them great pain; Horus responds by cutting off his mother's head. Fortunately, this proves to be just a temporary inconvenience, and Isis is restored, either by her own magic or by Thoth, who is able to give her a replacement cow's head, thus creating the first animal-headed deity. The New Kingdom *Harris Magical Papyrus*[56] tells an even darker tale which harks back to the tradition that the king must impregnate his mother to engender himself. Here Horus rapes his mother on the riverbank and causes her to weep so that her tears fall into the water. In retaliation, and because they are natural enemies, Seth then attacks the vulnerable eye, or eyes, of Horus. As always, accounts vary: Horus is either completely blinded, or one eye is damaged; the eye(s) is damaged by Seth's finger, is fragmented or is eaten; the eye is restored by Horus himself or, more usually, by Hathor, Isis or Thoth.

The attack on his eye(s) gave rise to two versions of Horus – the eyeless, irascible Horus Khenty-en-irty who relieved his anger by tormenting the evil dead, and the sighted and more peaceful Horus Khenty-irty. Once restored, the eye of Horus became the *wedjat* eye: a potent symbol of completeness or wholeness which, initially used to bring Osiris back to life, also helped more humble mummies be reborn. Illustrations invariably show the eye as a mixture of human eye and eyebrow with falcon-like facial markings.

The Horus-eye fraction

Educated Egyptians would have recognized that the six components of the eye of Horus resembled the hieroglyphic writing of the six fractions ½, ¼, ⅛, ¹⁄₁₆, ¹⁄₃₂, ¹⁄₆₄ of the *hekat* (the unit of volume used to measure grain). Any illustration of the eye therefore forms a mathematical sequence known as the 'Horus-eye fraction'. This allows the mathematically minded to read the historiola of the Eye of Horus as an equation waiting to be solved by simply adding ¹⁄₆₄ to ⁶³⁄₆₄ (the sum of the eye fractions) to make a whole number, or a whole or healed eye.

It is perhaps not surprising that we find the healed and whole eye of Horus featuring in the medical papyri, where myth and magic are routinely combined with more practical (to modern eyes) cures. So, in the Ptolemaic *Papyrus Hearst* we may read the protective spell:[57]

Hail to thee, O eye of Horus . . . The goddess Isis came forth, when joy was given to her before Geb, she (Isis) *having fought for it, and so on. Protect him against the shade of the male dead and the female dead. I am that Thoth, that physician of the eye of Horus. My father Osiris fought in the presence of Neith, mistress of life, and her attendants.*

Meanwhile, in an entirely different interpretation, an eclipse of the moon might be equated with Seth taking the form of a boar to swallow, and subsequently regurgitate, the eye of Horus.

SETH: THE RED ONE

The gods seem particularly appalled by the thought that Horus has enjoyed sexual intercourse with his uncle. In a land where homosexual rape was considered a means of degrading the unfortunate, it was the victim rather than the aggressor who was deemed to have brought shame on himself. This explains the shock when Horus's seed very publicly emerges from Seth's head, making it clear to everyone just who has been penetrated by whom. As homosexuality did not fit with the accepted ideal of the nuclear family (husband, wife and as many children as possible), it was more or less ignored in official writings. However, the New Kingdom funerary books make it clear that, however tempting homosexual intercourse may be, abstinence from it is a virtue. The author of the scurrilous story of Neferkare, the 6th Dynasty King Pepi II, was well aware of this.[58] He tells how Teti, son of Henut, sees his king slip out of the palace at night and decides to follow him. The king makes his way to the house of General Sisene, and throws a brick up at the window to alert the general that he has a guest. A ladder descends, and the king climbs up and through the window to spend four hours alone with

Sisene. No further details are offered, but it is made clear that Teti does not imagine that the two have been occupied with battle plans.

The earliest account of Seth's and Horus's uncle–nephew bonding comes from a damaged Middle Kingdom papyrus recovered from the pyramid workers' village of Kahun.[59] In this tale Horus is revealed as a manipulative, complicit partner prepared to yield to Seth's lust for his own gain. The story starts with Horus complaining to Isis that Seth has been admiring his buttocks and longs to sleep with him. Isis advises her son to tell Seth, 'It is too difficult for me because of my physique; because you are too heavy for me, my strength will not be equal to yours.' Only when Seth has agreed to make Horus stronger should the two sleep together and, as Isis happily observes, 'he will enjoy it exceedingly'. Seth agrees to Horus's terms, and the deed is done. Horus, however, following his mother's instructions, is careful to catch his uncle's semen in his hand. What he intended to do with it we do not know, as the papyrus breaks off at this point.

In later versions of the tale, as told in *Papyrus Chester Beatty I*, Horus is an adult who still consults his mother on important matters. Once again he sleeps with his uncle and catches his semen. Isis throws the semen into the water before assuming the role of God's Hand (a reminder of the first creation) to stimulate her son. She then exploits Seth's love of lettuce as a means of impregnating him. When the seed of Horus is summoned, Seth gives birth to the solar disk which Thoth then places on his own head. The story preserved on the wall of the Edfu temple, however, has Thoth himself emerging from Seth's head. A birth rooted in family discord seems appropriate for Thoth, 'the son of two lords, who came forth from a lock of hair', who will spend much of his time resolving domestic disputes.

Seth is not one to respect sexual taboos and, if we were to apply modern terms to ancient deities, we would probably classify him as voraciously bisexual. It comes as no surprise to learn that lettuce is his favourite food. He is married to his sister Nephthys, yet seduces his nephew Horus and has affairs with Taweret and the mysterious 'seed goddess'. *Papyrus Jumilhac* tells how he assumes the form of a bull to pursue his sister Isis – she in turn transforms into a dog with a knife on her tail, and runs away. Much to Isis' disgust, Seth then ejaculates on the ground, and his seed becomes a valuable crop (of watermelons?). His castration at the hands of Horus must have been a terrible punishment indeed; fortunately, in the divine world, it was a reversible operation.

The Egyptians interpreted Seth's rampant sexuality as a clear example of his chaotic or uncontrolled behaviour. Seth is sexually active, but his energies are in many ways wasted; he is not recognized as a fertility god and he has no children. Mild-mannered Osiris, in contrast, is a powerful fertility god and the father of at least one son, yet he demonstrates the ultimate in self-control during his famous coupling with Isis, when he himself remains inert (admittedly because he is dead) and Isis is left to play what the Egyptians would have regarded as the man's active role.

Seth, the 'Red One', god of the infertile desert and lord of foreigners, was an ancient, discontented being. As the epitome of confusion and disorder he should, perhaps, have been a direct affront to *maat* and the maintenance of the status quo. Fratricide, Seth's worst offence, would have been abhorrent to a people who placed a high premium on family loyalty. Yet, to classify Seth as the equivalent of the modern Satan is to make a vast over-simplification. A comparison with the Biblical Judas is perhaps more appropriate. Like the legend of Judas's treachery, the legend of Seth's infamy grew over time, so that only at the very end of the dynastic age is he recognized as a wholly evil being. In his earlier incarnations Seth is far from irredeemable and his most heinous crime is surely no worse than the matricide carelessly practised by Horus. Indeed, Seth's fratricide is a pivotal moment in the cult of Osiris: without it, there could have been no resurrection and no eternal life for the masses. For most of the dynastic age Seth was accepted as a maverick, whose chaos represented an aspect of real life; a recognition that things do not always go to plan. When real, eternal danger threatened – when, for example, the sun was attacked by the monstrous daemons of the underworld – Seth would always align himself on the side of virtue. And so, far from being shunned, Seth, or Seti, gave his name to three New Kingdom Ramesside pharaohs: the 19th Dynasty Seti I and Seti II, and the 20th Dynasty Sethnakht. It was understood that Seth had torn himself from Nut in a painful and chaotic birth in the southern Egyptian city of Nagada. However, during the New Kingdom he was primarily worshipped in the Delta town of Avaris, hometown of the Ramessides where, as the 'lord of foreign countries', he was equated with the Hittite god Teshub and the turbulent Semitic storm god Baal.

Seth's bizarre appearance reflects his confusing nature. His human-form body is topped by a head that appears to combine the rounded snout of an aardvark (unknown to the ancient Egyptians) with curious, straight, flat-topped donkey ears. When represented in fully animal, four-legged form, he also displays a long neck, a dog-like body and an erect, curiously forked tail. It seems highly likely that this fantastic appearance is deliberately chaotic; composite deities such as Taweret might display a selection of body-parts culled from different species, but they are the recognizable parts of known animals, not of invented creatures. Nevertheless, Egyptologists have struggled valiantly to identify Seth's component features: there is not enough space here to list all the suggestions, but the more imaginative include camel, long-nosed mouse, hare, antelope, pig, giraffe and boar.

Seth is, quite literally, a larger-than-life character. His weapon of choice is a huge animal-headed *was*-sceptre, a weapon so heavy that only he can lift it. His voice is a thunderous roar. When he transforms, as he quite often does to work his mischief, he assumes the forms of violent, uncontrollable and sexually voracious beasts including the crocodile, bull, pig, wild ass or hippopotamus. His colour of choice is the red of the desert: those with auburn hair (including, perhaps, the Ramesside royal family), animals with red fur, and desert animals in general, may therefore be considered to have an affinity with him. Red was not always chaotic, however. Hathor, mistress of the west, wore a red dress to welcome the deceased to the afterlife, while a pharaoh might take the form of the 'red king', a powerful being who has absorbed the powers of Seth.

Seth is born a younger brother. He is, in fact, the world's first younger brother, an unfortunate accident of birth which causes him great anguish, as he is expected to stand by and smile as first his elder brother and then his young and inexperienced nephew claim the throne of Egypt. Generally speaking, the gods, immune to the threat of child mortality, avoided fraternal conflict and the problem of surplus sons by restricting their families to one child. Mortals could not be so confident and children, boys in particular (as sons could best perform their parents' funerary rites), were welcomed – the more the merrier. Polygamy – a royal prerogative – ensured that the royal nursery remained full, and Ramesses II was not necessarily unusual in fathering up to 100 children: 45 to 46 sons and 40 to 55 daughters. Welcome and useful though younger brothers might be, the royal family could offer them no specific role and, unless some tragedy befell the eldest son, they were unlikely to inherit the throne. Younger sons therefore spent their earlier years as understudies to their eldest brothers, and those who did not eventually become king sank into obscurity once the succession was assured. The immediate royal family was effectively restricted to the king, his close female relatives (queen consort, mother, grandmother and sisters) and his children by the queen consort. Brothers and uncles were no longer regarded as fully royal, although they enjoyed a respected place in court life.

In our account of *The Contendings of Horus and Seth*, the case is settled quite suddenly when the gods decide to ask Osiris his opinion. Not unexpectedly, he sides with his son against his murderous brother. Backing up reasoned argument with a thinly veiled death threat, he is easily able to persuade his fellow gods to his point of view. The crown goes to Horus, and Seth is compensated with an honourable place in the solar boat: a highly suitable place for a storm god. He will spend eternity helping Re fight off the malevolent serpent Apophis, a role that will earn him the gratitude of the masses. A parallel version of the myth has the dead Osiris appearing in court to testify against his murderous brother. Vindicated by the tribunal, Osiris is carried back to the underworld by Seth.

A somewhat different case and outcome are detailed on the Shabaqo Stone. Here Geb serves as the president of the tribunal of the gods. Geb can hardly be an unbiased judge as he is both father to Seth and grandfather to Horus. This may explain his initial decision that Egypt should be shared, with Seth ruling southern Egypt and Horus ruling the north. Geb then changes his mind, decreeing that Horus, as the son of his first-born son, must have the whole land. Stripped of his crown by his father, Seth responds surprisingly well, and uncle and nephew are pacified and united in the house of Ptah.

Seth does not always get off so lightly, however, and the story may end with him banished to the desert, suffering a brutal punishment, or being killed. At the Edfu temple of Horus the conflict was commemorated in the annual Ptolemaic Festival of Victory, which included a re-enactment performed on the temple lake. The drama ended with Seth, in the form of a hippopotamus, mortally pierced by ten harpoons, which injured his snout, forehead, neck, head, ribs, vertebrae, testicles, haunches, legs and hocks. The temple wall shows Horus standing on Seth's back to stab him; here Seth is a diminutive hippo, his small size being a basic precaution against the magical animation of his image. At Isis' insistence Seth's body is dismembered and eaten – his bones are given to the cats and his fat to the worms – so that there are no remains for burial. The ritual accompanying the celebration included the sacrifice and dismembering of a donkey, an animal closely associated with Seth.

6

AT THE END OF TIME

Egypt was, and of course still is, a hot, fly-infested country. The dead were therefore not encouraged to linger over-long in the land of the living. Soon after death the corpse was taken by boat to the 'pure place': the undertaker's workshop. This passage over water was an important ritual, and a symbolic voyage might be undertaken even if it was not strictly necessary. For reasons of religion and hygiene the embalming houses were situated outside the settlements, part-way between the black land and the desert cemeteries. After over two months of gory, messy, manual labour interspersed with priestly magic rites – months which saw the deceased eviscerated, desiccated, oiled and bandaged – the mummy was ready for its funeral.

Just as the violence done to Osiris was kept hidden, so the violence done to the dead in the embalming house was left unrecorded. Our understanding of the practicalities of mummification is therefore derived from modern experimentation (which has its limitations, given the problems inherent in mummifying human corpses), the scientific investigation and occasional unwrapping of ancient mummies, and the works of the Classical authors. Herodotus is our expert here. Although it is unlikely that he ever witnessed the events he describes, his account agrees in many respects with modern scientific observations:[60]

The most perfect process is as follows: as much as possible of the brain is extracted through the nostrils with an iron hook, and what the hook cannot reach is rinsed out with drugs; next the flank is laid open with a flint knife and the whole contents of the abdomen removed; the cavity is then thoroughly cleansed and washed out, first with palm wine and again with an infusion of pounded spices. After that it is filled with pure bruised myrrh, cassia, and every other aromatic substance with the exception of frankincense, and sewn up again, after which the body is placed in natron, covered entirely over, for seventy days – never longer. When this period, which must not be exceeded, is over, the body is washed and wrapped from head to foot in linen cut into strips and smeared on the underside with gum, which is commonly used by the Egyptians instead of glue. In this condition the body is given back to the family, who have a wooden case made shaped like the human figure, into which it is put.

The ritual-religious elements of mummification are even harder to assess, although we know that the chief embalmer might wear the jackal-mask of Anubis, and are told that the embalmer-priest, who mutilated the corpse by drawing a long incision down the left flank, was forced to run away from colleagues, who threw stones to defend the dead against this violent outrage.

JOURNEY TO THE AFTERLIFE

In our modern, secular culture it may be argued that the funeral is for the benefit of the living rather than the salvation of the dead. The same cannot be said of ancient Egypt where the funeral, like the mummification that preceded it, was a vital stage in the regeneration of the deceased. But, important though the funeral undoubtedly was, a reluctance to record the rituals of death means that we know very little about royal funerals, and our somewhat scanty knowledge of mortuary rites is largely derived from elite (non-royal) New Kingdom sources. These make it clear, as we would expect, that the funeral is to be seen as a beginning rather than an end: it is the first stage in the final voyage.

The mummy travelled to the cemetery by sledge, the coffin being dragged by oxen across the desert sand. The accompanying cortège included the lector-priest who would read out the spells, the *sem*-priest who would perform the rituals, the widow (or a paid substitute), family, friends, servants and bands of professional mourners who grieved with ostentatious enthusiasm, beating their breasts and disordering their hair. A series of rituals was performed at the entrance to the tomb. The most important of these was the 'Opening of the Mouth', a ceremony said to have been designed by the craftsman Ptah to animate the eyes, ears, nose and mouth and, in so doing, convert mummies, statues and images into latent beings with a potential for life. The mummy was propped upright as the *sem*-priest touched it with a series of archaic sacred objects including the flint *pesesh-kef* knife (a knife similar to that used to cut the umbilical cord at birth), an adze and the leg of an ox. Meanwhile, the lector-priest recited the spells that would make the transformation complete.

Correctly performed, the mummification and funeral rituals re-animated the mummy, making it ready for the life to come. But, as the mummy transformed into an Osiris, the female dead experienced something of an identity crisis. For most of the dynastic age the deceased was equated with the male gods Osiris, Atum and Re, while rebirth was, to some extent, dependent upon male sexual potency. Only in Roman times do we find the female deceased being addressed as 'Hathor' rather than 'Osiris'. To achieve a proper rebirth women therefore had to undergo a subtle form of gender adaptation that would allow them to utilize male-orientated funerary myths and accessories. Experts are divided over the extent to which tomb scenes can be interpreted as sexual images, but it has been argued that almost everything, from the blatantly attractive, semi-naked dancing girls to the apparently innocent pouring of wine into a cup, was designed to arouse the male deceased.

With the funerary feast consumed, the mourners departed and the mummy sealed safe in the tomb, the deceased entered a stage somewhere between death and life. While the earliest mummies now faced eternity within the tomb, mummies from the later Old Kingdom onwards prepared for the ultimate big adventure. The time had come for the spirit to embark on the long and perilous journey to the afterlife, a journey which would invariably involve some form of test. The Middle Kingdom *Coffin Texts* describe the deceased appearing before a court or tribunal, very similar to the earthly civil court, where he or she can petition for entry into the next life. As time progresses there is increasing emphasis on separating the good from the bad, so the New Kingdom funerary texts describe a more lengthy journey and a more elaborate court appearance featuring the weighing of the heart of the deceased against the feather of truth. Our knowledge of this ordeal is largely derived from the *Book of the Dead*. Like the *Coffin Texts*, from which it is clearly descended, the *Book* is a diverse collection of spells packed with advice and essential knowledge for those wishing to achieve eternity.

The *Book* makes it very obvious that entry to the afterlife was dependent on knowledge rather than on purity, piety or bravery. Quite simply, anyone rich enough to be mummified and buried with a copy of the *Book of the Dead* was guaranteed entry to the kingdom of Osiris. As New Kingdom Egypt was a land without money it is difficult to value this ticket to eternity, but it has been estimated that a basic *Book* could have been purchased for roughly the equivalent cost of a bed. Mummification, a rock-cut tomb and appropriate grave-goods would have cost considerably more; an endowment for a priest and his descendants to make offerings to the dead in perpetuity, yet more still. It therefore seems unlikely that more than 10 per cent of the population could afford a full and proper burial, complete in all its aspects. Many of those who were mummified were able to cut costs by utilizing second-hand linen, so that some Egyptians appeared before Osiris wrapped in old sheets, towels and, in at least one case, the sail of a boat (which may, of course, have helped the deceased to make a pilgrimage to Abydos). The after-death expectations of the majority of the people, those who were buried unmummified in desert pit graves, are unknown although, given the obvious popularity of the cult of Osiris, it seems likely that they, too, had some hope of an eternal life.

Passing over the horizon, following the dying sun, the deceased travelled westwards until he or she came to a labyrinth guarded by a series of gateways or portals. While *Book of the Dead* spell 146 indicates that there were twenty-one portals, spell 144/147 lists just seven, each with a named doorkeeper, guardian and announcer.[61] In order to progress, the deceased had to be able to recite a set text before each doorway, and name the various doors, guardians and announcers.

THE COURT OF THE TWO TRUTHS

With the labyrinth safely negotiated, the spirit entered the 'broad court of the two truths' to stand trial before Osiris and the forty-two assessor-gods. The well-prepared spirit, equipped with the *Book*, already knew the names or epithets that these judges would use, their provenance or identification, and the specific crime that he or she would judge:

1. Far Strider, of Heliopolis (falsehood)
2. Fire Embracer, of Kherara (robbery)
3. Nosey, of Hermopolis (extortion)
4. Swallower of Shades, of the cavern (stealing)
5. Dangerous One, of Rosetau (murder)
6. Double Lion, of the sky (wasting food)
7. Fiery Eyes, of Letopolis (crookedness)
8. Flame, he who came forth backwards (stealing offerings)
9. Bone Breaker, of Herakleopolis (lying)
10. Green Flame, of Memphis (taking food)
11. You, of the Cavern of the West (sullenness)
12. White Teeth, of the Faiyum (transgression)
13. Eater of Blood, of the shambles (killing a sacred bull)
14. Eater of Entrails, of the house of Thirty (perjury)
15. Lord of Truth, of Maaty (stealing bread)
16. Wanderer, of Bubastis (eavesdropping)
17. Pale One, of Heliopolis (babbling)
18. Doubly Evil, of Andjet (arguing)
19. *Wememty*-Snake, of the place of execution (homosexuality)
20. See Whom You Bring, of the house of Min (misbehaving)
21. Over the Old One, of Mau (terrorizing)
22. Demolisher, of Chois (transgressing)
23. Disturber, of Weryt (bad temper)
24. Youth, of the Heliopolitan Nome (unhearing of truth)
25. Foreteller, of Wenes (creating a disturbance)
26. You of the Altar, of the secret place (hoodwinking)
27. Face Behind Him, of the cavern of wrong (copulating with a boy)
28. Hot Foot, of the dusk (neglect)
29. You of the Darkness, of the darkness (quarrelling)
30. Bringer of Your Offering, of Sais (over-active)
31. Owner of Faces, of Nedjefet (impatience)
32. Accuser, of Wetjenet (damaging the image of a god)

33. Owner of Horns, of Asyut (talkative)
34. Nefertem, of Memphis (wrongdoing)
35. Temsep, of Busiris (conjuration against the king)
36. You Who Acted Wilfully, of Tjebu (wading in water)
37. Water Smiter, of the Abyss (being loud-voiced)
38. Commander of Mankind, of your house (reviling the gods)
39. Bestower of Good, of the Harpoon Nome (doing ?)
40. Bestower of Powers, of the city (making distinctions for self)
41. Snake with Raised Head, of the cavern (dishonest wealth)
42. Snake Who Brings and Gives, of the silent land (blasphemy)

The names used by the tribunal often differed from their usual names, so that 'Far Strider, of Heliopolis' is likely to be Re, while 'Nosey, of Hermopolis' is probably Thoth. Standing before the gods, the deceased was called upon to justify his or her mortal life by reciting the 'negative confession': a list of diverse moral and ethical crimes that had not been committed. Here the emphasis was very much on the avoidance of sin rather than the active pursuit of virtue or piety, and specific, personal, sins were entirely excluded from the list. It was enough that the deceased had not deviated from the expected norm:[62]

I have not done falsehood against men,
I have not impoverished my associates,
I have done no wrong in the Place of Truth,
I have not learned that which is not,
I have done no evil . . .

The climax of the trial, the most dangerous moment, where the deceased could not simply rely on the *Book*, was the 'weighing of the heart' ceremony. Vignettes show Anubis leading the deceased forward; it is his duty to place the heart in the pan of the scales so that it might be weighed against the feather of Maat, the symbol of truth and justice. On top of the scales there squats a baboon, the representative of either Thoth or Khonsu. In the exclusively royal *Book of Gates*, the judgement scene which immediately precedes the sixth hour of night shows Osiris sitting on a throne before an empty, human-headed balance.

The heart, believed to be the seat of intelligence rather than emotion, was left in place during mummification rituals that saw the removal and preservation of the lungs, liver, stomach and intestines (organs that would be needed in the afterlife), and the removal and disposal of the brain whose function was un-appreciated (and which would therefore not be needed in the afterlife). No deceased could arrive at the weighing ceremony without a heart, so hearts which were accidentally removed were sewn back, not always in the correct place: Ramesses II was by no means the only Egyptian to meet Osiris with a heart, sewn with golden thread, on the wrong side of his chest. There was a very real danger that a disloyal heart might weigh heavy in the scales, condemning its pure and sin-free owner to permanent death. Fortunately, there were spells specifically designed to avert such a calamity. *Book of the Dead* spell 30 was often engraved on the flat base of the heart scarab, a large beetle-shaped amulet which was incorporated within the mummy wrappings to support and maybe even replace the flesh-and-blood heart, should it somehow be mislaid in the embalming house:[63]

> *O heart which I had from my mother, O my heart which I had upon earth, do not rise up against me as a witness in the presence of the Lord of Things; do not speak against me concerning what I have done, do not bring up anything against me in the presence of the Great God, Lord of the West ...*
>
> *Not dying in the west, but becoming a spirit in it.*

With the weighing complete, Thoth, Horus and the Ennead announced the verdict and Thoth recorded it in his scroll. The light-hearted, safe at last, were transfigured to become the blessed dead. They were now equated with Osiris and Horus, 'true-of-voice', and, as an effective *akh*, they gained immediate admittance to the Field of Reeds, where they would hope to live a version of their earthly life.

Those who lacked virtue, whose hearts weighed heavy in the balance, faced a horrific future of eternal chaos. During the Old Kingdom the impure dead might suffer perpetual hunger and thirst, or might be required to perform bizarre, chaotic behaviour such as walking upside down or consuming excrement or urine. As the Middle Kingdom developed, the damned were liable to suffer appalling punishment in the 'place of destruction': they might be burned in the lake of fire (a lake which soothes the virtuous but consumes wrongdoers), slashed by knives, cooked in cauldrons or eaten by an untameable beast. The New Kingdom funerary books introduce us to Ammit, the 'eater of the damned' or 'beast of destiny': a hideous composite monster with the head of a crocodile, the fore-parts and body of a lion or leopard and the hind-parts of a hippopotamus. As Ammit was equally at home on land or in water, the condemned spirit could not hope to run or swim away from his or her fate. Vignettes in the *Book of the Dead* show Ammit squatting beside the scales, ready to devour the hearts of those who fail the test. Of course, because the owners of the *Book* did not expect to fail, we rarely see scenes of Ammit fulfilling her mission. However, we know that, with the heart destroyed and, perhaps, the earthly mummy ripped apart by daemons, the guilty could never be transfigured. They were either doomed to haunt the living as malevolent, restless ghosts, or consigned to the outer darkness beyond the created world.

The virtuous passed straight into the Field of Reeds, a part of the *Duat* (the underworld familiar to us from Re's nocturnal adventures). The non-royal dead would then spend their days in the Field and their nights either resting in their tomb or, perhaps, assisting the solar boat of Re on its nocturnal journey. Meanwhile, kings, altogether different beings, would be united with the gods. Not everyone looked forward to this life beyond death. Taimhotep, wife of the high priest of Ptah, Pasherenptah III, died aged thirty during the reign of Cleopatra VII, leaving three daughters, a son and a grieving husband. Her funerary stela records her very personal fears:[64]

> The west, it is a land of sleep,
> Darkness weighs on the dwelling-place,
> Those who are there sleep in their mummy-forms.
> They wake not to see their brothers,
> They see not their fathers, their mothers,
> Their hearts forget their wives, their children.
> The water of life which has food for all,
> It is thirst for me;
> It comes to him who is on earth,
> I thirst with water beside me . . .
> Say to me 'You are not far from water.'
> Turn my face to the north wind at the edge of the water,
> Perhaps my heart will then be cooled in its grief.

Book of the Dead spell 109 hints at the strange grandeur of the Field of Reeds: a fertile land bound by walls of iron, where trees are made of turquoise, and barley grows five cubits tall. It would be a grave mistake to imagine this Field as the equivalent of our peaceful Christian or Islamic paradise. This was not a place where the blessed dead could rest for ever with friends and family, basking in the approval of a beneficent god. The Field was a more personal and challenging environment; a land specific to each deceased. There were waterways, fields, harvests and sunshine, but there were also more sinister regions: sandy mounds and caverns housing nameless, ancient gods. Every night, as Re sailed by, evil was defeated and light triumphed; every morning, as he left the *Duat*, they sprang back to life again. Barry Kemp has described the Field as a 'place of journeys, with multiple destinations and obstacles to overcome'.[65] Reading spells which allow the deceased to commandeer the solar boat, or to transform into a crocodile, snake or bird, it is hard to disagree with his summary.

The Field of Reeds was, of course, only a part of the afterlife existence. As the *akh* spirit journeyed forever onwards, the bird-headed *ba* spirit either haunted the land of the living or travelled across the sky with Re, before returning to the tomb at night. Meanwhile the weaker *ka* spirit sought nourishment – the usual formula demanded an offering of 1,000 loaves of bread and 1,000 jugs of beer – within the tomb. The living paid frequent visits to the houses of the dead, where they left offerings of food, drink and words, picnicked at festival times, and occasionally, if they felt that they were being unjustly haunted, wrote letters of complaint or supplication which generally took the form 'I was good to you during your lifetime, so why are you allowing bad things to happen to me now?' As everyone knew that ghosts could communicate with the living through dreams, specific spells protected the living from nocturnal hauntings by the evil dead. These hauntings could involve touching, kissing and more serious assaults, as the dead might still be sexually active.

THE TALE OF SI-OSIRI

The New Kingdom royal funerary books – the books which detail the passage of the sun through the underworld – confirm that those who have lived unjust lives will be classified as the enemies of the king/sun/*maat*. They appear in the *Duat* as opponents to be felled, they lie under the feet of the virtuous, and they fight in vain alongside those who would halt the solar boat. However, there is no equivalent of our modern concept of Hell, and no equivalent of Purgatory, where wrongdoers might eventually repent. By the end of the dynastic age, when Egypt was coming under increasing foreign influence, this perception of the afterlife had changed.

The Late Period text known today as *Setne II* preserves the myth of Si-Osiri, a powerful magician who takes his father, Setne, on a visit to the halls of the afterlife so that he may contrast the perpetually idyllic existence of the blessed dead with the tortures reserved for the wicked.[66] This is a story strongly reminiscent of the Biblical parable of Dives and Lazarus, and it is clear that Si-Osiri's version of the afterlife has absorbed elements of the Greek Hades as a place of divine retribution and perpetual torment. Missing pages and gaps in the text prevent us from appreciating the full horrors on display, but we know that in the fourth hall Setne sees men condemned to plait ropes which are immediately chewed apart by donkeys, and men who are suffering perpetual hunger and thirst because the food and drink they crave is suspended just out of reach and, as they struggle upwards, pits are dug at their feet. The fifth hall has the spirits of the deceased standing in rows; those who are accused of crimes plead at the door which is fixed in the right eye of a man who is pleading and lamenting his fate. The sixth hall is reserved for the gods of the tribunal of the inhabitants of the afterlife. It is here that the servants of the afterlife make their accusations. Finally, in the seventh hall, Setne sees the crowned Osiris seated on a throne of finest gold. Anubis is on his left, Thoth is on his right, and the gods of the tribunal of the inhabitants of the netherworld stand both to his left and right. Using a balance, the gods weigh the good deeds of the deceased against the bad deeds, and Thoth records one of three possible outcomes. Those who have more misdeeds than good deeds are given to the Devourer and are permanently destroyed; those who have more good deeds than misdeeds are taken in among the gods of the tribunal; those who have good deeds equal to their misdeeds join the spirits who serve the god Sokar-Osiris.

Si-Osiri makes the point that the virtuous poor man may not receive an elaborate funeral, but he will nevertheless enjoy the idyllic afterlife denied the wealthy, but morally bankrupt, man. This admirable moral stand is not necessarily true of a land where proper, and extremely expensive, mummification was a vital part of the journey leading to the land of Osiris. There then comes a neat plot twist. It becomes apparent that Si-Osiri is not actually the son of Setne; he is the legendary sorcerer Horus-son-of-Paneshe, who has returned from an earlier age to defend Egypt in a magical contest. The story ends in best pantomime tradition with the false son vanishing in a puff of smoke and a real son being born to Setne and his wife Mehusekhe.

If it was possible to live after death, it had to be possible to die after death. This time, however, death would be both irreversible and permanent. The Second Death would follow the destruction of the corpse and the death of the *ka*. This was a truly terrible fate, and the worry that the mummy might be either accidentally or deliberately destroyed was a constant and very real one. Spells for 'not perishing in the land of the dead' were included in tombs from the Old Kingdom onwards.

Tomb-robbing, the activity most likely to lead to the destruction of the mummy, was punished by the state with utmost severity: those caught stealing from the dead could expect execution by being impaled on a wooden stake, close by the scene of their crime. Usurping a tomb – future generations ejecting long-dead and probably already robbed occupants before using the tomb themselves – was less of a crime, but an equal threat to the well-being of the deceased. Fortunately, it was understood that, in an emergency, the *ka* could survive in a named statue or image, a written name or even a memory. Kings who carved their name throughout their land were therefore not only indulging their own propaganda, but were taking practical steps to ensure that they would indeed live for ever. Conversely, kings who attempted to erase the names of their predecessors from the official records were pushing those earlier pharaohs a step nearer to permanent obliteration.

The very real fear of permanent oblivion made the Second Death a suitable punishment for those who had committed unforgivable crimes. The most awful punishment that the state could inflict was execution either by impaling or by burning, both of which caused the destruction of the body. Stories which told of unfortunates being consumed by fire, eaten by dogs or snatched by crocodiles conveyed a real horror to their original audiences. Only those who drowned – accidental drownings being an unpleasant fact of life in river-based Egypt – were excused the normal funerary rites in order to claim their place among the blessed dead. Their drowning linked them to the early, undeveloped myth which saw Seth drown Osiris, and which allowed drowning to became recognized as a good death.

THE END OF ALL THINGS

Most of Egypt's gods were born in a fairly conventional way to divine parents. Some, like Horus-the-Child and Ihy son of Hathor, then lived their lives as eternal children, naked and sporting the side-lock of youth. Others were perpetual, ageless adults. Re was unusual in experiencing a full human lifetime as he crossed the sky, starting the morning as the young and vigorous Khepri, and ending the evening as the old and decrepit Atum.

But the world of the gods, like Egypt itself, was gerontocratic: the elder son could only inherit when his father died and passed on his role. How then could the immortal gods transfer power to their heirs? Some, the first god-kings of Egypt, chose to retire. Others, like Osiris, had to die. The death of Osiris was Egypt's best-known divine death, but it was by no means the only one. Osiris died just once and was to a certain extent reborn, although he could never rejoin the land of the living. Six of the Ogdoad of Hermopolis either died or retired when their work was done, and the divine snakes on the fantastic island visited by the Shipwrecked Sailor all died when they were consumed by fire. For a time Egyptologists believed that Seth might have been truly immortal, but later New Kingdom images of him as a mummy indicate that he too would eventually die. By now it was acknowledged that Thoth and Seshat, who were known to inscribe the reign lengths of the kings on the leaves of the sacred *ished* tree, might also assign fixed lifespans to the gods.

Death, of course, need not be the end of life. Given the Egyptian view of time as an endlessly repeating cycle, we might expect to find the gods dying and then being rejuvenated. But what would happen at the end of all things, when all the gods died and none was reborn? Given their avoidance of anything that might be interpreted as an affront to *maat*, it is not surprising that the Egyptians made few references to the end of the world. But we can piece together a few allusions. Time had erupted with a surge of water and a flash of life, as the primeval mound burst from the still waters of Nun. But Atum the creator understood that what could be created could also be ended. *Coffin Texts* spell 1130 predicts a bleak future. Millions of years after their coming into separate existence, Atum will become one with Osiris 'in one place' while the land returns to the waters:[67]

I possess life, because I am its lord, and my staff will not be taken away. I have passed myriads of years between myself and yonder Inert One, the son of Geb (Osiris); I will sit with him in the one place, and mounds will be towns and towns will be mounds; mansion will desolate mansion.

The first cry of the *benu* bird heralded the birth of the world; now it will announce the end of all things. *Book of the Dead* spell 175, a 'spell for not dying again', is brutally explicit:[68]

The Deceased speaks: *What will be the duration of my life?*
Atum speaks: *You shall be for millions on millions of years, a lifetime of millions of years. I will despatch the Elders and destroy all that I have made; the earth shall return to the Primordial Water, to the surging flood, as in its original state. But I will remain with Osiris. I will transform myself into something else, namely a serpent, without men knowing or the gods seeing . . .*

This final meeting of opposites, the solar creator of life and the king of the dead, is entirely appropriate as already, each midnight, they are temporarily united in the underworld. At the end of time Atum and Osiris will writhe together as twin snakes in the formless waters of chaos. And, perhaps, eventually, the cycle of life will begin all over again.

III

THE GREAT GODDESSES

I worship my mistress, for I have seen her beauty.

Coffin Texts *spell 484*

7

THE GOLDEN ONE

Egypt's first goddesses appear before her first kings and queens and, perhaps, before her first gods. The Predynastic cemeteries of the Nagada cultural phase have yielded large quantities of painted pottery decorated with images which we must assume had a deep significance for the grave-owners and their bereaved families. On these pots, amid scenes of rivers, boats, animals and stick-men, we see ample female figures whose long, curved arms, raised above faceless heads, remind us of the curved horns of a cow. The painted figures are paralleled by the simple pottery female figurines included in some Nagada graves. These, with rudimentary, bird-like faces but well-defined breasts and hips, again raise horn-like arms above their heads.

A firm link between cows and the sky has already been established.[69] The ceremonial Gerzeh Palette, which dates to the Nagada II cultural phase, shows a stylized cow's head decorated with five stars on the ears, the horns and the top of the head, and this symbolism is repeated in seal impressions and on a 1st Dynasty porphyry bowl recovered from Hierakonpolis, where we can see that the celestial cow has a human face. At the same time, parallel to the developing cow cults, cults were emerging to celebrate the fierce virility and fertility of the bull who was now associated with both gods and the king. The gods Ptah (Apis), Montu (Buchis) and Re-Atum (Mnevis) would each be associated with living bulls: their stories have been told in Chapter 2.

Given this wealth of evidence, it seems safe to assert that, by the end of the Predynastic Period, the cow had become a divine symbol of creation and fertility or rebirth, with strong stellar connections. She may even have been the embodiment of the Milky Way.[70] However, it is a step too far to deduce that all prehistoric Egyptians worshipped an archetypal earth-mother, a celestial cow who served as the common ancestor for all subsequent female deities. Given Egypt's strong polytheistic tradition, there is no reason to believe that the diverse goddesses whom we encounter in the dynastic age are merely aspects or manifestations of one original mother goddess.

SHE OF THE TWO FACES

We have already encountered the Narmer Palette, a carved ceremonial cosmetic palette that celebrates the first king of Egypt as he stamps his authority on his land. The Palette makes a clear statement of divinely authorized royal dominance. Even at this early stage in Egypt's history, *maat* must be seen to triumph over chaos. But alongside the brutal battle and post-battle scenes the Palette shows images of mythical creatures: twin serpopards whose long necks twist together, snake-like, to represent the newly entwined lands of Upper and Lower Egypt; a bird (possibly an early form of Horus) who leads a stylized prisoner by a rope threaded through his nose; a bull who attacks a walled city and gores a fallen enemy. This awareness that the animal and the divine may be closely entwined is particularly obvious on the upper register of each face, where we see two heads of an unnamed cow deity who is usually identified as Bat, but who has also been identified as the celestial cow Mehet-Weret.

Bat, 'female spirit', features in *Pyramid Texts* spell 506 as 'Bat with her two faces'. Reading this description literally, it seems that the goddess has two opposing yet complementary countenances that can, perhaps, look into the past and the future, or see both the living and the dead. In defiance of Egyptian artistic convention which decrees that human and divine faces will be shown in profile with just one eye visible, Bat looks directly at us so we can see her human face with its two large, cow-like eyes, and can observe her broad cow's ears and the two, prominent, inwardly curved horns that rise from her forehead. If we look closely at Narmer himself, we can see that his kilt is decorated with four miniature versions of the same, though not an identical, full-face cow's head. By the time of the *Pyramid Texts* this kilt-cow has become identified with Hathor.

Bat would remain an important goddess in southern Egypt for many centuries until, during the 11th Dynasty, her cult and mythology started to be absorbed by the increasingly powerful cult of Hathor. However, Bat's broad human face could still be found on the handle of the *sistrum*, the sacred rattle which, from the 5th Dynasty onwards, was shaken by women in praise of Hathor. It seems that the slightly metallic sound of the *sistrum* recalled the sound of the rustling of the papyrus thicket from which Hathor the divine cow emerged, and where Isis hid her infant son Horus from his furious uncle Seth. An equally pleasing percussive sound with divine connotations could be produced by shaking a beaded *menyt* necklace.[71] The women who dressed in bead or shell girdles – recovered from Middle Kingdom contexts, and illustrated in the banqueting scenes depicted on New Kingdom tomb walls – presumably generated a similar, seductive rattling noise as they danced.

Here, in the *sistrum*, we have a classic example of an artefact riddled with mythic allusions. Designs vary, but the top of the *sistrum*, a frame crossed by metal rods threaded with metal disks,

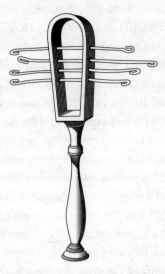

A simplified sistrum: *the beads that made the percussive sound have been lost*

often takes the shape of a temple *naos* (shrine). The handle of the *naos*-style *sistrum* is usually decorated with the Bat/Hathor head or mask, while a pair of 'horns' extends to flank the frame. Handle decoration might include a vulture and a cobra, both symbols of femininity and, in the case of the cobra, a reminder that gentle Hathor was also the fierce Eye of Re, whose irascible temper might be soothed by percussive rhythm. A cat motif might indicate that the *sistrum* was employed in the cult of the goddess Bastet. Plutarch, writing at the beginning of the second century AD when the *sistrum* had become closely connected with the cult of Isis, believed that the instrument was used to frighten away the evil Typhon (Seth). Plutarch offered his own explanation of its elements: for him the frame represented the lunar cycle, the four rods the four elements, the two Bat/Hathor heads life and death, and the often-encountered cat decoration the moon.

THE DAUGHTER OF RE

Hathor makes her first undisputed named appearance on the forecourt of the valley temple built as part of his Giza pyramid complex by the 4th Dynasty King Khaefre. Here she represents southern Egypt, while Bastet represents the north. Several hard-stone statues recovered from the mortuary temple of Khaefre's son and successor, Menkaure, show the king standing between a local nome goddess and Hathor, who is unlabelled, but who appears as a woman wearing a tight-fitting sheath dress, cow horns and a solar disk. Her popularity and importance then increase swiftly as she absorbs the mythologies of Bat and Mehet-Weret, so that, while she is a relatively minor character in the Old Kingdom *Pyramid Texts*, she has become a powerful figure in the Middle Kingdom *Coffin Texts*.

Her rapid rise in status has led to suggestions that Hathor was effectively invented (or re-invented with an enhanced mythology) as a suitable consort/daughter for Re, the dominant state god of the Old Kingdom. Motherless, it seems that she was created when the tears of Re fell either on to the first earth, or on to a lotus blossom. Her written name, a falcon within the box that represents a house, tells its own tale. Hathor is quite literally '*Hwt Hor*', the house or temple of Horus: she is the womb from which Horus is born; the sky in which the falcon soars; and the world that Horus rules. She is both a sky-goddess and a mother-cow who protects and nourishes either her own child or the child of Isis in the papyrus thicket and, by extension, who nourishes and protects all of Egypt's pharaohs.[72] She may even, on occasion, be the solar disk that houses and transports the solar child. At a more practical level she may be the divine personification of the building at Heliopolis where Horus the king was crowned. As

Hathor was associated with Horus, and Horus was associated with the living king, so Hathor herself was strongly linked with kingship. Her absorption of the cults of lesser local goddesses, who were transformed into versions of Hathor, therefore indirectly supported the Egypt-wide role of the king, who was himself supported by Hathor.

Hathor might also be the wife of Horus, and so be equated with the consort of the living king. This version of Hathor has strong healing powers, so that when, in the *Contendings*, Seth blinds Horus, it is Hathor rather than Isis who has the skill to restore his sight using gazelle milk. Hathor of Dendera is both the wife of Horus of Edfu and the great cow of the heavens who gives birth to the sun (her son Ihy) each day. Ihy, also known as Harsomptus, is a human-form child god who, like his mother, appreciates percussive rhythms; his name may be broadly understood to mean either '*sistrum* player' or 'calf'. However, Ihy has a complicated genealogy, and is also accepted as the son of Isis, Nephthys or Sekhmet, by either Horus or Re.

Once a year Hathor of Dendera was briefly united with her husband Horus of Edfu. At the Festival of the Beautiful Union, celebrated two weeks before the appearance of the new moon in the third month of summer, Hathor (in the form of her cult statue) left her temple, processed to the river and embarked on the lengthy journey south. Horus (also in the form of a cult statue) met his spouse at the quay, and the divine couple were presented with *maat* before travelling to the Edfu temple for a marriage ceremony. After fourteen days with Horus, Hathor returned to Dendera to await the birth of her son. Meanwhile, in a nod to northern tradition which accepted Hathor as the daughter of Ptah, the version of Ptah who lived within the precincts of the Edfu temple paid an annual visit to his daughter at Dendera. This was replicated in northern Egypt by the visit of Ptah of Memphis to his daughter Hathor of the Sycamore.

The opposing tradition was honoured when, during the ceremony of 'uniting with the sun', Hathor's statue was taken from the gloom of the temple sanctuary and placed on the roof, so that the goddess might communicate directly with, and be invigorated by, her father, Re.

SEKHMET AND THE DESTRUCTION OF MANKIND

Hathor's strong solar connections are made obvious by the solar disk, supported by two tall cow horns and augmented by a uraeus, which she wears on her head. Among her different solar personae she may be the wife, daughter or, occasionally, mother of Re. As the fierce uraeus she protects her father with a burning heat; as the Golden One she accompanies him on his daily voyage across the sky; as the Eye of Re she acts as his agent. But when the mild-mannered Hathor grows angry she transforms into Sekhmet, the 'powerful one', an uncompromising, fire-breathing lioness armed with an arsenal of pestilence and plague. Sekhmet's destructive female anger – the burning anger of the uraeus – is put to good use as she protects Egypt's pharaohs. This fierce defence of the king, and her skill with the bow and arrow, cause her to become closely associated with the army so that Ramesses II, valiantly fighting his solo battle at Kadesh, might claim to be 'like Seth great-of-strength; like Sekhmet in the moment of her rage'.

Sekhmet's personal life is relatively myth-free, although we know that she is the wife of Ptah of Memphis and the mother of his son, Nefertum (or, in some accounts, the mother of Heka). She may be equated with the lioness Mut of Thebes, daughter of Re, and also with Pakhet, 'she who scratches', a wild lioness who hunts by night in the deserts of Middle Egypt. As 'mistress of life', Sekhmet can cure all the ills that she inflicts, and her priests are recognized as healers with a powerful magic. In this capacity she is referenced frequently in the medical texts.

The story of Hathor and her alter ego Sekhmet is told in *The Destruction of Mankind*, the opening section of the New Kingdom royal funerary book known as the *Book of the Cow of Heaven*.[73] The story tells of a mortal rebellion against King Re, while the accompanying illustration shows his solar boat sailing along the body of the celestial cow Mehet-Weret, who is supported by Shu and eight divine assistants. Time, and the king, may also support the sky. It may be that the myth represents an attempt to understand disease and plague as a divine punishment for human sins; alternatively, it has been suggested that it seeks to explain the collapse of royal authority that occurred at the end of the Old Kingdom. Certainly, it provides a neat explanation for the separation of the sun from the earth.

The story is set in the time before history: a time when Re has not yet started his daily journey across the sky, and when gods and people live together in Egypt's equivalent of the Garden of Eden. Life should be idyllic, but the people have turned against their king. It seems that Re, who is gently fossilizing into precious metals and minerals, is considered too old to rule effectively. He may even be senile, although he is certainly capable of decisive action in this tale. Ancient Egypt was a relatively young society and, although Kings Pepi II and Ramesses II lived well into their nineties, each spending over sixty years on the throne, forty would have been considered a reasonable lifespan for those who managed to avoid childhood illnesses, accidents and the hazards of pregnancy. While the elderly were generally respected for their wisdom, long-standing kings were expected to prove their fitness to rule by participating in a *heb sed,* or jubilee celebration: a ceremony of renewal or rejuvenation performed (in theory) by individual kings after thirty years on the throne, and every three years thereafter. The *heb sed* rituals included a run which saw the king, or his representative, racing against an invisible enemy whom we may tentatively identify as old age or death.

Realizing that his people have turned against him, Re first demonstrates divine wrath, and then divine compassion. The outcome, however, is not satisfactory to him, and the story ends with his ascent into heaven. This, given the text's location in the royal tombs, may be equated with the rebirth and ascension of the dead pharaoh.

It happened in the time of Re, the self-created one, when he had ruled gods and humans together for many years. Re had grown old in his kingship and now his bones were turning to silver, his flesh to gold and his hair to true lapis lazuli. The people had grown dissatisfied and, ill concealed in the desert, rebels were daring to plot against their king. Aware of their treachery, Re started to think of leaving Egypt and retiring to the waters of Nun. But first he needed advice.

Re issued his orders: 'Summon my Eye, and the gods Shu, Tefnut, Geb, Nut and Nun and their retinues. But bring them to me in secret; do not let the people see them enter the palace.'

It was done, and the gods slipped quietly into the palace to stand in respectful ranks on either side of Re's throne. They bowed low in greeting and invited Re to speak before his father Nun.

Re could not hide his anger: 'My father, from whom I came into being, and respected ancestors: look at what is happening. The people, who grew from my tears, are plotting against me. I think of killing each and every one but I will not do this until I have heard your thoughts. Tell me what you would do in my place.'

Nun spoke: 'My son, you are indeed a great king. Keep your throne and remember how the people fear when your Eye is upon them. Set your Eye free, and she will smite the rebels for you. Release Hathor and the evil schemers will be destroyed.'

And so it was done. Re unleashed the fury hidden deep within his Eye, his gentle daughter Hathor. The Eye of Re transformed and Sekhmet the powerful one came into being. The desert ran red with blood as the Eye hunted the traitors and killed them, one by one. She did not stop until the sands were littered with bodies. Then, temporarily sated, she returned in triumph to her father to boast of her achievements. Re welcomed Hathor back with joy and gratitude, but his happiness was tempered with apprehension. For Re belatedly realized the true power of the force he had unleashed. The sight of so much killing had sickened him, and he had decided to spare the remainder of mankind. But the Eye of Re, had tasted human blood and liked it. She was determined to kill again.

Re devised a plan to thwart his headstrong daughter. Sending his swiftest messengers he ordered vast quantities of red pigment from the land of Yebu. The pigment was brought to Heliopolis, where it was ground to finest powder by the king's most trusted servant, the High Priest of Re. At the same time scores of serving maids were put to work grinding many hundreds of baskets of barley. The red pigment was then mixed with the barley, and 7,000 jars of blood-red beer were brewed. Re and his fellow gods inspected the blood-red beer, and were pleased.

The dark day dawned when Hathor-Sekhmet, the vengeful Eye of Re, planned to destroy the remainder of the people. Re rose early that day, and travelled to the killing fields ahead of his daughter. He emptied the 7,000 jars of blood-red beer over the fields so that they were flooded to a depth of three palms. The Eye of Re saw the foaming red liquid covering the land and thought that it was blood. Bending down, she saw her own beautiful face reflected in the liquid, and was entranced. Forgetting mankind, she drank the beer, became confused and returned to her father drunk and satisfied. Re welcomed his daughter in peace.

Re's problems were solved and he should have been happy, but his heart was still troubled. He found it impossible to forgive the people, and he no longer wished to rule on earth. Leaving his fellow gods behind, Re clambered on to the back of the celestial cow Mehet-Weret and rose into the heavens. From this lofty vantage point he was able to watch mankind still quarrelling beneath him.

Re has not created evil, but he does have to confront it. His knee-jerk response, crude but undeniably effective, is to wipe out mankind and start again. The idyll has ended as, for the first time, death visits Egypt. Parallels with Biblical, Mesopotamian and later Classical tales of destruction are obvious. But in Egypt the slaughter starts not with a flood – here floods are considered beneficial – but with the Eye of Re (Hathor as Sekhmet) who carries plague and burns her father's enemies with the fierce heat of the sun. Sekhmet has forgotten, or does not care, that her mortal victims are the product of the tears of Re, and are therefore, effectively, both her siblings and her children. A variation on this theme in *Papyrus Jumilhac* sees Isis transforming into a version of Hathor to slay the followers of Seth, while the Edfu temple records the drama of a rebellion in Nubia in Re's regnal Year 363, which ends with the execution of the rebel leader Seth.

Observing the carnage but not swayed by the plight of any specific individual, Re decides to halt the slaughter. Again we are not told why. Perhaps all the plotters, those who had fled to the desert, have already died and the murder that is scheduled to take place in the fields will involve the killing of the innocent, which would surely be an offence against *maat*. It may simply be that he is worried that the death of all the people will bring an end to the offerings which he craves. Whatever his reasoning, Re is now facing a dilemma. How will he stop his headstrong daughter?

While she is not the only drinker in the pantheon – Seth, too, is known to like a tipple and is considered the patron deity of wine – it is well known that Hathor has a deep and permanent thirst. She is the goddess of inebriation, whose temple rituals and festivals include the tellingly named 'Festival of Drunkenness', a Graeco-Roman celebration involving music, dance, happiness (misery was specifically banned) and the immoderate consumption of alcohol, which was enjoyed on day 20 of the first month of inundation. A text in the Edfu temple confirms her weakness, 'while all the gods live by incense burning, The Golden One [Hathor] lives by drunkenness', while, in a less than subtle reference to his mother's habits, her son Ihy bears the titles 'lord of bread' and 'master of brewing', brewing and baking being closely linked, grain-based tasks performed by women.

The answer, therefore, is a simple deception. Offer Hathor a potent drink which she will be unable to refuse, and she will be deflected from her mission. Re could have offered his daughter wine but instead he chooses beer, a diet staple, brewed in most houses, quaffed by men, women and children alike, presented to the gods in copious amounts in their daily rituals, used in medical recipes, and offered to the dead as the tomb nourishment of choice. Sweet and soupy, and so thick that it was occasionally drunk through a filtering straw, Egyptian beer was far weaker than modern beers. Re dyes his beer with an unspecified red pigment, which is probably ochre. It now resembles both the blood that Hathor craves, and the rusty-red floodwaters of the inundation. After consuming 7,000 jars of this potent cocktail, even the seasoned toper Hathor feels sleepy.

Hathor is distracted from her mission when she sees her own beautiful face mirrored in the shimmering surface of the liquid. Like most Egyptians, it seems that she is unaccustomed to seeing her own image. A polished metal 'see face' was a luxury item which, although undoubtedly used by both men and women when applying cosmetics, quickly came to symbolize femininity and female sexuality. Strongly associated with Hathor and with the sun's disk, and often decorated with the flat face of Bat, mirrors were used in Hathoric cult dances, while rituals recorded on Ptolemaic temple walls show the king presenting mirrors – a symbolic sun and moon – to Hathor and Isis. By returning the mirrors to the king, the goddesses confirm his authority over light.

The slaughter has been averted, but the weary Re knows that it is time for him to leave the earth. Nut assumes the form of a celestial cow, and Re withdraws to the sky either on her back or on her horns. As Egypt grows dark the frightened people urge him to stay. But Re will not change his mind. From now on he will make a daily journey across the body of Nut, who is supported by her father Shu and the newly created Heh gods of the dusk. Re appoints the wise god Thoth his night-time moon substitute, and appoints Osiris king of Egypt. With a king on the throne, he is sure to receive the offering of *maat* which he craves. Thus begins the formal separation of gods and mortals, a separation which directly reinforces the status of the king as the one man who can communicate with the absent deities using prescribed temple rituals.

THE DOOMED PRINCE

Hathor could be one, but she could also be seven. As the sum of three (plurality) and four (totality), seven was itself a significant number. The Seven Hathors were seven aspects of Hathor's personality who, at the birth of a child, could look into the future and see the timing and manner of that child's death. Their work ran alongside that of the other fate-determining goddesses,

Meskhenet who determined status and Renenutet who determined material wealth. The 6th Dynasty *Instructions of Ptahhotep* make it clear that fate, once foretold, could not be averted: 'His time does not fail to come: one cannot escape what has been decided.' This theme is repeated in the *Story of Sinuhe* when the eponymous hero attempts to explain to Senwosret I his precipitous flight as an uncontrollable impulse inflicted upon him by an unknown god.

Yet the predictions made by the Hathors were not always accurate and it was sometimes possible, with careful planning, bravery and sheer good luck, for an innocent person to prolong a seemingly blighted life. The *Tale of the Doomed Prince* is an 18th or 19th Dynasty fantasy which includes some elements familiar from our modern fairy stories, so that we can recognize parts of Sleeping Beauty (the bad fairy at the christening; although here the Seven Hathors are the innocent bearers of bad news, rather than its cause), Cinderella (the evil stepmother: a perennial fairy-tale favourite) and Rapunzel (the princess isolated from the world in a high tower), while the magical talking animals are a feature of many modern stories. The Egyptian audience would, perhaps, have recognized the use of strong drink to deflect a destroyer as a key plot element in *The Destruction of Mankind*. *The Doomed Prince* tells of the fates which haunt a young man who has done nothing to arouse the enmity of the gods and who is, as far as we can tell, the child of equally blameless parents. As it is strongly plot-driven, with few detailed descriptive passages, the story grips the reader's attention. It is therefore unfortunate that it is preserved on just one papyrus and that the end of the tale is missing, leaving us wondering whether the prince did indeed, as we might suspect, escape his fate.[74]

Once upon a time there lived a king who had everything that a man could desire except a son. The king prayed to his gods that he might be granted a son, and they decided that his wish should be granted. That night the king visited his wife in her bedchamber, and she conceived a child. And nine months later her son was born.

The Seven Hathors came to decide the baby's fate. Their words were not comforting: 'He will meet his death through a dog, or through a snake, or through a crocodile.'

The nursemaids rushed straight to the king, and told him of the prophecy. And the king was instantly plunged into a deep sorrow. Determined to protect his son from his fate, the king had a stone house built for him in the desert. The house was filled with staff, furniture, and food and drink from the palace kitchens. Here the prince would be raised in safety: he would never be allowed to venture outside.

The years flew by and the baby grew into a sturdy boy. One day, as he was sitting on the roof of his house, he saw a man walk by, closely followed by a greyhound. The boy was intrigued. He summoned his attendant, and demanded to know just what the strange four-legged creature could be.

'It is a creature called a dog. A greyhound dog, my lord.'

'Have one just like it brought to me!'

Troubled, the attendant went straight to the king. And the king, who had no wish to deny his son anything, reluctantly ordered that a small puppy be brought to the prince. And so it was done.

More years passed and the boy became a grown man. The prince sent a message to his father: 'What is the point of my sitting here all alone? My fates have been foretold, and I cannot avoid them. Let me go free, so that I may live as I wish until the gods decide to do with me as they will.'

Sadly, the king agreed. A chariot was prepared for the prince, equipped with an impressive range of weapons. And a servant was appointed to accompany him on his travels. The prince was ferried over the river to the eastern shore and, with his father's blessing ringing in his ears, 'Go wherever you wish', he set off, free at last. And his faithful greyhound went with him. The prince travelled northward over the desert, following no particular path but riding wherever his heart took him and living off the desert game. His travels took him eastwards out of Egypt, across the Sinai land bridge, to the faraway land of Naharin or Mitanni on the upper Euphrates River.

Now the Prince of Naharin had only one child, a daughter whom he loved very much for she was as clever as she was beautiful. Her father had built for her a stone tower, whose window was seventy cubits from the ground. The Prince of Naharin had then summoned his daughter's suitors to the base of the tower and spoke to them: 'Whoever jumps up to my daughter's window, he will win her hand in marriage.'

The princes immediately started to leap, competing to reach the window.

When they had been jumping for many days, the Egyptian prince arrived. The suitors made the newcomer feel very welcome; they took him to their lodgings, bathed him, rubbed him with oils, bandaged his feet and fed his horses, his dog and his attendant. Then they asked where he had come from. The prince, reluctant to reveal his true nobility, quickly made up a story:

'I am the son of an Egyptian charioteer. When my mother died my father took a new wife. My stepmother soon came to hate me. So I left home, fleeing from her harsh words.'

This sorry tale stirred the sympathy of the leaping princes. They hugged the newcomer and kissed him.

The prince in turn had a question for the leaping young men: 'What exactly are you doing here, lads?'

They told him the whole story of the Prince of Naharin, his beautiful daughter and her impossibly high window. The

Egyptian was eager to try to win the hand of the fair princess but his sore feet hurt too much. So he was forced to stand by and watch as his companions made their daily jumps. Unknown to him, high in her tower, the princess had her eye on the handsome newcomer.

When many days had passed the prince's feet were fully healed, and he was able to take his place among the leaping suitors. With one mighty bound he sailed through the air to reach the window of the Princess of Naharin. She was delighted. She kissed him, and held him in a close embrace. Meanwhile her attendants rushed to tell the king that his daughter's husband had been found.

'Which high-born prince has won my princess?' demanded the king.

His face fell as he realized that his precious daughter had been won by the lowly son of an Egyptian charioteer.

'Do you really expect me to give my daughter to an Egyptian fugitive? Make him go away!'

The attendants hurried back to the tower, and ordered the prince to leave Naharin immediately. But the headstrong princess heard their words, and grew angry: 'I swear by the great god Re-Horakhty. If he is taken away from me I shall not eat and I shall not drink. I shall die, straightaway!'

The attendants returned to their master and repeated his daughter's threat. The Prince of Naharin immediately sent men to slay the Egyptian, so that the matter would be resolved once and for all. But again the princess intervened: 'By the great god Re. If this man is killed, I too shall be dead before sunset. I shall not live a single hour without him.'

Hearing these words, the Prince of Naharin realized that his headstrong daughter had outsmarted him. He summoned the couple and, in spite of himself, was very impressed with what he saw. The Egyptian had a natural dignity; perhaps he would not make too bad a son-in-law after all? The prince embraced the Egyptian and kissed him: 'Tell me all about yourself, for now you are my son.'

And, for reasons best known to himself, the Egyptian repeated the invented story of the cruel stepmother and the flight from Egypt. Hearing this tale the Prince of Naharin gave his blessing to the match. And the happy couple were given a house, fields, cattle and all sorts of good things.

After many days the Egyptian told his wife the truth about his destiny: 'I am fated to die by one of three animals: the dog, the snake or the crocodile.'

Alarmed, the princess at once demanded that the prince's faithful greyhound be killed. But he refused to listen to her: 'Don't be stupid! I will not kill a dog that I myself have raised from a puppy. He is a lovely dog – he will never harm me.'

The wife, however, was not convinced, and she started to watch her husband closely and did not allow him to leave the house alone.

Unknown to the prince, the crocodile that was to be his fate had followed him from Egypt and was lurking in a lake in the village close by his house. There it was stuck, for a strong water spirit also lived in the lake. The water spirit would not let the crocodile leave the water, and the crocodile in turn would not let the water spirit go for its regular stroll around the village. Every day, as soon as the sun rose, the crocodile and the water spirit fought each other tooth and nail. And that had been happening for three months.

The next day was a feast day. The prince fell asleep that night as soon as his head touched his headrest. His wife, however, was still alert. She filled a bowl with wine, and a bowl with beer, then she sat and watched over her sleeping husband. Suddenly, a snake slithered out of a small hole. It intended to bite the young prince and so fulfil his destiny. But instead the snake drank from the bowls, and became drunk. As it collapsed in a stupor the wife hacked it to pieces with an axe. The noise woke the prince, and the wife was able to show him the remains of the snake: 'Look, your god has delivered you from one of your fates. He will surely deliver you from the others, and you will be safe at last.' Hearing this, the prince made an offering to Re. He continued to praise Re for many days.

A few days later the prince went for a stroll around his estate. Naturally, he took his faithful greyhound with him. His wife, however, chose to stay at home. Suddenly, his dog began to speak: 'I am your fate!'

The prince took to his heels, running away from the growling dog straight towards the lake. Jumping into the water he had just one second to think himself safe before the crocodile seized him in its powerful jaws. The crocodile then spoke: 'I am your fate! I have followed you from Egypt so that I might kill you. But for three months now I have been tormented by the water spirit that lives in this lake. I am prepared to strike a bargain with you. If I let you go, you must help me to kill the daemon that torments me daily.'

When the next day dawned the water spirit returned . . .

Hathor's solar connections are strong and obvious. But, as a sky goddess, the 'Lady of the Stars', she also had stellar aspects and might be recognized as the morning or evening star. By the Roman period she had also become a moon goddess. Her other, diverse roles are too numerous to list in full; indeed, in the Ptolemaic Edfu temple she was credited with as many forms as there are days in the year. At Thebes she was the compassionate Mistress of the West who welcomed the setting sun just as she welcomed the deceased to the afterlife; in travellers' tales she was the Lady of the almost mystical land of Punt; in the heat of the Sinai desert she was the Lady of the Turquoise (and, indeed, lady of all precious metals and gemstones); at Memphis she was the Mistress of the Southern Sycamore, who sustained the dead with food and drink. Egypt's tree goddesses, women with trees on their heads, or trees with female arms, or even trees with female torsos, heads and breasts, have a curious look to modern eyes. But trees offered both moist fruit and welcome shade, and in consequence were perceived as nurturing; the human-headed *ba* souls of the dead were often depicted perching in the branches of trees. The Southern Sycamore was an actual, sacred tree which grew in the temple complex of Ptah at Memphis during the Old Kingdom. Another sacred tree was the *ished* (probably a persea) which grew in the temple complexes of Heliopolis, Herakleopolis, Memphis and Edfu. As we have already seen, the *ished* tree was strongly associated with Re, and the well-armed 'Great Tom Cat of Re' liked to sit in its shade.

More generally, Hathor was celebrated as a goddess of pleasure, love and sexuality, a role which gave her a particular appeal to women and which led to her appearing as 'the Golden One' or simply 'the Golden' in New Kingdom love poems. That Hathor's was not an austere or spiritual love, but a sexual love in all its messy and uncontrolled forms, is made casually clear in the *Contendings*, when Hathor uses her charms, and 'uncovers her nakedness' to cure her father's depression. It seems likely that Hathor was the original 'Hand of Atum'; the hand with which Atum masturbated to create Shu and Tefnut. Many years later, towards the end of the dynastic age, her sexual expertise and her healing powers prompted those who longed to conceive to leave small votive phalluses at her shrines.

Hathor's sexual power was closely connected to her role as a guardian of the dead. The parallel between the grave and the womb would have been particularly obvious to the first Egyptians, who buried their dead in rounded pit graves in a contracted or foetal position. Sex, birth, life, death, rebirth and life beyond death soon became the accepted natural progression, and continuing sexual potency was considered essential for an effective afterlife. Simple bone and ivory figurines with emphasized pubic regions and rounded breasts recovered from Predynastic graves confirm that this principle was recognized long before it was committed to writing. As the art of mummification developed, great care was taken to ensure that mummies were interred with their sexual organs intact; false penises and nipples would be supplied if necessary and, in a few unfortunate cases where the gender of a badly damaged or decomposed body could not be determined, the undertakers hedged their bets by providing both.

Hathor's patronage of music and dance, her love of the *sistrum* and the *menyt*, is a manifestation of her sexual power, as music was known to stimulate the gods. We should remember that our earliest manifestation of Hathor is as a dancing female form with raised, horn-like arms, and the carved stone walls of the surviving New Kingdom temples confirm that dance played an important role in festival and processional ritual, and in particular in Hathoric rituals. The original audience who listened to the *Story of Sinuhe* would have recognized the Hathoric ritual performed by the queen and her daughters as they welcome the wanderer home with their *sistra*. Indeed, Sinuhe's name, Sanehat in the original Egyptian, itself suggests a link with Hathor, as Sanehat translates as 'Son of the Sycamore'.

The link between music, dance, sex and death is made obvious on the painted New Kingdom tomb walls, where we see the tomb owner and his wife attending magnificent banquets where they act as audience to troupes of nubile female musicians and acrobatic dancers whose skimpy costumes leave little, if anything, to the imagination. Originally, these scenes were interpreted as accurate snapshots of the tomb owner's actual life. Today, however, it is recognized that they are images anticipating the life to come which, as they appear to be riddled with veiled sexual references, will stimulate the tomb owner to retain his potency and so achieve his resurrection. The semi-naked dancing girls are the most obvious of these stimulating references, but elaborate hairstyles, lotus blossoms, perfume cones and mirrors may all be associated with female sexuality, while scenes involving the pouring of liquids, and hunting scenes, are likely to have had had a dual meaning, as the verb *seti*, 'to pour' or 'to shoot', might also mean 'to ejaculate' (or, with less relevance, 'to set alight').

Hathor's love of music and dance is one aspect of her sexual power; her motherhood is another. To modern eyes, heavily influenced by Judaeo-Christian traditions, the Egyptian juxta-position of motherhood and eroticism is a slightly uncomfortable one. The Egyptians, for the most part farmers who lived in cramped one- or two-roomed houses with very little privacy, were an intensely practical people with none of our modern hang-ups. With no notion of prudery and no great value placed on abstin-ence, there was no perceived need to keep sexual activities hidden. Indeed, the erect penis was included among the more commonly used hieroglyphic signs.

BASTET OF BUBASTIS

Late Hathoric mythology is preserved in the writings of the Classical authors and in the rituals recorded on the Ptolemaic temple walls. These reflect the traditions of an age when Hathor had become closely linked with both Isis and the Greek Aphrodite, acquiring many of their myths and attributes. By now, carefully controlled overt female sexuality had become an accepted aspect of state religion. Herodotus describes what happened when the women of the Delta celebrated the festival of the goddess Bastet of Bubastis (the modern Delta city of Zagazig), whom Herodotus equated with Artemis:[75]

The procedure at Bubastis is this: they come in barges, men and women together, a great number in each boat; on the way, some of the women keep up a continual clatter with the castanets and some of the men play flutes, while the rest, both men and women, sing and clap their hands. Whenever they pass a town on the river-bank, they bring the barge close in-shore, some of the women continuing to act as I have said, while others shout abuse at the women of the place, or start dancing, or stand up and pull up their skirts. When they reach Bubastis they celebrate the festival with elaborate sacrifices, and more wine is consumed than during all the rest of the year.

Herodotus knew Bastet, 'lady of the *bas*', or perfume jar, as a cat or cat-headed deity, the mild guardian of mothers and pregnant women. At Bubastis she was the nurturing wife of Re-Atum and the mother of the lion god Mahes, and was often depicted, with kittens frolicking at her feet, carrying the *sistrum* and *menyt* beads associated with Hathor. But the placid cat had started life as a far fiercer being: she was the lioness who nursed the dead king and who stood with three other lionesses – Sekhmet, Wadjet and Shesmetet – to guard the dead Osiris.[76] Bastet could be both the lunar Eye of the moon and the solar Eye of Re who, in her most fierce, fully feline form, might be the knife-wielding cat who killed the evil serpent Apophis. She might even be Hathor's fierce alter ego, Sekhmet.

8

ISIS: GREAT OF MAGIC

Isis, several centuries younger than Bat/Hathor, makes her first appearance in the *Pyramid Texts*, where she is initially recognized as the mother of Horus and only later becomes the devoted sister-wife of Osiris and a member of the Ennead of Heliopolis. Her name, Aset in the original Egyptian, is represented by the hieroglyphic sign of the throne. It is a name that connects her to her husband-brother, whose own name, Usir (Osiris), is written with the signs of the throne and the eye. Her diagnostic crown is a throne, worn either alone or, from the 18th Dynasty onwards, in conjunction with the cow horns and solar disk which she 'borrows' from Hathor. The link between Isis and the throne of Egypt is therefore a strong and unbreakable one. Isis, effectively, is the living throne. As both the throne and the mother and protector of Horus, she naturally becomes the mother and protector of all of Egypt's living Horus kings. We may therefore 'read' any image of Horus sitting on his mother's knee as an image of any king sitting on his throne. Conversely, any image of an Egyptian queen with her son may be interpreted as a representation of Isis and Horus.

Her resurrection of the vegetation god Osiris caused Isis to be associated with the resurrection of Egypt and the flooding of the Nile which was, in some tales, caused by the tears that she shed for her dead husband. In this role she was linked with the fertility god Min as either his consort and/or the mother whom Min, assuming the form of 'bull of his mother', impregnated to father himself. As we have already seen in the *Contendings*, Isis enjoys an unusually close relationship with her son Horus; he tells her his most intimate thoughts, while she does not baulk at stimulating him to release his sperm. Late tradition tells us that Isis slept with, or was raped by, her son Horus-the-Strong (the composite god Min-Horus). It may therefore be that Horus too, confirmed in his role as living king, needed not only to possess the throne (his mother), but to father himself.

WIFE OF OSIRIS

Isis' best-known role is that of the loyal wife of Osiris and protective mother of his son Horus-the-Child. We have already read the tale of the murder and resurrection of Osiris in its post-Ptolemaic form. This myth has been described, with dubious accuracy, as Egypt's earliest love story. Leaving love aside, the Isis of this tale epitomizes the ideal queen and, indeed, the ideal wife. She is wise, faithful, supportive and fertile. While things go according to plan she remains modestly in the background, supporting her husband and attending to the domestic tasks that are traditionally the wife's lot. Specifically, we are told, she teaches the women of Egypt the feminine skills of weaving, baking and brewing. This division of labour – the passive 'indoor' wife who cares for the household and its occupants, and her active 'outdoor' husband who supports his family by interfacing with the external world – is a well-balanced opposition that is reflected in formal art where, whatever their actual appearance, women are consistently depicted as pale and slender while the more muscular men have a skin tanned red or brown by the sun. Similarly, in formal sculpture, men almost invariably stride forward while their wives stand still and slightly sheltered beside them. Unfortunately, the traditional woman's work of childcare, cooking and laundry has little impact on the archaeological or historical record. Consequently, Egypt's women tend to be quite literally hidden behind the husbands, fathers and sons whose achievements are commemorated on stone walls. This bias is made worse by the shortage of domestic sites that might have helped us to understand the daily routine of women's lives. The few settlements that have survived have done so because they were built in atypical locations and are therefore, by definition, atypical sites. The best preserved of these are the Middle Kingdom workmen's village of Kahun, the New Kingdom workmen's village of Deir el-Medina, and the short-lived 18th Dynasty city of Amarna, which has its own subsidiary workmen's village.

Egypt was the most fertile, and therefore the wealthiest, country in the ancient world. A quick glance at the decorated tombs of the elite suggests a land of sunshine and plenty, where happy families might spend their days in the fields or sitting beside shaded pools, and their evenings feasting, listening to music and playing board games. This is of course, an illusion. Egypt may have been the best place to live – the Egyptians themselves, and many envious foreigners, certainly thought so – but things were far from perfect, and modern mummy studies have revealed that the Egyptians suffered constant, low-level illness, for most of their lives, with parasitic infestations, infected teeth and persistent coughs standard throughout all levels of society. The family unit provided the only dependable support mechanism for those threatened by sickness, disability or old age. With marriage a practical contract designed to create a viable economic unit, quite simply everyone was expected to marry and produce children.

It would be a serious mistake to underestimate Egypt's pallid, delicate wives. At first glance it seems that they are just too fragile to perform any useful role. A second glance shows that, in formal sculpture, it is the woman who consistently offers physical support to her partner by placing an arm around his waist or shoulder. Mothers, daughters and goddesses, too, might embrace others or stand with husbands and fathers to express solidarity and feminine protection so that Nut, who permanently embraces the dead in their coffins, becomes, in the *Pyramid Texts*, the 'great protectress'.

Legally, too, women could be strong. Men and women of equivalent social status were considered equals before the law; this meant that women could own, buy, sell, earn and inherit property. They could live alone, could raise their children alone, and could bring cases before the law courts. In theory those women who had time to spare from domestic duties could work outside the home; in practice, however, their lack of education and training, and the sheer amount of time taken to raise, feed and dress a household in a pre-industrial age, made this an impossibility for most wives.

Isis is obviously clever – cleverer, perhaps, than her trusting husband – and she is quite capable of independent 'outdoor' action when the need arises. It is Isis, not Osiris, who sees Seth for what he is and who, in consequence, poses the greatest threat to his ambition. When Osiris takes a sabbatical to travel the world, it is Isis, and not Seth, who is left to rule in his absence. When Osiris is lost, it is Isis who finds him and returns him to Egypt. And when Osiris departs to the land of the dead, it is Isis who rules on behalf of Horus. This reflects tradition in the real Egyptian world where queen consorts might be called upon to rule Egypt on behalf of an absent husband or, like Isis, to protect the interests of an infant son. Displacing Hathor and Horus, Isis and Horus would eventually come to symbolize all that was good and powerful about Egyptian motherhood. Their mythology survived beyond the Classical world, so that images of Isis suckling Horus served as inspiration for early Christian artists seeking to depict Mary and the infant Jesus.

SISTER OF NEPHTHYS AND SETH

Isis is not only an exemplary wife and mother, she is a good elder sister to the shadowy Nephthys. When she discovers that Nephthys has uncharacteristically seduced Osiris, she swallows her anger, does the right thing, and saves the life of her husband's illegitimate child. Her relationship with her brother Seth is more complex. Isis supports Horus against Seth; the *Contendings* show that she is prepared to strike him with her harpoon to protect her son. And yet, when Seth reminds her that he is her brother, she relents and releases him and in so doing incurs the wrath of Horus. When, in some versions of the *Contendings*, the defeated Seth is handed over to Isis for punishment she finds herself unable to hurt him. Clearly, Isis does not have the uncontrolled anger of Sekhmet; she is, at heart, a healer and peacemaker rather than an aggressor. It is only the late-dating sources, heavily influenced by non-Egyptian traditions, which see her as the implacable enemy of Seth who himself, by this stage, has become a one-dimensional, irredeemably bad character. So, *Papyrus Jumilhac* tells us that Isis, having transformed into the fiery Sekhmet (or perhaps the equally fiery Eye of Re), not only fights Seth, but has no compunction in killing him and burning all his companions.

Isis has such extraordinary magical healing powers that she experiences no difficulty in bringing the dead and dismembered Osiris back to a semblance of life, and reconstructing his penis so that she may conceive a son by him. The *Pyramid Texts*, recognizing this skill, accord her the power to halt putrefaction and preserve the corpses of all dead kings. This leads to her recognition as the mother of the 'Four Sons of Horus', the deities who guard the organs removed from the body during mummification. The Four Sons are usually considered to be the children of Horus-the-Elder, but occasionally they are the sons of Horus of Khem, or of Harsiese, while in alternative mythologies they grow from a lotus blossom. The human-headed Imseti (guardian of the liver), baboon-headed Hapy (lungs: not to be confused with the inundation deity of the same name), dog-headed Duamutef (stomach) and falcon-headed Qebehsenuef (intestines) were themselves associated with the four cardinal points, with the four pillars that hold up the heavens, and with the four goddesses – Isis, Nephthys, Serket and Neith – who guard the corpse. They are found in funerary literature from the Old Kingdom to the end of the dynastic age. In the *Pyramid Texts* they protect the dead king while eliminating his hunger and thirst, then help him to ascend into the sky. During the Middle Kingdom the Four Sons protect Osiris by fighting the Followers of Seth; in the New Kingdom they belong to the group of seven stars who help Anubis protect the dead Osiris.

How exactly does Isis restore Osiris to life? The *Pyramid Texts* tell us that Isis and Nephthys suckled their dead brother, Isis' milk being an essential element in the regenerative process. All divine milk carried potent magical powers. It is therefore not surprising that we find constant images of, and references to, kings (both living and deceased) being suckled by goddesses – Hathor, Isis, Neith, Weret-Hekau and others – who take the role of the king's mother and in so doing impart power, and the right to rule, to their 'son'. Normal human milk carried healing powers too, and so might be included in the medical recipes intended to cure burns and swellings, and heal eyes and noses. The milk of the mother of a male child was considered particularly effective in this respect. Meanwhile, other divine body fluids, such as urine or menstrual blood, carried their own restorative powers.[77]

Isis and Nephthys transform into kites (soaring birds of prey) to retrieve their dismembered brother, and Isis retains her bird form to conceive her son in a flash of lightning, allowing the wind from her beating wings to permeate her husband's nostrils and create the breath of life. Two- and three-dimensional images of Isis as a kite or a winged woman hovering over her husband's body, which is inert apart from an unfeasibly large erection, make the mechanics of this impregnation quite clear. This tradition of Isis and Nephthys as birds is reflected in later funerary ritual, where women playing the roles of the two goddesses take the form of kites to lead the mourning and sing lamentations to the dead. *Papyrus Bremner-Rhind* and *Papyrus Berlin 3008* detail the mourning hymns to be sung by the two women who play the parts of Isis and Nephthys in the celebration of the Festival of Osiris at Abydos:[78]

> *Here begin the stanzas of the Festival of the Two Kites which is celebrated in the temple of Osiris, First of the Westerners, the great god, Lord of Abydos, in the fourth month of Inundation, from the twenty-second day down to the twenty-sixth day. The entire temple shall be sanctified, and there shall be brought in [two] women pure of body and virgin, with the hair of their bodies removed, their heads adorned with wigs . . . tambourines in their hands, and their names inscribed on their arms, to wit Isis and Nephthys, and they shall sing from the stanzas of this book in the presence of this god.*

A brief extract from the ritual serves to express the grief of the two sisters – a grief that could be extended to every living mourner – as they lament the loss of their brother:

> *Isis sings:*
> *Even as I desire to see thee!*
> *I am thy sister Isis, the desire of thine heart,*

[Yearning] after thy love while thou art far away;
I flood this land [with tears?] today.

Duet:
Draw nigh, so please you, to us;
We miss life through lack of thee.
Come thou in peace, O our Lord, that we may see thee,
O Sovereign, come in peace,
Drive trouble [?] from out of our house,
Consort thou with us after the manner of a male.

MOTHER OF HORUS

Isis gave birth to her son after a ten-month pregnancy during which he was protected *in utero* by the gods. Safely delivered, Horus was raised in the Delta papyrus marshes, in a place known today as Khemmis (Akhbit in the original Egyptian). Although many authorities have attempted to pinpoint its location, it seems likely that Khemmis was a mythical place. But any earthly temple could in truth be said to represent Khemmis.[79] Herodotus, an indefatigable tourist, visited what he believed to be Khemmis and recorded some of its 'history':[80]

> . . . *what impressed me most was the island called Khemmis.*
> *This lies in a deep, broad lake by the temple, and the Egyptians*
> *say that it floats. I did not see it move, and it did not actually*
> *look as if it was floating, and I wondered very much, when I*
> *heard about it, if there could be such a thing as a floating island*
> *. . . The Egyptians have a legend to explain how the island*
> *came to float: in former times Leto, one of the eight original*
> *deities, lived in Buto, where her oracle now is, and having*
> *received Apollo, son of Osiris, as a sacred trust from Isis, she*

saved him from Typhon (Seth) when he came there in his world-wide search, by hiding him in the island. The Egyptians say that Apollo and Artemis are the children of Isis and Dionysos (Osiris), and that Leto saved them and brought them up. In Egyptian, Apollo is Horus, Demeter is Isis, Artemis is Bubastis.

Hidden in the papyrus thickets, Isis protected Horus with the help of the scorpion Serket, the warrior Neith and the Two Ladies, Wadjet and Nekhbet, who acted as his servants. Horus proved extremely vulnerable to accidents and sickness – as, indeed, were all of Egypt's children – and there are many tales of his illnesses and recoveries. A typical example tells of the day that Isis returned home to find Horus lying unconscious on the riverbank. As she was overwhelmed by grief her self-control snapped and she wailed aloud, lamenting her unfortunate life, dead husband, disloyal brother and sick child. Alerted by her cries the men of the Delta arrived, but they could do nothing to help. Then a lady from the city was able to diagnose the illness as poisoning. Next Nephthys turned up, not to offer first-aid, but to wail alongside her sister. Finally Serket made a practical suggestion. Isis should stop the solar boat, halting the sun's voyage across the sky until she received the help of the gods. This Isis did. Faced with a disruption to the solar journey, Atum quickly sent Thoth to cure Horus with a magic spell. There are several variants on this tale: one has Horus himself suggesting that Nut may be able to cure his sickness, another has the naughty Horus falling ill after he deliberately eats a sacred fish. In the latter case, Isis is able to use her own medical skills to cure her son.

Amuletic stelae known as *cippi*, or 'Horus on the crocodile stelae', became popular during the New Kingdom and remained in use until the end of the dynastic period. As their name suggests, these are plaques or stelae which show images of Horus-the-Child or Horus-the-Saviour (Horus-Shed) standing naked and slightly bow-legged on the back of a submissive crocodile, with a bundle of snakes clutched in each babyish fist. Often Horus is surrounded by a host of malign creatures: snakes, scorpions and daemons. The benign dwarf Bes may hover, protectively, nearby. The stelae, which are often carved from a dark grey or green schist (a stone imbued with its own magical powers), are inscribed with elaborate spells and stories designed to repel snakes, scorpions and other dangerous creatures and, should the worst happen, to treat their bites and stings. The same stories appear on the stelae, in slightly different form, over and over again. These were not primarily designed to be read. Instead, it was understood that water poured over the *cippus* would serve as both a preventative and a cure: the water could either be drunk, or the sufferer could bathe in it. This reflects the widely held belief that spells could be effective when ingested, either 'dissolved' in water or beer or by licking the inscribed hand of a magician-healer.

The 30th Dynasty Metternich Stela is a large, elaborately carved temple *cippus*.[81] Its text preserves the tale of the stela itself; from this we learn how, during the reign of Nectanobo II, the priest and historian Nesuatum visited the burial ground of the Mnevis bulls to copy the inscriptions that he found there. He had the inscriptions carved on to a splendid stela, which he intended to set up in honour of both the Mnevis and his king. His stela includes, among other tales (including a spell for warding off snakes, a spell to exorcize poison from a cat and a spell for repelling crocodiles), the myth of *Isis and the Seven Scorpions*, a myth which is also known from New Kingdom contexts:

Acting on Thoth's advice, Isis decided to take the baby Horus and flee from Seth. She was protected on her journey by seven scorpions; the seven children or aspects of Serket. Three scorpions preceded her, two scuttled under her carrying chair, and two brought up the rear. The bizarre party reached the Delta town of the Two Sisters, and sought a night's lodging at the house of a rich woman. Perhaps understandably, given the curious nature of the party, the woman closed her door on them. Taking refuge at the home of a poor but generous-hearted woman, the scorpions plotted their revenge.

Six of the scorpions lent their stings to the seventh, a large, bold scorpion named Tefen. Tefen scuttled back to the house of the rich woman, crawled under the door and stung her young son. Immediately, the house burst into flame and water poured down from the sky, even though it was not the season for rain. Distraught, the mother ran round the village seeking help for her dying child, but no one came to her aid. Just as she had rejected a plea for help, so her own plea went unanswered.

Eventually the gentle-hearted Isis relented and restored the child's breathing by rubbing his throat while reciting the names of all seven scorpions: Tefen, Befen, Mesten, Mestetef, Petet, Thetet and Maatet. As the child recovered the rains stopped and the fire was extinguished. The rich woman, now realizing the folly of her ways, gave away all her wealth.

The story ends with the news that Horus, too, has been stung, and Isis rushes off to lament over her own son. Roman period re-enactments of this myth saw devotees of Isis handling live scorpions.

The scorpion goddess Serket, 'she who causes the throat to breathe', is another Eye of Re: an ancient goddess with a fierce demeanour, limited mythology and strong healing powers, whose priests are accomplished healers. As a scorpion sting can cause breathing problems which may prove fatal for the old, the young or the unfit, it is not surprising that Serket, who quite literally takes the breath away, also has the power to help the deceased to breathe again. Variously described as the sister of Isis, the wife of Horus and the mother of the benign snake god Nehebu-kau, 'he who harnesses the spirits', she usually appears as a woman whose scorpion headdress has a threatening raised tail, yet, in order to protect the observer, may be missing the sting, a leg or a claw. In animal form Serket may be a scorpion, a rearing snake, a crocodile or a lioness.

Isis understands that the personal name, an integral and inseparable part of the identity, carries its own powers. In the myth of *Isis and the Seven Scorpions* it is her ability to recite the names of all seven scorpions that weakens their combined sting and allows her to effect a cure. This principle was accepted in the living Egypt, where knowledge of a name conferred authority over the name's owner, and where the memory of a name might prevent the Second Death if all other earthly trace of the deceased had vanished. In order to avoid dying unnamed – effectively, to avoid dying without ever having been – children were named by their mothers at birth. In the criminal courts, wrongdoers were stripped of their names and identities; this was particularly true if they happened to bear the name of a god. The gods themselves bore multiple names and titles which reflected their diverse interests and abilities, and their priests used these names again and again in deliberately repetitive temple rituals.

Re, the ultimate creator, has the ability to name himself. In so doing, he reinforces his own powers. The myth of *Isis and Re* tells how Isis, as a great magician and an even more ambitious woman, decides to divert the great power of Re's most secret name to her own advantage.

One evening, as the elderly Re enjoyed a stroll, his mouth fell open and he drooled a little spit on to the ground. Isis collected the saliva, mixed it with mud, and formed it into a live snake which she left at a crossroads.

When Re next shuffled by, the snake reared up and bit him. Suffering the very great heat of his own venom, Re let out a scream which brought the other gods running. Re explained that he had been bitten by a creature unknown to him, and begged Isis the healer to relieve his pain. She, however, claimed to be unable to act unless she knew the sun god's true name.

At first Re refused to tell her: he recited a list of his many names and titles – each reflecting a different aspect of his being – but did not reveal his most private name. Then, as the pain grew worse, he agreed to speak as long as Isis and Horus vowed to keep his secret. Satisfied, Isis administered the cure, casting the fiery poison out of Re's body. Her knowledge of the true name of the sun god gave her immense wisdom: she now knew everything that could be known, and was truly 'Great of Magic'. Her son Horus, in possession of the same knowledge, was destined to rule Egypt.

Unfortunately, none of our sources – a series of Ramesside documents recovered from Deir el-Medina – actually reveals the secret name of the sun god. But they do tell us that Isis' cure was made from herbs mixed with either beer or wine. A parallel and somewhat confusing story preserved in a healing spell in Turin Museum starts with Seth being bitten and Horus seeking to help him. Like Re before him, Seth lists a number of names, but it is only when he reveals his very personal name, 'Evil Day', that a cure can be effected, and so 'he who was bitten shall stand up, being sound for his mother, as Horus stood up sound for his mother on the night when he was bitten; the protection is the protection of Horus'.[82]

QUEEN OF HEAVEN

Isis gradually absorbed the attributes, mythology and regalia of Hathor, Mut, Maat and doubtless scores of ill-recorded local goddesses until she became Egypt's dominant female deity. In her earliest appearances Isis had been a typically slender, eternally young woman who wore the throne-crown and bore the *ankh* sign and the papyrus staff carried by many other goddesses (or, occasionally, she appeared as a woman with winged arms, or as a kite, cobra, scorpion, cow or sow). As the dynastic age progressed she began to carry the *sistrum* and *menyt* and to wear the sun disk and cow horns of Hathor, so that the two goddesses became near-identical in appearance.

In funerary art Isis displaced Hathor in the solar boat of Re, where she recited a magic spell which would helps Seth to defeat Apophis. At Sakkara, she replaced Hathor as the Lady of the Beautiful West, and in the 18th Dynasty tomb of Tuthmosis III in the Valley of the Kings she took the form of a sycamore tree to suckle the king. This, an obvious usurpation of Hathor's role as Lady of the Sycamore, had a particular personal relevance for Tuthmosis as his birth-mother was named Isis. During the Late Period, Isis was revered at Giza as Mistress of the Pyramid. By the start of the Ptolemaic Age she had also assimilated several prominent, and purely anthropomorphic, Greek goddesses. Demeter, Persephone, Athena, Hera, Artemis and Aphrodite all donated aspects of their mythology, allowing Isis to develop into a versatile being accepted far beyond Egypt's shores. She was now both queen of heaven and mistress of the sea. In Alexandria she was the consort of the new city god Serapis and, while Isis Pelagia protected the sailors entering and leaving the safety of the harbour, Isis Medica cured the sick in temple-hospitals outside the city walls. In Rome, the first temple to Isis was raised on the Capitoline Hill in *c.*80 BC. It was destroyed almost immediately, then quickly replaced, a pattern which continued for many years.

Back in Ptolemaic Alexandria, all queens felt a close bond with Isis. Cleopatra III and Cleopatra VII, two particularly strong queens who ruled on behalf of fatherless sons, even proclaimed themselves her living incarnation. Cleopatra VII is rumoured to have dressed as Isis when she sailed to Tarsus for her first, fateful meeting with Mark Antony. As Mark Antony considered himself the living Dionysos, one of the many recognized consorts of the Hellenistic Isis, her choice of costume was particularly apt. Although we have no eyewitness account of their meeting, we can guess that Cleopatra wore a crown incorporating the solar disk and horns, and a multicoloured robe covered by a black cloak tied with the Isis knot.

Isis was a universal goddess, yet for most of the dynastic period she had no dominant cult temple. Instead she was worshipped alongside Hathor at Cusae, Min at Koptos and Osiris at Abydos. During the 30th Dynasty two large temples to Isis were built: the Iseion at the Delta site of Behbeit el-Hagar and the temple of Isis on the southern island of Philae. This temple was then developed by the Ptolemies and the Romans so that it eventually covered most of the island. While most of Egypt's pagan temples were shut in AD 391, the temple of Isis at Philae continued in use until it was closed, on the orders of Emperor Justinian, in AD 535–7. However, the cult and mythology of Isis proved strong enough to survive the loss of her temples, and today pagan cults throughout the world continue to revere Isis as an earth-mother of many aspects.

9

WARRIORS AND WISE WOMEN

All formal images of kings and their families carry a mixture of propaganda and myth. At the most obvious level there is the myth of the perfect royal family. Kings appear young, fit and good-looking; their queens are slender, pale and beautiful. If they are depicted at all, their daughters are perfectly formed miniature adults. Their sons are generally invisible. None of these 'portraits' can be assumed to be true-to-life, nor were they intended to be. In a land lacking the concept of purely decorative art, all royal images were designed to convey selected aspects of kingship, and so the kings of the Old Kingdom appear as the remote embodiment of semi-divine authority; the Middle Kingdom kings are the careworn guardians of their people; the New Kingdom kings show a renewed confidence in their role; and the Late Period kings reflect on their country's glorious past. Conformity to this stereotype was extremely important as any deviation might imply a challenge to *maat*. And so we find the 19th Dynasty King Siptah appearing as a healthy young man while his mummy proves that he had a deformed left foot, and the 18th Dynasty Hatshepsut appearing with a man's body even though she is a woman.

A closer look at the royal images reveals a sub-text. The royal family is the earthly representative of the divine family. Every living king represents Re or his son Horus; every king's wife plays the part of Maat or Hathor (for a living king), or Isis (for a dead king who would himself take the role of Osiris); royal daughters assume a protective role, mirroring the role played by the various daughters of the sun god. There is no place in this intimate family group for sons and brothers, or for children of either sex born to lesser queens, and so they rarely appear. Not only is it difficult to differentiate between individual kings, it is difficult to distinguish between the royal women and, increasingly, between queens and goddesses. We have already noted the physical similarity between the human queen and Maat, the constant companion of the king. As the dynastic age progresses it becomes increasingly difficult to distinguish between the human queen, Hathor and Isis, as all three now wear the solar disk and cow horns that were once the exclusive property of Hathor. This confusion is deliberate. It seems that, just as the king could represent either all or one of the gods, so his queen could represent either all or one of the goddesses. Together king and queen formed a perfect balance of male and female that would serve the gods, rule Egypt and confound chaos – at one and the same time. For a king to rule without a woman by his side was unthinkable.

Although the badly fragmented Graeco-Roman tale of *Prince Pedikhons and Queen Serpot*[83] tells of a Syrian 'land of the women', whose highly effective female warriors are inspired by Isis and Osiris and who are prepared to fight to the death (or, rather, until their queen falls in love with Pedikhons), mortal Egypt had no tradition of female soldiers. The gods, however, had a different tradition, and gods, kings and the dead were happy to harness the protective feminine loyalty – and the highly effective weaponry – of Egypt's goddesses. Some goddesses were adept at brandishing axes, spears, sharp knives or bows and arrows, while others included fire, pestilence and plague in their arsenal. Mother goddesses – the fiercest of all goddesses – shunned weapons, preferring to manifest as dangerous animals: rearing snakes, stinging scorpions, hippopotami, crocodiles and lions. Here we will meet some of ancient Egypt's fiercest female fighters.

THE COBRA GODDESSES

Male snake deities might be either good or bad; they might appear as bizarre mutants equipped with multiple limbs and heads, as insignificant, slender, wriggling worms, or as long, fat, python- or dragon-like creatures. Generally speaking these monsters dwelt in the *Duat*, and did not trouble the living Egyptians overmuch. We have already met the malignant serpent Apophis and his counterpart, the benign Mehen, and the snake god Nehebu-Kau, son of either Serket or Renenutet, who, impervious to magical trickery, protects and feeds the dead king in the underworld.

Female snakes, invariably cobras, played a more important role in daily life. Cobras were considered exceptionally good mothers and it is no coincidence that Isis and Neith, who were also considered good mothers, occasionally assumed cobra form. The Egyptian cobra, *Naja haje*, can grow to be nine feet long and can, when angry or threatened, raise a third of its body from the ground, and expand its 'hood' (cervical ribs). A rearing cobra is a frightening sight. This, coupled with a strong filial devotion to the sun god, made the female cobra a useful royal bodyguard. A rearing cobra (the uraeus) worn on the brow watched over the gods and the royal family, cobra amulets incorporated in mummy wrapping protected the deceased, and a painted pottery cobra, placed in the corner of a room, was a tried and tested means of warding off evil ghosts and spirits.

As, each year, the rising Nile waters caused a rise in the number of snakes attracted to the settlements by the increased numbers of vermin flushed from the low-lying ground, cobras also came to be associated with the fertility of the Nile. In some traditions the mysterious cavern which served as the font of the Nile was guarded by a serpent who controlled the water level. Renenutet, 'she who nourishes', lived in the fertile fields where, as goddess of the harvest and granaries, she ensured that Egypt would not go hungry. As a divine nurse Renenutet suckled and raised babies in general and the king in particular; as the fierce uraeus she protected the adult king in life; as a fire-breathing cobra she also protected him in death. While Renenutet was generally recognized as the mother of the corn god Neper, or of Nehebu-Kau, in the Faiyum she was celebrated as the wife of Sobek and the mother of Horus.

Meretseger, 'She who Loves Silence', served as the guardian of the Theban cemetery where she gained a loyal following among the residents of the village of Deir el-Medina, which was, un-usually, situated in the desert rather than on the edge of the cultivated area. In this extract from his votive stela, the hapless draftsman Neferabu reflects on his folly in annoying Meretseger, 'Peak of the West', the Peak being a reference to the snake-infested pyramid-shaped desert mountain overshadowing the Valley of the Kings, which served as one of the entrances to the underworld:[84]

> I was an ignorant man and foolish,
> Who knew not good from evil;
> I did the transgression against the Peak,
> And she taught a lesson to me.
> I was in her hand by night as by day,
> I sat on bricks like the woman in labour,
> I called to the wind, it came not to me,
> I libated to the Peak of the West, great of strength,
> And to every god and goddess.

The accompanying illustration on the stela shows Meretseger as a snake with two serpent heads and one human head. Fortunately, this time Neferabu's story has a happy ending.

The goddesses Nekhbet and Wadjet, the 'Two Ladies' who guard the king, his name and his double crown, may be represented as twin cobras. Nekhbet, 'Lady of Nekheb' (Hierakonpolis), is the vulture goddess of southern Egypt and, as such, is closely associated with the white crown. She is a very ancient being: we can see a vulture hovering protectively over the head of Egypt's first king on the Narmer macehead, a ceremonial artefact recovered with the Narmer Palette from the remains of the ancient temple of Horus at Hierakonpolis. Vultures, like snakes, were considered to be good mothers; indeed, the vulture hieroglyph represented the word *mut*, or 'mother'. By extension, Nekhbet herself was recognized both as a good mother and as the mother of the pharaoh, and in the 5th Dynasty mortuary temple of Sahure she takes human form to suckle the king.

Nekhbet's counterpart, Wadjet of Buto (the ancient Delta city of Pe/Dep), the 'Green One', was a cobra who lived in the marshy thickets of northern Egypt. As Nekhbet personified the white crown, so Wadjet was associated with the red crown. While Nekhbet was mother to the king, Wadjet was his protector. She was the fire-spitting uraeus, the rearing cobra with an expanded hood who, as 'Lady of the Devouring Flame', helped Re to defeat his enemies including Apophis. Wadjet, too, suckled the king, feeding him the right to rule along with her divine milk.

The cobra (or occasionally lioness) Weret-Hekau, 'Great in Magic', personified the magic of the royal crowns. As she, too, served as the uraeus she might also be considered an aspect of Wadjet, or of Hathor/Sekhmet. Weret-Hekau is featured on a beaded pendant found inside the small golden shrine recovered from the tomb of Tutankhamen; here we see her in her human-headed snake form suckling the king to prepare him for his coronation. The shrine itself, essentially a gilded wooden box with a double door, is decorated with scenes of the king and his sister-wife Ankhesenamen. The young queen shows a conventional wifely concern for her husband as she accompanies him on hunting and fishing trips, entertains him with her *sistrum* and *menyt*, and ties his necklace firmly in place. Howard Carter, the first to view the shrine in over 3,000 years, was charmed by what he saw:[85]

> ... *a series of little panels, depicting, in delightfully naïve fashion, a number of episodes in the daily life of king and queen. In all of these scenes the dominant note is that of friendly relationship between the husband and the wife, the unselfconscious friendliness* ...

The images on the shrine certainly appear to be domestic, rather than funerary, in nature. But analysis by a variety of experts has demonstrated convincingly that the simple, intimate scenes should actually be read as confirmation of the queen's role in supporting her husband in his royal duties. More specifically it seems that she is preparing him for his coronation and for his participation in the New Year rituals.[86] While Ankhesenamen here serves as the earthly representative of Maat, or of Hathor/ Sekhmet, Tutankhamen is the son of Ptah and Sekhmet, the son of Amen and Mut, and the image of Re.

At the end of the dynastic age the Ptolemaic capital city of Alexandria mixed Egyptian and Hellenistic tradition to develop its own protective snake deity. *The Alexander Romance*, a legendary account of the life of Alexander the Great, compiled some five centuries after his death, tells how the workmen building the city were worried by a snake. Alexander had the snake killed, then, perhaps regretting his order, built a shrine where it had died. Soon the shrine filled with snakes, which started to infest the neighbouring houses. These were the *Agathoi Daemones*, the 'good spirits' who would protect the city and bless its inhabitants. They are perhaps a version of the earlier snake deity Shai, the personification of destiny, who determined both lifespan and the means of death. Shai was often linked with Renenutet and the birth-goddess Meskhenet, and all three could appear as a human-headed birthing brick.

NEITH

One of the oldest known depictions of an Egyptian shrine is inscribed on an ivory label recovered from the Abydos tomb of the 1st Dynasty King Aha, son of Narmer. The shrine is an open compound with a simple hut at one end and what appear to be two flagpoles at the other. The 'flagpoles', which are actually poles wrapped with cloth, form the hieroglyphic word *netcher*, or 'god'. Standing in front of the hut are the crossed arrows and shield which symbolize the warrior Neith, a goddess whose name has been translated as either 'the terrifying one' or 'that which is'. Later, Neith's symbol will evolve two stylized bows that the goddess might wear as a crown.

Even at this early date, Neith is strongly linked with royalty in general, and with queenship in particular. Several of the 1st Dynasty royal women bear names compounded with 'Neith', including Neithhotep, 'Neith is Satisfied', wife of Narmer and mother of Aha, and Meritneith, 'Beloved of Neith', the daughter of King Djer and widow of King Djet who ruled as regent for her infant son Den, and who was rewarded with the honour of a regal tomb in the royal cemetery at Abydos. At the same time, we know of several priestesses of Neith. Yet this obviously important goddess makes only a fleeting appearance in the *Pyramid Texts*, where she is classed with Isis, Nephthys and Serket as one of the four female guardians of the deceased king. A thousand years later, these same four goddesses will protect coffins, canopic chests and the four corners of the royal sarcophagi.

Neith is widely acknowledged as either a warrior or a hunter, yet she is consistently depicted in a linen sheath dress so tight that, if we were to take the representations literally, it would have been difficult for her to walk, let alone function effectively on the battlefield. Human-form, wigless and bald, from the 5th Dynasty onwards she wears the red crown of Lower Egypt.[87] Her accessories are far from conventional feminine equipment, and they lead directly to her titles 'mistress of the bow . . . ruler of arrows'. Beyond this, however, she has a surprising shortage of warrior-based mythology, although texts in the temple of Khnum at Esna, a temple which includes a celebration of the cult of Neith, do describe the Roman festival which celebrated Neith's use of her bow and arrows to save Re and defeat the enemies of the sun. This lack of epic tales of fighting and adventure suggests that Neith's role as a warrior should not be over-emphasized, but regarded as just one aspect of her multiple personae. Plutarch was writing under a misapprehension when he informed his readers that 'In Sais the statue of Athena, whom they believe to be Isis, bore the inscription "I am all that has been, and is, and shall be, and my robe no mortal has yet uncovered."'[88] Athena of Sais was Neith rather than Isis. Nevertheless, his statement, and Neith's statue inscription, contain more than a grain of truth. It seems that no one has yet managed to strip away the veil of privacy which shrouds this goddess.

Like all goddesses Neith has a family and, while her partner is uncertain (he may, perhaps, be Seth), she is recognized as the mother of the crocodile-headed Sobek (or in some cases Re, Horus, Osiris or even Apophis). In this role, she may appear as a woman suckling one or two miniature crocodiles. She might also be the daughter, and Eye, of Re.

Her title 'mother of the gods' identifies Neith with the creative force present at the beginning of the world, and it may even be that she invented birth: the 18th Dynasty King Amenhotep II tells us that he has been moulded by Neith, while the sarcophagus of the 19th Dynasty King Merenptah tells us that she is the mother of both Re and Osiris. In the New Kingdom funerary text known as the *Book of That Which is in the Beyond* she appears at the fourth, tenth and eleventh hours of the night. Here, at the eleventh hour, she is simultaneously identified as a child, the two queens of Upper and Lower Egypt, and the pregnant goddess through whom the sun will be reborn. On the wall of the temple of Khnum at Esna we see Neith emerging from the primeval waters as a cow-goddess. As she rises she creates the land by speaking just seven words: 'Let this place be land for me.' Neith is now father and mother of the gods; like all other creator gods, she has male and female aspects. She first creates thirty gods, then the great god Re, who in turn creates mankind from his tears. Finally Neith travels north to found the Delta city of Sais. Meanwhile, back at Esna, Neith is able to call forth the waters of the inundation – a role that she shares with Khnum and which associates her with the celestial creator-cow Mehet-Weret.

Neith is an intellegent goddess. As such, she is one of the few divinities to be treated with any degree of respect by the author of the *Contendings*. Indeed, her opinion is held in such high regard that she is asked to rule in the tedious dispute between Horus and Seth. Her judgement is both legally and morally sound: while Horus must be placed on his father's throne, Seth must be compensated for his loss (she suggests that he be given Anath and Astarte, the two daughters of the sun god, as his wives). Her ability to judge the dead is made clear in *Coffin Texts* spell 630, where we learn that 'Judgement has been made in the presence of Neith.' Her role as patroness of weavers reinforced this link with the deceased, who required vast amounts of linen for their bandages.[89]

Neith was worshipped throughout Egypt. There were important Neith temples at Mendes and Memphis, but she was particularly associated with the western Delta town of Sais (modern Sa el-Hagar) where her temple became known as the 'house of the bee'. Her cult waned slightly during the Middle Kingdom and early New Kingdom, only to revive in the later New Kingdom: when the 19th Dynasty pharaoh Ramesses II was crowned at Karnak, Neith was present as a witness. During the 26th Dynasty, a time when Sais served as Egypt's capital city, she became the dominant state deity and the kings were buried in the grounds of her temple. Unfortunately, her temple is now ruined and inaccessible; the royal tombs are therefore lost and we cannot confirm the claim of the philosopher Iamblichus, writing in *c*.AD 300, that the temple walls were carved with the secret of how the soul may unite with God.

MUT

As the vulture hieroglyph is read as *mut*, or 'mother', Mut of Thebes is, quite literally, a mother goddess. More specifically, she is the consort of Amen and the mother or adoptive mother of the lunar deity Khonsu. Meanwhile, in Memphis, she might be the consort of Ptah. She is a relatively late-dating deity; her first reference is found in Middle Kingdom sources and we know little of her story before she displaces Amaunet from Amen's side during the New Kingdom. Although it is difficult to tell the ages of subjects in Egyptian art (the convention being that almost everyone should appear as eternally young and fit), Mut's image is often interpreted as that of a more mature woman; if this is the case, we may guess that, in flaunting convention, the artists are reflecting her political authority and wisdom. Mut usually wears a brightly coloured sheath dress, a long, heavy wig, and the feathery vulture headdress that takes the form of a limp bird draped over the wearer's head.[90] Her regalia, royal sceptres and either the white crown of southern Egypt or the double crown of the united land, again emphasize Mut's political authority.

Curiously, Mut never appears as a vulture. As the daughter of the sun god, however, she may be a lioness, a snake or the knife-wielding cat who slays the serpent Apophis in the shade of the *ishtar* tree. As the fierce Eye of Re she is Mut-Sekhmet, the wandering goddess who quarrels with her father and has to be persuaded to return to Egypt so that she might give birth to the divine king. This form of Mut is a powerful healer who can both cause and cure sickness. As the mother of the pharaoh, Mut, like the uraeus, defends Egypt, and the king, with her flame; enemies were symbolically (and, some have argued though with little supporting evidence, literally) burned on braziers within her temples. As yet another creator deity she may appear as a mummiform lion-headed (or three-lion-headed) goddess with an incongruous erect penis: this syncretized transgender being, Mut-Min, was a potent deity 'Great of Magic'. Alternatively, she might be Mut-Sekhmet-Bast, a fearsome being equipped with wings, a penis and three heads: one human, one lion and one vulture.

ANATH AND ASTARTE

Anath and Astarte were fierce Semitic warrior goddesses who offered an effective protection against dangerous animals, enemies and daemons. As atypical, foreign women capable of violent, chaotic behaviour and, or so it was rumoured, sexual aggression, they made suitable partners for the unconventional Seth, who was himself equated with the Canaanite storm god Baal.[91]

The impetuous, Amazon-like Anath was the daughter of the great Canaanite god El and the sister-wife of Baal. As an unmarried girl on the brink of womanhood, she was allowed to participate in male activities such as hunting, which would be denied to a sexually mature or married woman. Anath arrived in Egypt during the late Middle Kingdom, at a time when increasing numbers of easterners, or 'Asiatics', were settling in the Delta. She was accepted as 'the woman who acts like a warrior', a loyal daughter who protected both her divine father (and perhaps husband) Re and all of Egypt's kings, with her axe, spear and shield. She was afraid of nothing and no one; impressed by her strength, Ramesses II named both his daughter (Bint-Anath, 'daughter of Anath') and a favourite dog ('Anath-in-Strength') after her. A historiola used in several healing spells, including *Papyrus Chester Beatty* VII,[92] was initially interpreted as telling the tale of Seth's rape of Anath. However, it is now apparent that the otherwise unidentified 'Seed Goddess' was Seth's victim. Re, enraged by Seth's villainy, poisoned him. Only when Anath pleaded on Seth's behalf did he relent and allow Isis to effect a cure.

Astarte, the equivalent of the Babylonian goddess Ishtar and the Sumerian Inanna, arrived during the Second Intermediate Period and became particularly associated with horses and chariots, which had just been introduced to Egypt. She was often depicted naked, wielding a weapon or weapons, and either riding a horse or driving a chariot. As yet another daughter of Re she was identified with the fierce leonine form of the solar Eye; alternatively, she might be the daughter of Ptah. The disjointed 18th Dynasty story known today as *Astarte and the Insatiable Sea*, is almost certainly derived from a story originally told in the Syrian port of Ugarit (modern Ras-Shamra):[93]

In the beginning, the world was created. But the sea, Yam, challenged the authority of the creator god and demanded tribute. The gods were frightened and Renenutet, goddess of the harvest, was sent with the tribute – boxes of silver, gold, lapis-lazuli and turquoise – to placate Yam. This was not enough. Yam was displeased, and Renenutet sent an urgent message, via a bird, to Astarte asking her to bring more. Astarte was reluctant, and wept, but she did as she was asked. Arriving at the seashore she sang and danced for Yam before sitting on the beach. Entranced by her beauty, Yam decided that he wanted Astarte for his wife. The Ennead collected a dowry for Astarte, but when Yam came to collect it, he was challenged by Seth . . .

The end of the tale is lost, but comparisons with the Ugaritic version, which features Yam, Astarte and the storm god Baal, suggest that Seth would have defeated Yam and claimed Astarte as his prize.

IV

HEROES AND VILLAINS

Now my heart turns this way and that, as I think what the people will say. Those who shall see my monuments in years to come, and who shall speak of what I have done.

From the obelisk inscription of the female pharaoh Hatshepsut

IO

DIVINE KINGS

Egypt's earliest myths were either set deep in the past, at the very beginning of time when gods ruled the earth, or far in the future, at the very end of time when mankind had already perished. As the dynastic age progressed humans started to play an increasingly important role in the tales as the gods lost some of their remote splendour, and the mortal world mixed tentatively with the divine. Disparate though they may at first appear, all the major myths were united by one underlying message. Each, to a greater or lesser extent, reinforced the right of the divinely appointed king to rule his land. The creation myths stressed the need to ward off chaos while placing kings on newly created thrones; the extended tale of Osiris, Isis, Seth and Horus confirmed the right of the son to inherit his father's throne; funerary mythology promoted the existence of an afterlife which, mirroring the land of the living, was ruled by a divine king. Above all, the concept of *maat*, which underpinned almost every aspect of official life, emphasized the need to maintain the status quo. In Egypt, of course, maintaining the status quo essentially meant maintaining the role of the king, whose primary duty was always the preservation of *maat*. Without the king *maat* would fail; without *maat* the gods would grow dissatisfied and might, perhaps, leave. Then, who knew what would happen? In offering *maat* to the gods, the king offered security against the chaotic unknown. It therefore goes without saying that the king headed the three interlinked state-run institutions designed to keep chaos at bay: the army (which defended Egypt against foreign chaos), the bureaucracy (which defended Egypt against internal chaos) and the priesthood (which defended Egypt against divine chaos).

The king of Egypt was neither fully human nor fully divine. He was born a mortal son to a mortal mother, just one among many king's sons who might, eventually, become king. In his official persona, however, he was recognized as the holder of a divine office, and was an *ex-officio* god on earth. This royal divinity was acquired on the death of his predecessor when the old king became associated with Osiris, and the coronation rituals allowed the new king to become both the son of Re and the living Horus. This newly acquired status separated the king from his subjects and allowed him to speak directly to the gods. Essentially, each successive king was both a new beginning and a continuation of all the kings who had gone before.

PAPYRUS WESTCAR

All kings expected to acquire full divinity with death. Some kings, however, were reluctant to wait. They believed that, as the child of a divine parent, they were already at least partially divine, and were keen to share this good news with their people. The earliest surviving royal birth myth is preserved in *Papyrus Westcar*.[94] This is an anthology of at least five independent fictional tales concerning kings past and present. Set during the Old Kingdom 4th Dynasty, the stories are told by four princes who have been called upon to entertain their father, the Great Pyramid builder Khufu. Unfortunately the first story is almost entirely lost, although we do know that it was set in the time of Djoser, the first king of the 3rd Dynasty and builder of the Sakkara Step Pyramid.

The Second Story: The Magic Occurring in the Time of King Nebka, Told by Prince Khaefre

I would like to tell Your Majesty of another wonder. This marvel occurred at the time when your ancestor, King Nebka, was visiting the temple of Ptah at Memphis.

Webaoner the priest was a respectable married man who owned a spacious villa with a green garden, shady trees and a calm blue pool. He should have been the happiest man in Egypt. But his beautiful young wife had become infatuated with a handsome man whom she had glimpsed in the street. So obsessed was she that she despatched a servant to the object of her desires, carrying a chest filled with the most luxurious of garments. The handsome man, overwhelmed with the generosity of her gift, returned with the servant to thank his benefactor in person. Having seen her beauty, he desired her greatly.

Several days passed by. Then the man sent a message to the beautiful wife of Webaoner.

'I know that there is a secluded gazebo in your garden, close by the pool. Would it not be pleasant for us to spend some time together, relaxing in the gazebo?'

The faithless wife needed no persuading. Immediately she summoned the household steward, and ordered that the gazebo be cleaned, and stocked with food and drink. This was done. The next day saw the wife and her lover secluded in the gazebo, eating, drinking and 'relaxing'. And, at the end of the day, the lover went down to the pool to bathe.

But the loyal steward was troubled by this turn of events, and reported the matter to his master. Webaoner was devastated by his wife's betrayal. He ordered the steward to light a fire. Then, sending for his chest, a beautiful wooden box inlaid with gold and ebony, he extracted a lump of wax and fashioned it into the form of a crocodile seven fingers long. As he worked he muttered magical words over the wax figure. Then he turned to his steward.

'Tomorrow, when the man goes down to the pool to bathe, throw this crocodile in after him.'

The steward agreed, and took the crocodile away with him.

The next morning the wife again asked the steward to prepare the gazebo. This was done, and she spent the remainder of the day secluded with her lover. But that evening, when the man went down to the pool to bathe, the steward threw the wax crocodile into the water after him. At once it grew into a living beast seven cubits long. The crocodile seized the horrified lover and dragged him under the water.

Webaoner worked for six days at the court of King Nebka. For all this time his wife's lover remained under the water with the crocodile, without breathing. On the seventh day Webaoner led King Nebka to his house. Standing on the edge of the pool, Webaoner called his creation forth. And the water bubbled and foamed and surged, and out of the depths the crocodile emerged with the lover, still alive, in its jaws. Webaoner called on the crocodile to release its victim, and the crocodile placed the shivering man next to the king. Then Webaoner picked up the crocodile. Instantly it turned to wax in his hands.

Webaoner told Nebka the full story of his faithless wife and her handsome lover. The king then issued a stern judgement. The crocodile was to take what belonged to him. At once the wax figure came to life and, picking up the man, slithered into the water. It was never seen again. As for the wife, she was to be taken from the house and burned, and her ashes scattered over the pool. And this is the marvel that happened in the time of Nebka.

This story visits the 3rd Dynasty court of the little-known King Nebka. It is told by Prince Khaefre, who is destined to rule Egypt as the fourth king of the 4th Dynasty. Unfortunately, there are some large gaps in the original text, and this version has been heavily reconstructed. The story tackles an often-repeated theme of Egyptian literature: the danger of approaching married women. The great didactic texts, guides to life aimed at young men, constantly warn against this folly. The danger is not that a pure young boy might be tainted by proximity to immorality or vice, but the more practical concern that a wronged husband will seek revenge. There were many, Herodotus for one, prepared to believe that the wives of Egypt were incorrigibly promiscuous. Here he tells the sorry tale of fictitious King Pheros:[95]

> [Pheros] was blind for ten years, and in the eleventh he received an oracle from the city of Buto to the effect that the time of his punishment being now ended, he would recover his sight if he washed his eyes with the urine of a woman who had never lain with any man except her husband. He tried his wife first, but without success; then he tried other women, a great many, one after another, until at last his sight was restored. Then he collected within the walls of a town, now called Red Clod, all the women except the one whose urine had proved efficacious, set the place on fire, and burned them to death, town and all; afterwards he married the woman who had been the means of curing him.

However, the interest in Khaefre's tale is not in the adultery, which is somewhat commonplace, but in the wonders worked by the cuckolded husband. Webaoner possesses a magic so powerful that he can control the crocodile, the untameable destroyer that lurks on Egypt's riverbanks menacing those, including boatmen and washermen, who work on or in the river and canals. His choice of agent is a deliberate one. The Egyptians often used the crocodile to symbolize destiny and, as we have already seen, the crocodile is one of the three fates in the *Tale of the Doomed Prince*. Webaoner's is a large, but not unfeasibly large, beast – a cubit measured just over 20.5 inches (52.5 cm), and so his crocodile must have been 12 feet (3.6 metres) long.

Pyramid Texts spell 317 describes how the dead king might become one with the divine crocodile Sobek: [96]

> *I have come today from out of the waters of the flood; I am Sobek, green of plume, watchful of face, raised of brow, the raging one who came forth from the shank and tail of the Great One who is in the sunshine. I have come to my waterways which are in the bank of the flood of the Great Inundation, to the place of contentment, green of fields, which is in the horizon. I make green the herbage which is on the banks of the horizon, that I may bring greenness to the Eye of the Great One who dwells in the field. I take my seat which is in the horizon, I appear as Sobek son of Neith, I eat with my mouth, I urinate and copulate with my phallus, I am the owner of the seed who takes women from their husbands whenever he wishes, according to his desire.*

Here we see the two contrasting sides of Sobek. On the one hand he is a life-enhancing fertility god who represents the fecund waters of the Nile flood, and who, closely linked with kingship and royal power, inspires the pharaohs of the 12th and 13th Dynasties. When syncretized with Re he becomes the universal creator Sobek-Re. On the other hand, however, he is the self-confessed merciless one 'who takes women from their husbands whenever he wishes' and who, through his association with Seth, becomes 'the rebel' who mutilates Osiris' corpse. Particularly revered in the watery and fertile Faiyum, Sobek was the son of Neith and, in later tradition, the husband of either Hathor or Renenutet. Although he started life as a full crocodile or a crocodile-headed man who wore the *atef* crown, Sobek later assumed many forms. In his role as 'Lord of Bakhu' (the mountain of the horizon), he owned a splendid temple built of carnelian; in his role as 'Lord of the Nile', he was the patron deity of fishermen. The *Coffin Texts* tell us that when Re wished to retrieve Horus's severed hands from the Nile, Sobek invented a fish trap to catch them.

Wronged though he has been, Webaoner is careful not to take the law into his own hands. Adultery is a moral crime but it is not a capital offence, and it is only when he has the full approval of the king that he allows his crocodile to claim its reward. The king, of course, is Egypt's ultimate judge. Here he pronounces the most severe penalty that the state can inflict: death followed by the loss of burial rites. With no mummified body the lover's *ka* will perish and he will effectively be barred from the afterlife. Webaoner's unfaithful wife meets an equally unpleasant end. She is to be incinerated, although it is not clear whether she is to be burned alive or cremated after death. Either way she, too, is denied an afterlife.

The Third Story: The Magic Occurring in the Time of King Snefru, Told by Prince Bauefre

Now I will tell Your Majesty of yet another wonderful event, one that happened at the court of your esteemed late father, Snefru.

One day Snefru was deeply bored. He wandered through all the rooms in the palace, seeking amusement, but found none. Finally he summoned the priest Djadja-em-Ankh, and sought his advice. Djadja-em-Ankh did not fail his king: 'Your Majesty, proceed to the palace lake. Fill a boat with all the beautiful girls in your palace. Your heart will be refreshed at the sight of them rowing up and down the lake.'

Snefru eagerly agreed: 'Indeed, I shall go boating. Bring me twenty oars of gold-plated ebony with electrum handles. Bring me twenty young women with the shapeliest bodies, firm breasts and fine braids; virgins who have not yet given birth. And bring me twenty nets and give these nets to the women in place of their clothes!'

And so it was done. Out on the sunlit water the maidens rowed with a slow, steady stroke. They sang as they rowed, their golden skin glistening with sweat, their braids swinging in rhythm with their songs, and their net dresses tracing exciting patterns on their bare flesh. Never had Snefru been so happy. But suddenly the tranquillity was broken. The leading maiden cried out in distress. A turquoise charm had fallen from her hair and was lost in the water. The rowers laid down their oars in confusion and the boats stopped moving. The king quickly promised to replace the turquoise charm, but the maiden could not be comforted. She wanted her own charm, not a new one, and she was too sad to continue.

Again Snefru sent for Djadja-em-Ankh. He explained the situation, and asked for help. The priest did not hesitate. He spoke some magical words, then bent down and folded one side of the lake's water on to the other. Djadja-em-Ankh found the charm lying on a piece of broken pot on the lake bed. He picked it up and returned it to its owner. A second spell then restored the lake to its watery form, and the maidens took to their boats again.

Snefru was mightily impressed by what he had seen. The priest's triumph was celebrated that evening with a great feast lasting well into the night. And Djadja-em-Ankh was rewarded with many valuable gifts.

This third magical happening occurs in the recent past, at the court of Snefru, father of Khufu and builder of three pyramids (the collapsed pyramid at Meidum and the two Dahshur pyramids). The story is told by Bauefre, a prince who has left no known tomb but whose name is recorded on a list of royal names carved during the Middle Kingdom in the Wadi Hammamat. He might perhaps be the Prince Babaef who was buried in the Giza cemetery.

Like Khufu, Snefru is infinitely rich and infinitely bored – boredom being a privilege of the elite. Snefru seems to have been particularly prone to attacks of ennui, and the Middle Kingdom story known today as the *Prophecies of Neferti* [97] tells of a separate (fictional) occasion when the king sends for a sage famed for his entertaining oratory. The sage Neferti allows the king to choose whether he hears about the past or the future and, perhaps unwisely, Snefru elects to learn 'what will happen'. Acting as scribe, Snefru is then forced to record an horrific account of civil war (the First Intermediate Period) followed by the reunification of the country under 'Ameny' who, it seems safe to assume, is the founder of the 12th Dynasty, Amenemhat I.

Back at *Papyrus Westcar*, Snefru's myth, like Nebka's, is centred on a pool. But this is a well-controlled pool under royal authority; there is no life-threatening crocodile here, and the tale itself is an innocuous confection of hot weather, cool water, pretty girls, mild voyeurism and, of course, spectacular magic. A nice touch is the storyteller's insistence that the king designed the women's garments himself. These are usually translated as fishing-net dresses but are more likely to represent the beaded over-tunics that have been found in funerary contexts. The turquoise fish-shaped ornament that falls out of the maiden's hair may well have been a charm against drowning. If so, we can understand her reluctance to continue rowing without it.

The Fourth Story: The Magic Occurring in the Time of King Khufu, Told by Prince Hardjedef

Prince Hardjedef stood up and spoke: 'You have listened to three tales of powerful magic performed by great men who are now dead: but who can tell if these wonderful events truly happened? Yet there is a man living today, one of Your Majesty's own subjects, who is truly a superb magician. A man named Djedi lives in the town of Djed-Snefru. He is a man already 110 years old, yet he eats five hundred loaves of bread and half a cow every day, and he washes his meal down with one hundred jugs of beer. And this man can rejoin a severed head. He can tame a lion so that it walks behind him like a cat, its lead trailing on the ground. And he knows the number and plan of the secret chambers in the sanctuary of Thoth.'

Khufu was greatly intrigued by his son's words. For he had long been fascinated by the riddle of the chambers of Thoth, and had spent many years researching their secret in the hope that he might be able to copy them in his own pyramid complex. He ordered Hardjedef to bring the magician to him at once.

The young prince had a fleet of boats prepared, then sailed upriver to Djed-Snefru. When the fleet had moored he disembarked to travel overland, seated in a carrying chair carved of ebony, whose poles were decorated with gold. When the son of Khufu reached the house of Djedi the magician he clambered out of his carrying chair. He found the wise old man lying on a mat in the courtyard of his house. One servant squatted beside his master, massaging his bald scalp with scented oils; a second servant squatted to rub his feet. Hardjedef was amazed. For Djedi was a man so old that death must surely be looming near, yet he had all the vigour and health of a young man with no sign of illness, not even a cough, to betray his true age.

The prince hailed the old man courteously: 'Greetings, O great sage. I have come to welcome you to the court of my father, King Khufu. There you may eat the finest of foods, and drink the best of wines. And when the time comes, my father will ensure that you have an honourable funeral with burial in the cemetery of your forefathers.'

The old man addressed the prince with equal respect: 'Welcome in peace, Hardjedef, beloved son of Khufu. May your father shower you with praise. May he promote you above all your brothers. May your spirit triumph over all your enemies, and may your soul lead you safely, at the right time, to the dark doorway that allows entry to the eternal life.'

Then the prince held out his hands and pulled the old man gently to his feet. Arm in arm they walked together to the mooring place of Djed-Snefru. Here Djedi stopped.

'Allow me a boat to carry my children and my books to the palace.'

Hardjedef allocated the magician two boats and their crews for the transportation of his goods and chattels, but he insisted that his guest should sail in the greater comfort of his own royal boat. And thus Djedi the magician sailed downstream to the court of King Khufu.

When they reached the palace, Hardjedef reported to his father: 'My lord, I have brought Djedi to you.'

Khufu could hardly wait: 'Bring him to me!' And he rushed to the great hall of the palace.

When Djedi had been brought in, Khufu started to question him: 'How can it be it that I have never seen you before, Djedi?'

With great wisdom, the old man replied: 'Only he that is summoned can respond, my king. You have summoned me, and I have come.'

'Is it true what they say, that you can rejoin a severed head?'

'Yes, my king, I can.'

In great excitement Khufu ordered that a prisoner be brought from the gaol, so that he might be beheaded and restored to life. But Djedi halted him: 'Surely there is no need to execute anyone, my king. For murder is forbidden by our law. Let us kill an animal instead.'

And so a goose was brought into the hall, and its head was cut off. Its body was placed on the west side of the hall, and its head was placed on the east. Djedi uttered his magical spell. And at once the body of the goose stood up and waddled towards its head, while the head started to jerk and roll towards its body. The two halves of the bird met and were joined, so that the goose was whole and live and cackling again. Djedi then repeated his magic, first with a long-legged ibis and then with a full-grown bull.

Then Khufu spoke again: 'They tell me that you know the number of the hidden chambers in the sanctuary of Thoth.'

But Djedi shook his head: 'I do not know the number, O king, but I do know where it may be read.'

'Where is that?'

'There is a chest carved from flint in the building known as the Inventory in the city of Heliopolis. It is in that chest.'

Khufu was beside himself with excitement: 'Then go and bring it to me.'

'Alas, my king, it is not I who shall bring it to you.'

'Then who will bring it to me?'

'Only the eldest of the three unborn sons in the womb of the Lady Redjedet can bring this chest to you.'

The king's face fell. For he greatly desired to open the chest: 'But who is this Lady Redjedet?'

'She is the wife of a priest of Re, Lord of Sakhbu, my king. She is destined to give birth to the three mortal sons of Re. They will hold the highest office in the land, and the eldest son will become high priest at Heliopolis.'

On hearing this prophecy Khufu's heart grew sad, for he had assumed that his own sons and grandsons and their sons and grandsons in turn would occupy his throne. Djedi noticed his king's abrupt change of mood: 'Why this sorrow, my king? Is it because I have told you of these three children? Do not worry – first your son will rule, then his son, and only then will one of the three take his place.'

Slightly consoled, the king asked: 'When will Redjedet give birth?'

'She will go into labour on the fifteenth day of the first month of winter,' the magician replied.

Khufu spoke: 'The sandbanks of the Two Fishes Canal will be dry at that time. Otherwise I could perhaps have gone to visit the magnificent temple of Re, Lord of Sakhbu.'

'Do not worry, my king. When the time comes I will make sure that there is water four cubits deep on the sandbanks of the Two Fishes Canal.'

Khufu retired to his private quarters. Djedi had proved to be everything that Hardjedef had claimed for him, and more. Khufu commanded that the magician should dwell for the rest of his life as an honoured guest among Hardjedef's household. His rations were to be set at one thousand loaves of bread, one hundred jugs of beer, one ox and one hundred bundles of green vegetables. And as the king had commanded, so it was done.

This fourth tale brings the listeners up to date, for it is set in the time of Khufu himself. Unlike his brothers, Hardjedef does not actually tell a story. Instead he asks permission to bring a real live magician to perform at court. Djedi lives at Djed-Snefru, the town associated with the late King Snefru's pyramid complex. His magic is the most impressive yet: not only can he tame wild beasts, he can bring the dead back to life. But Khufu is only really interested in the plan of the secret chambers of Thoth – a theme that is introduced to the story and then tantalizingly dropped. This casual mention of lost chambers has led to much speculation, as both conventional and alternative Egyptologists attempt to understand its meaning and locate (what they imagine to be) the esoteric knowledge of the wise Thoth.

The Fifth Story: The Magic Occurring in the Future

The day came when Redjedet, wife of Rewoser, felt the first sharp pangs of childbirth and took to her bedchamber. There she stayed for many hours, for her labour was long and very painful, and nothing could be done to help her. The great god Re, seeing her plight, summoned Isis, Nephthys, Meskhenet, Heket and Khnum to him. He begged the four goddesses to assist Redjedet: 'For, eventually, they will build shrines and make magnificent offerings to those who helped at their birth.'

The gods departed for Egypt, the four goddesses disguised as dancing girls, with Khnum dressed as their servant and carrying the birthing stool. When they reached the house of Rewoser they found him standing outside, his kilt disordered and his mind preoccupied with thoughts of his wife's suffering. The goddesses showed him their necklaces and their *sistra*, and he asked for their help at once: 'For my wife is in much pain, and her labour is very difficult.'

'Let us see what can be done. For we understand childbirth.'

The goddesses entered the house and went straight to Redjedet, locking the door of her room behind them.

Isis stood in front of Redjedet, Nephthys stood behind her, and Heket hastened the delivery. Isis greeted the first child: 'Do not be so strong in your mother's womb, you whose name means Strong.'

And a baby boy slipped into her arms; a sturdy child, one cubit long, with golden flesh and a headdress of real lapis lazuli.

13. Osiris depicted on a Third Intermediate
Period private stela from Deir el-Bahri.

14. The jackal-headed god Anubis.

15. Seth's distinctive head, on a New Kingdom block at Memphis.

16. Horus the falcon-headed king drives his harpoon into Seth, who takes the form of a hippopotamus, on the wall of the Ptolemaic Edfu temple.

17. The eye of Horus; painted on the side of a Middle Kingdom coffin, this would allow the deceased to look into the tomb.

18. The 4th Dynasty king Menkaure stands
between Hathor (on his right) and a local goddess.

19. The lion-headed Sekhmet tops a pole carried by her devotee, the fortress commander Neb-Re.

20. Hathor, recognizable by her cow-ears, is featured on this stone replica of the processional boat of Mut.

21. The traditional Egyptian Isis, in the New Kingdom tomb of Siptah.

22. Isis or Nephthys in the form of a kite.

23. The crocodile-headed Sobek. A Ptolemaic image from his temple at Kom Ombo.

24. Pottery vessel in the shape of the dwarf Bes.

25. The female pharaoh Hatshepsut presents herself in the form of a stereotypical male king on the wall of the Red Chapel, Karnak.

The umbilical cord was cut, and the baby was washed and placed on a cushion. Meskhenet approached him to confirm his fate:

'A king who will rule over the entire land.'

Then Khnum, the creator god, gave him the gift of health.

Again Isis stood in front of Redjedet, Nephthys stood behind her, and Heket hastened the delivery. Isis greeted the second child: 'Do not kick in your mother's womb, you whose name means Kicker.'

And a baby boy slipped into her arms; a sturdy child, one cubit long, with golden flesh and a headdress of real lapis lazuli. The umbilical cord was cut, and the baby was washed and placed on a cushion. Meskhenet approached him to confirm his fate:

'A king who will rule over the entire land.'

Then Khnum, the creator god, gave him the gift of health.

For a third time Isis stood in front of Redjedet, Nephthys stood behind her, and Heket hastened the delivery. Isis greeted the third child: 'Do not be dark in your mother's womb, you whose name means Dark.'

And a baby boy slipped into her arms; a sturdy child, one cubit long, with golden flesh and a headdress of real lapis lazuli. The umbilical cord was cut, and the baby was washed and placed on a cushion. Meskhenet approached him to confirm his fate:

'A king who will rule over the entire land.'

Then Khnum, the creator god, gave him the gift of health.

Having delivered Redjedet of three children, the gods left the room. They said: 'Give thanks, Rewoser, for your wife has given birth to three fine sons.'

Rewoser was overjoyed, and filled with gratitude. He offered the dancing girls a sack of barley in payment for their help for, as he said, this was a most valuable gift that they could use to make beer. Khnum picked up the sack, and they set off from the house. Then Isis had second thoughts: 'Why did we come, if it was not to perform wonders for those three children, and to report back to their father who made us come?'

So they made three royal crowns, and hid them in the sack of barley. And then, having conjured up a fierce storm, they returned to shelter at the house of the high priest. They asked Rewoser to store the sack for them: 'For we are going north to dance, and do not want to be burdened with a heavy sack.'

The sack was locked in an unused room.

Redjedet rested in bed for fourteen days, then resumed her household duties. She asked her maid: 'Is everything in the house in good order?'

'Everything is prepared, my lady, except for the beer – we don't have any jars of beer.'

'Why don't we have any jars of beer?'

'Because we have no grain in the house to make beer, except for one sack of barley which now belongs to the four dancing girls and their servant, and which is now locked in the unused room.'

Redjedet ordered the maidservant to open up the sack and take some of the barley, for she knew that her husband was an honourable man who would replace anything that she had borrowed when the musicians returned from the north.

The maid unlocked the door of the chamber and heard music, singing, dancing and shouting – all the noises that are made for a king. She ran to her mistress and told what she had heard. Redjedet entered the room. She too could hear the noise of celebrations, but could not tell whence it came until she put her ear against the sack of barley. Redjedet locked the sack in a box that was itself sealed in a larger chest and bound with a leather strap. Finally the chest was locked in the secure room that contained her own most precious belongings. When

Rewoser returned from work, she told him what had happened. His heart was filled with great happiness and they celebrated with a day of feasting.

Many days later, Redjedet had reason to find fault with her maid, and punished her with a beating. Then the maid said to everyone in the house: 'Who is she to treat me this way? She has given birth to three future kings in secret. I will tell King Khufu what is being plotted in the house of Rewoser.'

The maid left the house. Her path took her past the farm where she found her half-brother binding bundles of flax. Surprised to see his little sister, he asked where she was going. She told him all that she had seen and heard. Her brother turned on her: 'Is this a good thing for you to do? Involving me in your dangerous gossip?'

He lashed out at her with his bundle of flax. Then the maid went to draw a bucket of water and was snatched by a crocodile.

The brother went to tell Redjedet what had happened to his sister. He found his mistress hunched in her chair, weeping.

'My lady, why are you so upset?'

'I am upset because I am thinking of the little girl who grew up in this house and who became my maid. Just now she ran off to tell all she knew . . .'

The brother felt shame: 'My lady, she did indeed run to tell me. I hit her a hard blow. Then, as she drew water, a crocodile took her . . .'

Sad to say, this brief and entirely fictional tale provides our most complete account of childbirth in ancient Egypt. With little practical help available, childbirth was a time for unofficial female magic rather than official male medicine and, although gynaecological texts and what appear to be obstetric implements have been recovered from male tombs, the vast majority of women relied on the services of family members and female midwives to get them through their ordeal. These women were unable, or unwilling, to write down what, after all, every woman already knew. In *Papyrus Westcar* Re selects Isis, Nephthys, Heket and Meskhenet to help the stricken mother. We have already met Isis and Nephthys who, although strongly associated with death and mourning rituals, are also regarded as agents of healing and rebirth. The frog-headed Heket, wife of Khnum, carries the gift of life. In a role which reflects the widespread belief that frogs were spontaneously generated from the thick Nile mud, she both helps living women to give birth and helps the deceased to be reborn in the afterlife. Meskhenet is a goddess of childbirth who decides the destiny of the new-born.

The goddesses bring nothing in the way of specialist equipment save for a birthing stool, a simple stool with a hole cut in the seat. As an alternative to the birthing stool, many women squatted or knelt on birthing-bricks (personified in the form of Meskhenet) for their delivery; birth-bricks were also included among elite tomb equipment to aid the rebirth of the deceased. Rewoser is barred from the birth chamber, but Khnum is allowed admittance. With the door firmly closed, Heket is somehow able to hasten the delivery; we are not told how she accomplishes this. Then the umbilical cord is cut with a sharp obsidian or flint knife that parallels the knife used in the embalming ritual. While human midwives almost certainly recited prayers and spells to help the mother through her ordeal, the three goddesses do not need to do this. Similarly, they do not use the curious boomerang-shaped 'magic wands', which should probably be reclassified as 'magic knives', that we find in Middle Kingdom contexts. Carved out of hippopotamus teeth and decorated with figures of grotesque demi-gods, daemons and spirits, the precise purpose of these wands is unknown but, in the absence of any obvious practical application, they may have been used to draw a protective circle around mother and baby, and used again in the tomb to facilitate the rebirth of the deceased. The grotesque beings who dance along the wands presumably reflect an oral, female-based mythology which is today lost.

The 'wands' were not the only magical implements available to the midwife. The lack of practical medical equipment was balanced by an abundance of amulets and charms, many of them bearing the figures of the pregnant hippopotamus Taweret. While male hippopotami were regarded as dangerous, chaotic beings associated with Seth, Taweret, the 'Great One', simultaneously comforted mothers-to-be while scaring evil spirits away from the birthing chamber. Blessed with the head and body of a pregnant hippopotamus, the heavy breasts of a nursing human mother (or of the Nile god Hapy), the paws of a lioness and the tail of a crocodile, Taweret stood on her hind legs, freeing her front paws to carry the tools of her trade: the symbol for 'protection' and a sharp knife. Physically she was composed of the same body-parts as Ammit, eater of the damned, but while Ammit was feared and loathed, Taweret was welcomed into the home, where she was so important to the ordinary people that even during the Amarna Age, when most of the traditional pantheon was banned, she was allowed to prosper.

Plutarch tells us that Taweret was, for a time, Seth's concubine, but that she abandoned him to side with Horus. This moment of domestic drama aside, Taweret has little known mythology and no specific cult centre or priesthood. However, away from the birthing chamber she, like the other hippopotamus goddesses, Opet 'the nurse' and Reret 'the sow', is associated with the Nile floods as 'the one who is in the waters of Nun'. These three, alongside Nun and Mehet-Weret, can be regarded as the mothers of the solar creator god, while Opet, who gave birth in the secret chambers of her Karnak temple, may also be accepted as the mother of Osiris.

Bes was another grotesque who brought comfort and protection to mothers and children of all classes: his image was found both in the bedroom of the Malkata palace, home to Amenhotep III and his wife Tiy, and in far humbler workers' houses. A part-comical, part-sinister dwarf with plump body, prominent breasts, shortened legs, bearded face, flat nose and protruding tongue, Bes was regularly shown full-face in two-dimensional representations. He might be either fully human, or half-human, half-animal (usually lion), and might have a mane, a lion's tail, and wings. He often wears a plumed headdress and carries either a drum or tambourine, or a knife. As his name is not firmly linked to his distinctive image until relatively late in the dynastic period, it may be that the Bes whom we recognize today is a composite of early named and unnamed protective dwarf-deities including Aha ('the fighter') who was known to strangle snakes with his bare hands. In the later New Kingdom Bes was joined by Ptah-Pataikos, another protective dwarf deity, but one without facial hair. Dwarfs were often featured in scenes of craftsmen and metalworkers, hence their connection with the craftsman god Ptah.

Bes offered a welcome protection against snakes. But his primary role was as a dancer and musician who used his art to frighten away bad spirits during childbirth, childhood, sex and sleep. Bes featured on bedroom walls where, we may deduce, he supervised both conception and labour. He also appeared, either tattooed or painted, on the upper thigh of dancing girls; we cannot tell if this was simple body art, the mark of a prostitute, or a charm intended to protect against sexually transmitted disease. During the Late Period Bes and his feminine counterpart and consort Bestet (a replacement for his earlier wife, Taweret) came to be associated with the twins Shu and Tefnut. Bestet, who occasionally appeared naked, and/or pregnant, could also be equated with Isis, while Bes might be associated with Horus-the-Child either as his protector or as Horbes (an aspect of the

renewed sun). In some incantations Bes had, by the end of the
dynastic age, evolved into a perversely huge dwarf whose body
stretched from the underworld to the heavens.

A unique damaged and flattened painted mask found in a house
in the 12th Dynasty workmen's village of Kahun may have been
a prop used in a Bestet-based ritual.[98] The mask has eye- and
nose-holes, but no mouth, so its wearer could not speak with any
clarity. This was, presumably, deliberate. In the mortal world
dwarfs and pygmies were valued for their ritual dances rather
than their utterances; they performed at funerals and in temples,
they danced for the king, and they featured in the *Pyramid Texts*,
where their dance formed part of the mortuary ritual. When
the 6th Dynasty child-king Pepi II wrote to thank the courtier
Harkhuf for bringing him a real, live, dancing dwarf, Harkhuf
was so pleased that he incorporated the king's letter in the lengthy
autobiography carved on the façade of his Aswan tomb:[99]

A letter from King Neferkare Pepi II:
Day 15 of the third month of inundation, Year 2.
Written under the king's own seal.
The king writes to the Sole Companion, Lector Priest, and
Chief of Scouts, Harkhuf. The despatch that you sent to the
palace, informing me that you and your army have returned
in safety from Yam, has been received. In that despatch you
mention that you have brought with you many precious gifts;
gifts that Hathor has provided for the spirit of King Neferkare
Pepi, may he live forever. You specifically state that you have
obtained a pygmy, one of the god's dancers, from the land of
the horizon-dwellers. And you add that this pygmy is like the
pygmy that the God's Seal Bearer Wer-Djed-Ba brought from
the land of Punt during the reign of King Isesi. But, as you
point out, your pygmy is the first of his kind to come to Egypt
from Yam.

This is excellent news indeed. You really know how to please your Lord. Truly, I think that you must spend all your waking hours working out how best to serve me. I will reward you and your family for many generations for this good deed. Everyone, when they hear of my generosity, will say: 'Can anything ever equal the favours that were heaped on the Sole Companion Harkhuf, when he returned from Yam, as a reward for his irreproachable service to the king.'

Make your way northwards to the palace, at once. Hurry, and bring with you the remarkable pygmy from the land of horizon-dwellers, so that he might perform the dances of the god and delight my heart. Guard this pygmy with your life! When he is on board the ship, make sure that he is well supervised lest he fall into the water and drown. When he is in bed at night, have your loyal men care for him in his tent. Check on him at least ten times each and every night! For I long to see this remarkable pygmy more than I covet all the precious gifts of Punt.

If the pygmy is still alive and well when you reach my palace, I will do great things for you. More, even, than was done for the God's Seal Bearer Wer-Djed-Ba during the reign of King Isesi, for so great is my desire to see the pygmy that you bring. Orders have been issued to the chief of the new towns and the Companion, Overseer of the Priests, to ensure that supplies be provided from the storage depots and temple warehouses under their command. No one will be exempted from this.

Returning to *Papyrus Westcar*, the words uttered by Isis as the triplets are born are puns that the Egyptian audience would have recognized. 'Do not be so strong in your mother's womb, you whose name means Strong' identifies Userkaf, first king of the 5th Dynasty, whose name translates as 'his spirit is strong'. 'Do not kick in your mother's womb, you whose name means Kicker' refers to the second king of the 5th Dynasty, Sahure, a name which means 'well-endowed by Re' but which includes the element *sahu*, 'to kick'. 'Do not be dark in your mother's womb, you whose name means Dark' is spoken to Neferirkare-Kakai, third king of the dynasty. The element *keku* within his name implies darkness.

Papyrus Westcar is obviously not an accurate account of events at the beginning of the 5th Dynasty. It is a piece of royal propaganda designed to stress the divine birth of the three 5th Dynasty Kings Userkaf, Sahure and Nyuserre, and in so doing it leaps from the reign of Khufu to that of Userkhaf. We can fill in the missing history from more conventional sources. Khufu was succeeded by his sons Djedefre and Khaefre, and then by his grandson Menkaure, builder of the third Giza pyramid. Menkaure was followed by Shepseskaf, the final king of the 4th Dynasty. His successor, the 5th Dynasty King Userkaf, is a man of mysterious origins who may well have been a descendant of Djedefre or Menkaure; the dynastic break that so troubled Khufu may therefore not have signalled the end of Khufu's line.

The 5th Dynasty kings certainly felt a great devotion to their father Re. The triplets incorporated Re's name within their own, and each built both a pyramid and a sun temple dedicated to his 'father'. This close relationship leaves their mother Redjedet in the unusual position of a non-royal woman who has enjoyed an intimate relationship with a god. Although she is a fictional character, it seems likely that Redjedet is based on the 5th Dynasty Queen Khentkawes I, the probable wife of Userkaf. Khentkawes I was the owner of an unusual Giza tomb (known to archaeologists today as LG 100), which was built on natural outcrop of rock so that it looked like a combined mastaba-pyramid. Her titles, carved on the granite doorway leading to the tomb mortuary chapel, included one important, ambiguous phrase which can be translated with equal validity either as 'Mother of Two Kings of Upper and Lower Egypt', or as 'King of Upper and Lower Egypt and Mother of the King of Upper and Lower Egypt', while her door-jamb shows her sitting on a throne, wearing a false beard and uraeus and carrying a sceptre. Combined, this evidence suggests that Khentkawes served as a temporary ruler of Egypt, acting as regent for one or more of her sons.

As the centralized Old Kingdom collapsed, Egypt fragmented into a series of independent kingdoms. Scribe Ipuwer writes of an horrendous, *maat*-less time of chaos and violence: a time when crime was rife, the cemeteries were desecrated and the wealthy starved as the River Nile ran red with blood.[100] Ipuwer, however, was deliberately promoting the legend of the horrific, kingless age in order to stress the ordered calm of the Middle Kingdom. Although there were occasional food shortages, the First Intermediate Period was by no means the political and cultural Dark Age that Egyptologists once supposed, and archaeological evidence from the provincial cemeteries confirms that life actually improved for many at this time.

Slowly but surely the local governors of the Valley and the Delta started to form alliances until two dominant dynasties emerged: a northern dynasty based at Herakleopolis and a rival southern dynasty based at Thebes. Both aspired to reunite Egypt but that honour eventually fell to the Thebans under the leadership of Nebhepetre Montuhotep II, 'Unifier of the Two Lands'. Montuhotep II could not claim a chain of distinguished ancestors to reinforce his right to rule. Instead, he established prominent links with the state gods and, in particular, with Hathor. Montuhotep was now the self-proclaimed son of Hathor, and his wives were priestesses in her cult. Meanwhile, images of Hathor, as both a cow and a woman suckling Montuhotep, emphasized the mythology of the king as Horus who was suckled by Hathor in the papyrus marshes. Montuhotep built a small temple to Hathor at Dendera[101] and a large, unique and now sadly ruined mortuary temple-tomb in the Deir el-Bahri bay at Thebes, a site already sacred to the goddess. This link between Hathor, Deir el-Bahri and kingship would continue into the New Kingdom, with Hatshepsut and Tuthmosis III building their mortuary temples alongside the temple-tomb of Montuhotep II.

DIVINE BIRTHS

The New Kingdom monarchs Hatshepsut, Amenhotep III and Ramesses II made their divine status more explicit. Each, claiming Amen-Re as their father, carved the narrative myth of their conception into their stone temple walls. Unlike *Papyrus Westcar*, their stories concentrate on the moment of conception rather than the mechanics of birth; they are romantic yet eminently practical tales involving disguised gods and beautiful queens. In all three, the divine father-to-be makes his initial approach disguised as the queen's absent husband. These birth myths are very specific; they deal with named individuals rather than the divine origins of all kings. Because of this, and because they make the physical relationship between the mother-to-be and the god very clear, they boost the religious profile of the king's mother – the earthly equivalent of the goddess Nut – who now becomes one of the few mortals able to communicate with the gods.

Hatshepsut's myth, the earliest of the three, is told as a cartoon-like sequence of images and descriptive texts carved on the north side of the middle colonnade fronting her mortuary temple. Here, it takes its place alongside real events from the queen's reign: her brief but effective military adventures, her trade missions, and her raising of obelisks in honour of her father Amen-Re. Although both images and texts were severely defaced after Hatshepsut's death, and then further damaged by Ramesside 'restorations', we can still follow most of the birth story. The opening scene shows a council of the gods:[102]

Amen-Re is seated on his throne. He has summoned the twelve great deities of Egypt (Montu, Atum, Shu, Tefnut, Geb, Nut, Osiris, Isis, Nephthys, Seth, Horus and Hathor), for he is about to make an important announcement. He has decided to father a female king, and wants his fellow gods to offer her their protection: 'I will join for her the Two Lands in peace . . . I will give her all lands and all countries . . . ' In his role as scribe and messenger of the gods Thoth announces the name of the mother-to-be: she is Ahmose, queen of Tuthmosis I, and she is more beautiful than any other woman. As Ahmose is as virtuous as she is beautiful, Amen-Re will assume the appearance of Tuthmosis I when he impregnates her. Thoth then takes Amen-Re by the hand, and leads him to the palace.

The beautiful Ahmose, sleeping alone in her bedroom, is woken by the perfume of Amen-Re. She believes him to be her husband. They sit face to face on a bed supported by the goddesses Neith and Serket, and Amen-Re reveals his true form. He tells Ahmose that she is to bear a daughter whom she will name Khnemet-Amen Hatshepsut (The One who is joined with Amen, the Foremost of Women). This daughter will rule Egypt and will guide the living. He then holds out the *ankh*, sign of life, to the queen's nostrils while passing her the hieroglyphs for life and dominion. As their legs tangle suggestively together, Ahmose smiles at her 'husband'.

Next we see the royal infant and her identical *ka* being fashioned on Khnum's wheel. Both have unmistakably male bodies. Amen-Re watches anxiously as Khnum promises that the newly formed baby will be all that any father could desire: 'I will shape for you your daughter . . . I will make her appearance above the gods, because of her dignity as king of Upper and Lower Egypt.' As Khnum finishes his work the frog-headed midwife Heket offers life to the two inert forms. Khnum now makes a promise: 'I have come to you to create you higher than all the gods. I will give you all life, all purity, all stability, all joy within me.'

Back at the palace, Thoth appears before Ahmose. He tells the queen of the glories and titles that await her unborn child: '. . . in thy high dignity of princess, the head of the favourite and head of the preferred, the well-pleasing mistress, very affectionate and loving, who sees Horus [and Seth] who loves the sacred ram . . . '

Nine months later the pregnant queen is led to the birth bower by Khnum and Heket. Twelve deities wait to assist at the birth; the lengthy text which originally accompanied this scene is now destroyed. When next we see Ahmose she is sitting on a throne, holding the new-born Hatshepsut in her arms. She is surrounded by divine nurses and midwives, and Taweret and Bes are present as is Meskhenet, who is to be chief nurse.

Finally Hathor, the royal wet-nurse, presents the baby to her father. Amen-Re is overwhelmed with love. He addresses Hatshepsut: 'Daughter of my loins, sacred form, my first issue . . . as king you take possession of the Two Lands on the throne of Horus like Re', then takes her from Hathor, kisses her, and presents her to the assembled gods, who greet her with great joy: 'Come to me, come to me in peace, daughter of my loins, beloved Maatkare [Hatshepsut], you are the king who takes possession of the diadem on the throne of Horus the living, eternally.'

The story now slowly starts to move towards the real world. Hatshepsut travels north to visit the ancient shrines of the gods of Egypt accompanied by her earthly father, Tuthmosis I. This is followed by a coronation before the gods and then by a subsequent earthly coronation by Tuthmosis, who formally nominates his daughter as his co-regent and intended successor.

As this text makes quite clear, Hatshepsut was an anomaly: a female king. The daughter of a king (Tuthmosis I), widow of a king (Tuthmosis II) and step-mother of a king (Tuthmosis III), she took the throne soon after her husband's death, ruling for twenty-two successful years alongside the young Tuthmosis III who was, for most of her reign, insignificant and virtually invisible. Female rule was not forbidden. It was acceptable for a woman to rule where there was no male heir, and the brief 12th Dynasty reign of Sobeknofru had been regarded as a plucky but ultimately doomed attempt to continue her failing family line. As the myth of Osiris and Isis shows us, it was also acceptable for a queen to rule as temporary regent for her fatherless son. But Hatshepsut, who had been required to rule on behalf of a step-son rather than a son, broke this rule when she retained the throne long after Tuthmosis had come of age. We are never told why she took this unprecedented step, and can only guess that it was precipitated by a crisis, either political or theological, which required a fully adult king. Her birth myth, however, does offer some justification for her actions. Hatshepsut is entitled to the throne because she is not only the beloved daughter of the great king Tuthmosis I, she is also the daughter of the great god Amen-Re and, as such, is predestined to rule. Her unswerving love for, and loyalty to, her divine and earthly fathers was to be a constant theme of her reign.

Amenhotep III reigned almost seventy years after Hatshepsut's death. His birth myth is so similar to Hatshepsut's – indeed, portions of the text are identical – that it is impossible to escape the conclusion that he copied it wholesale. But why did he feel the need to re-tell the story? As the son of Tuthmosis IV, albeit by the secondary queen Mutemwia, Amenhotep III had a strong claim to the throne. It therefore seems likely that his myth was intended not to confirm his own right to rule – that was already accepted by all – but to confirm his own personal divinity. His story is told in the 'birth room', part of a suite of two rooms in the Luxor temple, a temple dedicated to both Amen-Re and to the celebration of the divine royal soul, where it features alongside his coronation and the celebration of one of his jubilees.

Amenhotep's father, Tuthmosis IV, had enjoyed his own divine encounter. Born a lesser son of Amenhotep II, he had several older brothers and no realistic hope of inheriting the throne. Then, one day, hot and tired after a day's hunting in the Giza desert, he made the fateful decision to rest in the shade offered by Egypt's largest statue: the Great Sphinx. The sphinx was a solar symbol of divine royal power whose name, derived from the Egyptian '*shesep ankh* [Atum]' or 'living image [of Atum]', linked it with the creator god.[103] Sphinxes invariably have the body of a lion and the head or face of a different creature: the Great Sphinx, which crouches beside the pyramid complex built by the 4th Dynasty pharaoh Khaefre, has the head of a man who is generally agreed to be Khaefre himself. Impressive though it undoubtedly was, the Great Sphinx was gradually neglected so that it became buried beneath Egypt's ubiquitous wind-blown sand. During the New Kingdom it enjoyed a resurgence of power when the isolated head poking through the dunes was recognized both as a powerful variant of the god Khepri-Re-Atum and as a form of Horemakhet (Horus in the horizon).

Exhausted by the thrills of the hunt, Tuthmosis fell into a deep sleep. In a vivid dream Horemakhet-Khepri-Re-Atum appeared to implore his 'son' to restore his neglected statue. This Tuthmosis did, employing labourers to clear away the sand that almost entirely covered the statue, and repairing a broken paw and a hole in the chest. Soon the Sphinx was as good as new. When the grateful god rewarded Tuthmosis by making him king of Egypt, the equally grateful Tuthmosis recorded his curious dream on a red granite stela (the Dream Stela) which formed the back wall of a small open-air chapel built between the newly restored forepaws. The stela was decorated with a scene showing two mirror-image sphinxes lying on a plinth or pedestal with an open doorway. The pedestal was perhaps an artistic device used to bring the recumbent beast up to the level of the standing king. However, Tuthmosis' door has led to centuries of speculation that there might be an unknown chamber within the body of the Great Sphinx. No major chamber has yet been found but there is a blind passageway which leads downwards from the Sphinx's rump, coming to an abrupt stop in the bedrock. There is no indication of when, or why, this passage was cut.

A watered-down, unillustrated version of the divine birth is presented in the coronation inscriptions of the final 18th Dynasty monarch Horemheb, which is preserved on the back of a seated statue of the king and his consort, Mutnodjmet. From this text we learn that the commoner-born, former general Horemheb is actually the son of Horus of Hansu (Hansu, or Henes, being Horemheb's home town). Horus travels to Thebes to present his son to Amen-Re, and Horemheb is immediately crowned king.

The childless Horemheb was succeeded by General Ramesses, who became the first king of the 19th Dynasty. Ramesses I was in turn succeeded by his son, Seti I, and his grandson, Ramesses II. Ramesses II was therefore an entirely legitimate king, the son and grandson of previous kings. But, because he had been born before Ramesses I was adopted as heir to the throne, he was not a king born to royal parents. The 18th Dynasty royal birth myth would have been familiar to him as his workmen conducted restoration work at both Deir el-Bahri and the Luxor temple. His decision to plagiarize the myth neatly provided him with a divine father while confirming his predestined right to rule. The story of Ramesses' divine conception was told in a chapel dedicated to his mother within the Ramesseum. Unfortunately the text is ill-preserved, but enough remains to show that once again a queen (Mut Tuya) sits unchaperoned on a bed facing

Amen-Re who holds the *ankh* in his right hand while stretching out his left hand towards the mother of his unborn child. Across the river, scenes in the Karnak temple complex show the divine infant Ramesses being suckled by a goddess and, in an image which is repeated in the temple of Seti I at Abydos, being moulded on the potter's wheel of Khnum.

The *Blessing of Ptah upon Ramesses II*, a text dating to his regnal Year 35, which is preserved at the Abu Simbel temple in Nubia and at Karnak, also includes details of the divine birth of Ramesses II. In this case, however, it is the creator god Ptah who is the father:[104]

> *Words spoken by Ptah-Tatonen, he of the tall plumes and sharp horns, who begot the gods: 'I am your father, who begot you as a god to act as king of South and North Egypt on my seat. I decree for you the lands that I created, their rulers carry their revenue to you. They come to bring you their tribute, because of the greatness of [your renown] . . .'*

As Ptah creates asexually using the spoken word, there is no role for the queen mother in this tale. Ramesses now becomes 'King of Upper and Lower Egypt, Usermaatre Setepenre, son of Re, who came forth of Tatonen [Ptah], born of Sekhmet the mighty, Ramesses II given life'.

Amenhotep III and Ramesses II enjoyed unusually lengthy reigns of thirty-eight and sixty-six years respectively. These, in a land where the majority of the population would not see their fortieth birthday, were surely divinely inspired reigns. As the years passed by, and jubilee followed jubilee, it seems that both kings started to believe their own propaganda. In Nubia there was no pretence: both kings were overtly worshipped as living gods. In Egypt, their position was less clear-cut. Both kings commissioned many colossal statues of themselves. These statues, placed either in front of the temple gateways or within the public temple court, were far more than enormous works of art. Each statue, like the king it represented, was an intermediary between the people and their gods; each therefore became the focus of an individual cult with its own priesthood. The priests who made offerings to the statue may have understood that they were offering the office of kingship personified in the form of the statue; whether the ordinary people understood this is debatable.

EGYPT'S LAST KINGS

An inversion of the royal birth myth evolved around ancient Egypt's last native king, the 30th Dynasty Nectanebo II. Nectanebo had but a tenuous grasp on his throne and so, in an attempt to strengthen his position, he promoted the propaganda of himself as 'Nectanebo the falcon', the living manifestation of Horus. Invoking the glorious old days, he embarked on a spree of conspicuous piety, building or restoring temples to the native gods and, in so doing, boosting the temple economies which would eventually feed back to the crown. This tactic, however, failed. Following the 343 BC Persian invasion Nectanebo fled Egypt for an unknown destination, leaving behind the impression of a mysterious, almost semi-legendary heroic figure. The Nectanebo who features in *The Alexander Romance* is a cunning magician who befriends the snake-loving Queen Olympias of Macedonia and, assuming the role previously played by Amen-Re, transforms into a serpent to impregnate the queen and to father Alexander the Great. In so doing, Nectanebo confirms Alexander's divine right to rule Egypt as the son of a previous, Egyptian-born king. When Nectanebo dies by Alexander's hand, his remorseful son buries him in Macedon.

In 332 BC Alexander the Great conquered Egypt and, in a

traditional ceremony, was crowned king by Egyptian priests in the temple of Ptah at Memphis. Certain of his own divinity, but wishing to prove it to others, he then trekked 300 miles across the Libyan Desert, guided by friendly crows and talking snakes, to consult the oracle of Zeus-Ammon in the remote Siwa Oasis. The oracle spoke and, as he expected, Alexander was confirmed a living god. His successors, the Ptolemies, did not bother with the oracle: they had the confidence to announce their own living divinity. The Ptolemies spoke the Macedonian-Greek dialect rather than Egyptian, and were unable to read the scrolls in the temple libraries, yet it is clear that they, or their advisers, had a sound knowledge of traditional Egyptian mythology.

The astute Ptolemy I deliberately developed the link between the new royal family and the ancient gods by instigating a programme of temple building and restoration throughout Egypt. One move appears particularly cynical. Realizing that the new capital city of Alexandria needed a patron deity, he summoned the Egyptian priest Manetho of Sebennytos and the Greek priest Timotheos of Athens, and invited them to design a new god with no pre-existing allegiance to either a city or a dynasty, and no powerful, long-established priesthood. Such a god, if he appealed to both Egyptians and Greeks, might go some way towards uniting Alexandria's religiously mixed population. The result was Serapis, a combination of Osiris and the Greek Dionysos, Hades (god of the underworld), Asklepios (god of medicine), Helios (the sun god) and Zeus (king of the gods). An anthropomorphic deity – animal and animal–human hybrid gods being unacceptable to non-Egyptians – Serapis personified divine kingship, healing, fertility and the afterlife. His name was derived from the name of the Memphite god Osor-Apis, himself a fusion of Osiris and the deceased Apis bull, and he borrowed heavily from their mythology. Serapis was married to the universally popular Isis who, as the wife of Osiris, was already acceptable to both Greeks and Egyptians. The triad of Serapis, Isis and their son Harpocrates quickly came to be associated with the ruling Ptolemaic dynasty. While the native Egyptians showed little interest in their new god, Serapis enjoyed a huge success throughout the Greek and Roman worlds.

Ptolemy II first deified his dead parents, then declared himself and his sister-consort Arsinoë II the living 'Brother-Sister Gods' (*Theoi Adelphoi*). From this time onwards, Egypt's royal family would enjoy official living divinity. This was enhanced by their habit of relating their already divine selves to specific gods. Ptolemy XII, for example, announced to the world that he was *Neos Dionysos*, or the new Dionysos. This was an astute choice of patron. In Alexandria, a city where the Greek concept of *tryphe* (undisciplined luxury and ostentatious display) underpinned many aspects of official life, Dionysos was considered both a protective deity and a royal ancestor as Arsinoë, mother of Ptolemy I, was believed to have been a descendant of both Heracles and Dionysos. So, by identifying himself with Dionysos, Ptolemy XII was effectively allying himself both with his Ptolemaic ancestors and with Alexander the Great, who had revered Dionysos as the conqueror of much of the eastern world. At the same time Ptolemy was distancing himself from the restrained and conservative Romans, who favoured the more austere Olympian gods. Unfortunately, the citizens of Alexandria were not convinced; they preferred to refer to their king as either 'Nothos' (the bastard) or 'Auletes' (the flute player). The former was undeniably true: Ptolemy XII was illegitimate. The latter may have been a flattering reference to the king's musical ability, or to the fact that his rounded cheeks were permanently plumped like the cheeks of a flautist, but is more likely to have been a decidedly unflattering reference to his sexual proclivities.

Ptolemy's daughter, Cleopatra VII, was the living incarnation of Isis and, as the mother of the fatherless Ptolemy XV Caesar, seems to have felt a particular affinity for Isis and Hathor.

Although Ptolemy Caesar was universally assumed to be the illegitimate son of Julius Caesar, his father was never officially announced. Parallels between the divine triad of Isis, Horus and the absent father Osiris, or Hathor, Ihy and the absent father Horus, and the earthly triad of Cleopatra, Ptolemy Caesar and the absent Julius Caesar, were clear and ripe for exploitation by a queen who wished to confirm her own right to rule.

THE AMARNA AGE

With one notable exception, all of Egypt's kings – even those, like the Ptolemies, who were of foreign extraction – manipulated the traditional pantheon to support their right to rule. The one exception was the 18th Dynasty monarch Amenhotep IV, son of Amenhotep III and Queen Tiy. In a daring and highly dangerous challenge to *maat*, Amenhotep IV dedicated himself to the worship of one solar deity whom he manipulated to emphasize the divine role of the king. The object of his worship, the Aten (literally 'the Disk'), seems to have been the light of the sun, rather than the sun itself. This was not a new god. During the Middle Kingdom the Aten had been respected both as a physical manifestation of Re and as a symbol of divinity closely affiliated with the king. However, the Aten had never achieved anything approaching national prominence.

By the end of Amenhotep's regnal Year 5 the Aten had become the dominant state god and the offerings which would normally have gone to the traditional temples were being diverted to the new Aten temples. Amen, who was both 'father of the gods' and, according to his father's birth myth, Amenhotep's own grandfather, was declared anathema and the king adopted a new name. He was now Akhenaten, or 'Living Spirit of the Aten'. As the old temples closed the decision was taken to move the court from Thebes to the new, purpose-built capital city of Akhetaten, 'Horizon of the Aten' (modern Amarna), in Middle Egypt.

Akhenaten's Aten was a faceless sun disk equipped with long rays tipped with tiny hands, which reached down from the sky to present the *ankh* of life to the royal family. He was an asexual and androgynous creator god with no anthropomorphic association and no spouse, and his lack of a body excluded him from traditional offering scenes so that he always hung in the sky above the royal family. This elevation of the god, and his relatively small size, allowed the king to become the most prominent figure in any religious scene. As the 'Beautiful Child of the Disk' Akhenaten literally stood between his god and his people. In many ways this was a continuation of the old theology, and most Egyptians would have experienced little challenge to their personal beliefs. The biggest change must have been felt by Akhenaten's elite, who were compelled to worship the Aten via Akhenaten and his consort Nefertiti.

The old gods had been swept away, and so had their mythologies. There was now no equivalent of the mother goddess who, in various forms, had been worshipped and loved since Predynastic times. More importantly, Osiris had gone, and so had his kingdom of the dead. The Aten now took full responsibility for the deceased. His was a grim regime for courtiers who had expected to dwell for ever in the Field of Reeds. While the king, queen and royal daughters might leave the tomb to unite with the sun, the non-royal dead would spend their days haunting the altar of the sun temple while their nights would be spent sleeping in tombs decorated with images of the royal family. These images – scenes of the royal family going about their business, driving through their city, enjoying banquets and participating in rituals – replaced the old funerary images and writings, and were clearly intended to have a divine sub-text.

Atenism has frequently been interpreted as the world's first monotheistic religion. But, although the Aten was far and away the most prominent Amarna deity, the new pantheon also included the solar deities Re and Maat while, crossing the divine–mortal divide, the Aten, Akhenaten and Nefertiti formed a triad, with the king and queen assuming the roles traditionally allocated to Shu and Tefnut. The connection between Nefertiti and Tefnut is emphasized by the queen's flat-topped blue crown, which resembles in shape the flat-topped crown worn by Tefnut. Meanwhile, Nefertiti's revealing garments – diaphanous linen robes sometimes worn completely open to display her body – and her six children, who are accorded an unusual prominence in official art, emphasize her role as a fertile woman/goddess.

The Aten is a mythless god. The closest that we come to an Amarna myth is the *Great Hymn to the Aten*, a long poem carved on the east wall of the unfinished tomb of the courtier Ay, where it is one of three prayers directed towards Akhenaten and his god. If not composed by the king himself, the *Great Hymn* was certainly inspired by his religious beliefs. It is not, however, an innovative piece of work and it does little to explain the appeal of Akhenaten's god to the modern reader.[105]

> *Glorious, you rise on the horizon of heaven,*
> *O living Aten, creator of life.*
> *Dawning on the eastern horizon,*
> *You flood every land with your perfect light.*
> *You are dazzling, wonderful and radiant,*
> *High over every land.*
> *Your rays embrace all the lands,*
> *All the lands that you have made.*
> *You are Re and so you reach their borders,*
> *Defining them for your beloved son.*
> *Though you are far away, your rays light the earth.*
> *Though you are seen, your movement is not.*

When you set on the western horizon
The land grows dark, as if death had come.
Dark night must be spent asleep in a bedroom with
   a covered head,
One eye cannot see the other.
In the dark no one would notice
If the possessions under their heads were stolen.
At night every lion comes out from its den,
And every serpent bites.
Darkness falls and the earth is hushed,
Because its maker rests on the horizon.

But the earth lights up when you rise from the horizon,
Shining bright, the Aten of the day.
You banish the darkness as you release your rays.
The Two Lands celebrate,
They grow lively and aroused.
You have awakened the people.
With bodies cleansed and clothing donned,
They raise their arms to praise your rising.

Now the whole land starts to work.
Cattle graze on their fodder,
Trees and plants grow.
Birds fly up from their nests,
Their wings stretched in praise of your spirit.
The flocks gambol in the fields,
And everything that flies and perches
Lives because you have dawned for them.
Ships sail to the north and to the south,
Roads open at your rising.
The fish in the river leap before you,
For your rays reach the middle of the sea.

You make the seed grow in women
And create mankind from sperm.
You feed the son in his mother's womb,
You comfort him and stop his tears.
You are the nurse within the womb,
Who gives breath to all that he has made.
On the day the baby is born, when he takes his first
*   breath,*
You open his mouth and supply all his needs.
When the chick in the egg chirps in his shell,
You give him the breath to live.
When his time has come to break free
He hatches and proclaims his birth.
Walking on his legs he leaves the shell.

You do so many things,
Things that are hidden from my view.
O sole god, you are without compare.
You created the world as you desired,
And you created it alone.
All the people, all the cattle, all the flocks,
Everything that walks with its feet on the earth,
And everything that flies with its wings in the air.
Khor, Kush, and
The land of Egypt herself.
You have set every man in his place,
And you have met his needs.
Everyone has his food,
Everyone has his allotted life span.
Tongues vary in their speech,
And characters and skins also vary,
For you have differentiated mankind.

You created the Nile in the Netherworld.
You bring him forth at your will,
To feed the people
That you made for yourself.
Master of all, you toil for them.
Lord of all lands, you shine for them.
For them the daytime Aten dawns,
Glorious and great.
You make all distant lands live.
For you have made a heavenly Nile come down for them,
To make waves on the mountains like the sea,
To water the fields of their towns.
O Lord of eternity,
How excellent are your designs.
A Nile from heaven for the foreigners,
And all their creatures that walk the lands.
And a Nile for Egypt springing from the Netherworld.

Your rays suckle every field.
When you shine they live, and they grow for you.
You made the seasons to nurture all you made
Winter to cool them and Summer that they may feel you.

You made a distant sky,
In which you might shine.
From there you see everything that you have made.
There you are alone,
Shining as the Living Aten.
Risen, dazzling, far away and yet near by.
You have manifested yourself many times.
Towns, villages, fields, roads and waterways;
Every eye sees you upon them,
For you are the Aten of the daytime ...

You are my beloved.
No other knows you as I do,
Only your son Neferkheperure Waenre.
You have taught me of your plans and your power.
The creatures of the earth exist in your hand as you have
    made them
When you dawn they live,
When you set they die.
You are a lifetime; it is by you that men live.
Eyes may look upon your beauty until you set,
But when you go down in the west all work must cease.
You who rise and make everything grow
For the king, and for those who hurry on foot.

You raise them up for the son who came forth from your body,
the King of Upper and Lower Egypt, Living in Maat, the Lord
of the Two Lands Neferkheperure Waenre, son of Re, living in
Truth, Lord of the glorious appearings, Akhenaten, the long-
lived. And for the King's Great Wife whom he loves, the Mistress
of the Two Lands, Neferneferuaten-Nefertiti, may she live and
flourish forever and ever.

Soon after Akhenaten's death the traditional pantheon, and its
traditional mythology, were restored by Tutankhamen.

II

TALES OF GODS AND MEN

Egypt has left us a small library of entertaining legends and stories which, 2,000 years after the end of the dynastic age, are still a pleasure to read. Here we meet heroes whose bravery is matched by their loquacity and occasional magical prowess.

THE HERDSMAN AND THE GODDESS[106]

Twenty-five lines of this ill-preserved 12th Dynasty tale have survived on the back of the complex lament known as *The Man Who Was Tired of Life*, a dialogue between a man who longs for death and his *ba*, or soul. This would, however, appear to have been an altogether more cheery story:

> . . . The herdsman tells of what he has seen: 'One day I decided to take my charges down to the marshy land. There I saw a woman, who did not look like other, ordinary women. My own hair stood on end when I saw the woman's hair, because it was such a beautiful colour. But I will never do what she asked me to do, because I am terrified of her . . .'
> . . . But, when the night sky grew light with the dawn, what he had related did happen. The goddess met him at the

pool, and she had removed all her clothes, and unbound her hair . . .

THE TALE OF THE ELOQUENT PEASANT[107]

The Eloquent Peasant is a Middle Kingdom composition preserved in snatches on four separate and incomplete papyri, two of which also tell the *Story of Sinuhe*. Here all four have been combined to re-create the whole story. The tale is full of literary flourishes, repetitions and puns designed to appeal to an educated elite readership. In order to spare the modern reader the full weight of Khun-Anup's lengthy oration, his court appearances have been condensed.

The tale has none of the excitement of magic, or travel to foreign lands and long-gone times; it sets out to instruct rather than entertain. It is saved from dullness by the extreme loquaciousness of Khun-Anup, an innocent and ill-educated man of humble origins who knows his rights and never shuts up. Khun-Anup is a frustrated, over-emotional peasant making a fuss about a relatively trivial matter. In contrast, the High Steward Rensi son of Meru is a restrained, self-controlled member of the elite who, acting under strict royal orders, communicates through silence. His silence serves as a spur to Khun-Anup's speech-making, and Rensi knows this. The story carries a twofold message. In Egypt, justice or *maat* will always prevail; the king will ensure that this happens. And, as we have already seen in *The Shipwrecked Sailor*, there will always be an appreciation of eloquent speech.

Here we are shown a darker side to the glowing, sunny Egypt so often pictured on tomb walls. It is an Egypt of casual thefts, corruption and careless brutality, a land where the elite think nothing of ordering a beating for the inferior who has offended them. This land needs a firm legal system to uphold the rights of the downtrodden. Ancient Egypt recognized two broad classes of crime. Criminal offences – regicide, theft from the temples and palaces, tomb-robbing – were serious matters. As such they would be dealt with by the state, which had a formidable array of physical punishments at its disposal. In this story, however, we are looking at a civil offence, a crime against a private person which would not, under normal circumstances, be of any interest to the state. Ideally, a downtrodden private person would have an influential patron to support his cause. But Khun-Anup, a stranger to the Nile Valley, stands very much alone, and it is only by chance that the First Intermediate Period King Nebkaure becomes involved in his case. Nebkaure is a monarch who, like Snefru before him, seeks amusement through the spoken word. There is a certain amount of cruelty in Nebkaure's justice; although he has the common sense to realize that the peasant's family must be in need of food, he appears completely indifferent to the mental stress caused to poor Khun-Anup.

Khun-Anup and his family live in the Wadi Natrun, an oasis famous for its precious natron salt, a key ingredient in mummification. He is probably more of a trader than a farmer or peasant, and he is clearly wealthy. He owns a valuable string of donkeys and has an impressive range of luxury goods. But he dwells on the outskirts of Egypt – the very edge of the civilized world – and so he appears as something of a country bumpkin to the sophisticated city-dwelling officials he meets in his quest for justice. In the absence of coinage, Khun-Anup is obliged to barter his produce for foodstuffs. His journey takes him from the Wadi towards the Middle Egyptian city of Neni-Nesut (Herakleopolis), the capital city of the 9th and 10th Dynasties. Medenit is the twenty-second nome, or province, of Upper (southern) Egypt. Per-Fefi is today unknown.

Once upon a time there lived a simple farmer named Khun-Anup. Khun-Anup dwelt in the Wadi Natrun with his wife Merit and their children. He was a hard-working and decent man; his children were well fed, his wife was happy and his barn was filled with home-grown produce. One day Khun-Anup called his wife to him.

'Our supplies of food are getting low. The time has come for me to travel to Egypt to trade my produce for food. Go to the barn, and see how much barley we have left from last year's harvest.'

So Merit went to the barn, and measured out twenty-six gallons of grain. This Khun-Anup divided into two unequal heaps. Twenty gallons would provide ample food for his family while he was away. The remaining six gallons were to be made into the bread and beer that would serve as his rations for the journey. And this was done.

Khun-Anup set off southwards on his travels, heading towards Neni-Nesut. His heart was light though his load was heavy, and his donkeys were making good speed under the weight of a vast array of goods. There were rushes, grasses and rare plants, natron and salt, precious woods, animal pelts including panther and jackal skins, pigeons and ostriches, and much, much more besides. Eventually the small caravan reached the district of Per-Fefi, to the north of Medenit. And there, standing on the riverbank, Khun-Anup encountered the man named Djehuty-Nakht, an employee of the High Steward Rensi son of Meru.

Djehuty-Nakht, an unscrupulous and incurably lazy man, ran a practised eye over Khun-Anup's merchandise. He recognized the value of the load at once, and wished with all his greedy heart that he had a magic charm which would allow him to hijack the goods there and then. But he had no such charm, and so would be forced to rely on his wits if he wanted to commit such an outrageous crime. Which of course he did.

After a great deal of thought Djehuty-Nakht smiled in triumph. He had devised a plan cunning enough to strip the naive peasant of all his precious goods and his donkeys as well. Running ahead of Khun-Anup, he spread a shawl across the narrow public road that ran in front of his house.

Khun-Anup, happily jogging along on the lead donkey, found that his path suddenly narrowed until it was no wider than a shawl. To one side of him there ran the waters of the canal; to the other there was a field of barley; in the distance there was a house – the house of Djehuty-Nakht. And in front of him there was indeed a shawl, spread across the road so that its fringe dipped into the canal water and its hem lay on the earth of the barley field. Standing beside the shawl was Djehuty-Nakht, an unpleasant smile on his lips. Djehuty-Nakht spoke first, his tone carelessly offensive:

'Take care, peasant. For I absolutely forbid you to step on my valuable shawl. And,' he added, as Khun-Anup attempted to reverse his donkeys so that he might go round the garment via the field, 'I also forbid you to step on my precious barley.'

As the other side of the road was bordered by the canal, Khun-Anup now had no way forward. He tried to reason with Djehuty-Nakht:

'My way is completely blocked. I cannot go into the water, the field is forbidden to me, and you are obstructing the road with your shawl. Will you not lift it, so that I may pass by?'

But even as Khun-Anup spoke, one of his donkeys lowered its head and ate an ear of barley from the field. This was exactly what Djehuty-Nakht had been hoping for.

'This is an outrage! You have deliberately allowed your miserable donkey to eat my valuable barley. Now, peasant, I will seize your donkey as compensation. It will pay for its crime by working for me.'

Khun-Anup, baffled by this ridiculous turn of events but

still courteous, immediately made an offer of reasonable payment for the ear of barley eaten by his donkey. But Djehuty-Nakht was deaf to reason. Seizing a green tamarisk rod he thrashed poor Khun-Anup until he cried out in pain, then he drove all the donkeys and their goods away to his own stables. The peasant was left alone on the road, his loud sobs stifled by Djehuty-Nakht's threat of murder should he make a fuss about his treatment.

Djehuty-Nakht expected to hear no more from the intimidated peasant. But Khun-Anup knew his rights and was not prepared to let the matter drop. After a week spent pleading with Djehuty-Nakht for the return of his property he travelled to the town of Ninsu to appeal in person to Rensi son of Meru, High Steward and employer of Djehuty-Nakht. Khun-Anup met Rensi as he came out of his house and told him – at some length – all that had happened. Rensi was appalled by the injustice. He laid the matter before the local magistrates expecting them to support Khun-Anup, but they were inclined to take a different view:

'This story can't possibly be right. Djehuty-Nakht is one of us, a gentleman. He would never steal from an honest man. This miserable complainant must be one of Djehuty-Nakht's own peasants, who has been caught out in wrongdoing and who is trying to gain revenge on a decent master. Why should we punish a good man like Djehuty-Nakht over such a trivial matter? If he is asked to replace a few grains of salt, he will surely do so.'

Rensi son of Meru listened to this unfair judgement, but made no comment.

The peasant Khun-Anup lodged a formal appeal with Rensi son of Meru. He spoke with great eloquence before him:

'If you go down to the river of truth you will sail on it with a fair wind. Your boat will remain sound and whole, and you will not capsize. You will not have to look upon the dark face of fear. Instead fine fish will swim to you and plump birds will fly to you. For you are the guardian of the unprotected. You are father to the orphan, husband to the widow, and brother to the abandoned wife. And your name will be remembered for ever. For you are a great man, free of all avarice and greed, who ensures that right triumphs over evil. Allow me justice, O Lord. Take away my grief and listen to my plea, for I have been sorely wronged.'

Rensi, amazed by what he had heard, referred the matter straight to King Nebkaure.

'Your Majesty, I have discovered an amazing thing: an un-educated peasant who is nevertheless capable of truly beautiful speech. This man came before me because he had been robbed and he wanted justice. I thought that it would amuse you to hear his words.'

The king, fascinated by Rensi's tale, replied:

'If you wish me well, detain this talkative peasant. Do not respond to his pleas, for if you do not reply, he will be forced to carry on speaking. Have his words written down, and send them to me so that I may learn everything that he says. But do not be cruel. Make sure that the peasant is well fed – give him food without letting him know who provides it. And send food to his family, for peasants come to Egypt to trade their goods only when their larders are empty at home.'

So Khun-Anup was detained. He was provided with ten loaves of bread and two jugs of beer every day. This ration came not direct from the hand of Rensi, but via a friend so that the peasant would not know who was feeding him. And Rensi wrote in secret to the mayor of Wadi Natrun, asking him to provide Khun-Anup's family with three baskets of grain each day.

The time came for the peasant Khun-Anup to made a second

appeal before Rensi son of Meru. This time Khun-Anup spoke with equal fluency but in less flattering terms:

'Great High Steward, richest of the rich, you are the dependable rudder of heaven and the plumb-bob of the scales that carry the weight of truth. Do not be swayed from justice. A truly great man will take only ownerless property, and you have all you need for your own satisfaction. Surely you will agree that it is wrong that a balance may be allowed to tilt, or a plumb-bob stray from the straight and narrow? But look around you. Justice flees from you, the magistrates are dishonest and all speech is twisted away from its original meaning. He who should punish the wrongdoers is now causing trouble himself . . .'

At this point Rensi interrupted the speechmaker with a threat of arrest which Khun-Anup, unstoppable in mid-flow, ignored.

'Yes, you are strong and mighty. But your heart is greedy and you show no mercy. How miserable is the wretched man whom you have destroyed. You are a messenger of the crocodile, you are worse than Sekhmet, Lady of Pestilence. The wealthy man should always be merciful. Violence should be left to criminals, and robbery to those who have nothing. We cannot reproach the poor robber as he is merely seeking to provide for himself (as indeed I myself may need to provide for myself if I lose all my goods). But you have enough food to make you vomit, and enough beer to make you drunk. You are rich in all kinds of treasure . . . Straighten your tongue, don't tell lies, and warn the magistrates to behave. Wisest of all men, do not ignore my case.'

Rensi, following the king's orders, heard this remarkable spate of words without making any response, and declined to make any sort of judgement. Khun-Anup, growing increasingly frustrated and bitter, was driven to following Rensi on a daily basis, appealing again and again against his harsh treatment at the hands of the court. On one occasion, pushed too far, Rensi ordered a casual beating for his impolite petitioner, but otherwise he remained impassive and gave no sign of listening. Eventually the desperate Khun-Anup found himself making his ninth appearance before the silent Rensi. And all this time, unbeknown to him, his words were being copied down so that they might be sent to the king. On this occasion the desperate Khun-Anup did not mince his words:

'My Lord, High Steward, the tongue is a scale that will always betray men's deficiencies. Truth will out. He who benefits from falsehood has no heirs; his boat will not harbour at the mooring place. Do not be heavy, and do not be light. Do not be late, yet do not hurry. Do not turn your face away from one you know, nor be blind to one you have seen. Above all, do not betray the one who petitions you now. Abandon your reticence and speak. I have spent many hours pleading with you, but you have not listened to me. I shall now go and plead about you before Anubis.'

On hearing this, Rensi sent two men to bring the peasant to him. Khun-Anup was afraid that he had said too much too often, and that he would be punished for his rudeness. But Rensi, speaking at last, quickly set his mind at rest:

'Do not be afraid my friend, but stay here with me and listen to all your petitions.'

And to Khun-Anup's great amazement a scribe read out his words just as they had been copied down on nine lengthy papyrus scrolls. The scrolls were then sent to the court, where they gave King Nebkaure great pleasure.

The king ordered Rensi son of Meru to pass judgement. And Rensi found in Khun-Anup's favour. Djehuty-Nakht was arrested, and all his goods confiscated and passed to the peasant whose eloquence had earned him the respect of the king.

It is finished . . .

THE TALE OF THE TWO BROTHERS[108]

Just one version of this remarkable story survives, recorded on a 19th Dynasty papyrus by the scribe Ennana. It starts out as a simple, almost believable account of two brothers and a faithless woman; a story highly reminiscent of the Biblical tale of Joseph and Potiphar's wife, which is also set in Egypt, and not too different from the story of the high priest Webaoner and his faithless wife that we read in *Papyrus Westcar*. But from the point our hero leaves the controlled land of Egypt, the story evolves into a complex fantasy involving travel, gods, magic, another faithless woman and the resurrection of the dead.

The two brothers have the names of gods. Anubis is the jackal-headed funerary deity of the cemeteries and mummification rituals, while Bata is a version of Seth who is here heavily equated with the Canaanite storm god Baal. Bata's self-emasculation is perhaps a reminder of the castration of Seth which follows the blinding of Horus.

Their story is partly set in Canaan, with Bata travelling from his homeland to the Valley of the Cedar before returning to become king of Egypt. The Valley is a real place – the story of the *Battle of Kadesh* tells us that Ramesses II also passed through the Valley of the Cedar en route to war. While Egyptologist Wolfgang Wettengel has suggested that the tale should be read as the story of the descent of Egypt's Ramesside kings from the divine entity Seth/Bata, others have argued, with equal persuasion, that it is a parable, telling the story of the sun's twenty-four-hour journey across the sky. The Ramesside kings certainly felt a very personal bond with Seth, the Red One, god of their eastern Delta hometown of Avaris. At least one of them – Ramesses II – is likely to have had red hair.

Hair certainly plays an important role in this story. As in our own culture, a clean, well-groomed head of hair – or an elaborate wig – was considered attractive and socially desirable in a woman, but the neat plaits would be loosened and the wig would be removed for comfort when the woman lay down to sleep. Neat hair signified control and the presence of *maat*, whereas disordered or unbound hair indicated chaos. This is made clear in the few illustrations showing women in labour – the ultimate loss of control, when the forces of life and death breach the security of the home – where the mothers-to-be adopt wild-looking, archaic hairstyles. Those in mourning tousle their hair, while women preparing to abandon themselves to wild love-making liberate their locks. Thus hair became inextricably linked with sexuality and lust and references to hair may be read as veiled references to eroticism. Bata's faithless, anonymous wife is an Egyptian Pandora: purpose-made by the gods, she is fatally tempted by the luxuries offered by palace life. So seductive is the god-given scent of her hair that the king of Egypt is prepared to search the whole world for its owner.

Towards the end of the story Bata transforms into a bull who, by rather roundabout means, is able to impregnate the queen, who then gives birth to himself in a non-bull form. The link to the theology of the creator god as the 'bull of his mother', who effectively sires himself, would not have been lost on the original audience.

Once upon a time there were two brothers, born to the same mother and the same father. The elder brother was named Anubis, and the younger brother was named Bata. Anubis was a prosperous man with a house and a wife. Anubis cared for Bata as a father cares for a son, and Bata in turn worked hard for his brother, herding his cattle, ploughing his fields and harvesting his grain. Bata was an excellent and exceptionally handsome young man with the strength of a god; there was none so fine in the whole of Egypt.

Bata had a simple daily routine. He would rise at dawn and head for the fields with the cattle. Returning home at nightfall he would bring armfuls of good things; vegetables, milk and wood. These he would give to Anubis as he sat with his wife in the house. Bata would eat his evening meal, then leave to sleep in the barn with the animals. But Bata was no ordinary herdsman. He had an unusual and secret gift: he was able to speak to the cattle. By listening to their conversation he was able to find the best grazing lands, and so the cattle under his charge became the fattest and most fertile cattle in the land. Anubis did not know this secret, but was very pleased with the way his brother cared for the cattle.

When the time came to plough the fields Bata made all the preparations. Then Anubis left the house to work alongside his brother. They ploughed with light hearts, happy to be working together. But then Anubis realized that they had not brought enough seed with them and so he sent Bata home to collect some. Arriving at the house, Bata found his brother's wife languidly plaiting her long hair. Disconcerted, he blurted out his instructions: 'Get up and fetch me some seed, for Anubis is waiting in the fields. Don't dawdle.'

But the wife did not move. 'Go to the grain-store and fetch what you need yourself. Don't make me leave my hairstyle unfinished.'

And so Bata went to the store and filled a large sack with barley and wheat seed. Hoisting the load on to his shoulder, he turned to leave the house. Once again he had to pass close by his sister-in-law.

'How much grain are you carrying there?' she asked.

Puzzled, Bata replied: 'Three sacks of wheat and two sacks of barley, that is all. Why?'

'Mmm . . .' the wife continued, running an appraising glance over his sweating torso, 'what well-developed muscles you have, and how strong you must be. I have been watching you work in the fields for many days, your bare chest exposed to the sun . . .'

To Bata's intense alarm, she jumped to her feet and took hold of his arm.

'Come, let us spend an hour lying together. You will enjoy it. And afterwards I will make you some fine new clothes.'

This proposal filled the honest Bata with the rage of a leopard, and his wanton sister-in-law was filled with fear.

'How can you say such things? You are like a mother to me, and my beloved brother is my father. My older brother took me in as a child, and raised me. What you have suggested is repugnant to me. Never mention it again. And I in turn swear that I will not let one word of this disgraceful matter pass my lips.'

And turning on his heels he ran to the fields and resumed his work alongside Anubis. When evening came Anubis returned to the house. And Bata tended the cattle and drove them back to their barn.

Back at the house, the faithless wife had grown increasingly frightened. What if Bata were to tell Anubis of her attempted seduction? Quickly she smeared fat and grease over her body so that she looked like the victim of an assault. And when Anubis returned home he found his wife lying down, feigning illness. She did not bring the water to wash his hands and she had not lit the lamp, so the house was in darkness. Peering through the gloom, Anubis found his wife retching and groaning on her bed.

Anubis was horrified. 'Who has done this terrible thing to you?'

'No one has spoken to me except your brother Bata. When

your brother came to collect some seed for you he saw me sitting alone. He suggested that I lie with him, and asked me to loosen my hairstyle, but of course I refused. I reminded him that I have raised him as a mother, and that you have raised him as a father. Hearing this he became frightened and beat me, to stop me telling you this sorry tale. Now, if you let him live, I shall surely die. You must kill him at once, when he comes home.'

Anubis was filled with the hot rage of a leopard. He sharpened his spear to a fine point, then stood patiently behind the barn door, waiting for Bata's return. As night fell, Bata made his way back to the barn, his arms loaded with produce and his cattle walking before him. But as the first cow entered the barn she stopped, and spoke.

'Be very careful. Your brother is hiding behind the door, and he intends to kill you with his spear. You must run away.'

A second cow entered behind the first, and spoke the very same words.

'Be very careful. Your brother Anubis is hiding behind the door, and he intends to kill you with his spear. You must run away.'

Mystified, Bata looked under the door, and caught a glimpse of his brother's feet. Realizing that the cows were speaking the truth, he dropped his load and fled. And Anubis, enraged, charged after him brandishing his spear.

Bata prayed aloud as he ran: 'Great God Re-Horakhty, you can distinguish right from wrong. Help me now.'

And Re, moved by Bata's plight, caused a great river of crocodile-infested water to spring up between the two brothers. They now stood facing each other in the gathering gloom, one on the left bank, and one on the right. Anubis was furious with himself, for he had failed to kill Bata. Then Bata shouted across the watery divide. 'Wait there, and when the Aten rises we will sort this matter out, with the sun as our witness. Then I shall leave your house and be with you no more, for I shall travel to the Valley of the Cedar.'

Eventually the long night ended and Re-Horakhty rose. The two brothers stared at each other across the waters, and Bata asked his brother why he had attempted to murder him without listening to his side of the story: 'For when you sent me to fetch the seed, your wife attempted to seduce me and I resisted her, yet somehow, in your eyes, the true sequence of events has been distorted.'

He told Anubis the whole sorry tale, ending with an oath shouted out before Re-Horakhty: 'You have no reason to kill me, save the word of a dirty whore.' And taking a reed dagger, Bata hacked off his own penis and threw it into the water. A catfish swallowed the penis, and Bata grew weak from loss of blood. Anubis, stranded on the opposite bank of the crocodile-infested river, could only weep for his young brother, for now he believed his story, but could not cross the waters to comfort him.

Then Bata cried out again: 'You find it easy enough to believe ill of me – can you not search your heart and remember some good deed that I have done for you instead? Go back to your home, and look after your cattle. For I can no longer live with you, but must go to the Valley of the Cedar. I ask just one thing of you. If you learn that something bad has happened to me, come and look after me. I shall take out my heart, and place it in the blossom of the topmost bough of the tallest cedar tree in the Valley. If that tree should fall, come and search for my heart. Do not stop looking, even if it takes you seven years or more. And when you find it, place it in a bowl of cool water. For thus I will live again to avenge those who have wronged me. You will know that something bad has happened to me when the jug of beer in your hand starts to foam and froth. Do not ignore this sign, but come at once to help me.'

Bata turned away from his brother, and set off on his lonely journey to the Valley of the Cedar. And Anubis wiped away his tears and returned home grieving, his hands raised to his head and his skin smeared with the mud of mourning. He killed his faithless wife and threw her body to the dogs. Then he sat for many days mourning his loss.

Many days later Bata reached the Valley of the Cedar. All alone, he spent his days hunting game in the desert. At night he always returned to sleep beneath the great cedar tree that held his heart. Soon, his strength restored, he started to build himself a house besides the great pine, for he longed to start a family.

One day Bata met the Ennead – the nine great gods – as they walked about, ruling the entire world. The gods stopped to speak to him.

'O Bata, the lies told by your brother's wife have caused you to flee your home town, and now you live here all alone, isolated from your family and friends. But cheer up, Anubis has killed his faithless wife, and thus you are avenged.'

Understanding Bata's loneliness, Re-Horakhty ordered Khnum to make a companion for him, and this the god did. The woman made by Khnum for Bata was more beautiful and more fragrant than any woman in the entire land. Then the seven Hathors came to forecast her fate: 'She shall die by the executioner's blade.'

The beautiful woman moved into Bata's splendid house, and into his heart. He desired her with every fibre of his being but he had cut off his penis, and was impotent. On his orders the woman spent her days in the shade of his house while he went out into the hot sun, hunting game for them both to eat. The woman chafed against her confinement, but Bata would not allow her to go outside, for he was worried that she might be snatched by the cruel sea and 'If that were to happen, I could not rescue you, for I am a woman just like you. I tell you this. My heart lies in the blossom of the topmost bough of the tallest cedar tree in the Valley. If anyone finds it there, I shall fight him to the death.'

One hot, dull day, while Bata was, as usual, out hunting, the woman strolled in the shade of the great cedar tree. Then she saw the sea surging towards her. She ran for the safety of the house, and nearly made it, but the sea called out to the cedar tree, 'Catch her for me.' And the cedar tree snatched a lock of the woman's hair, and gave it to the sea. The sea carried the hair all the way to the Nile, and dropped it in the waters used by the palace washermen. And thus the scent of the woman's hair perfumed the king of Egypt's clothes. No one knew what the exotic new scent could be. The king quizzed the washermen, who angrily denied using any new products. Everyone remained baffled until the chief laundryman discovered the lock of perfumed hair still floating in the waters of the washing pool. The king's most learned scribes soon identified the tress: 'It is the hair of the most beautiful woman ever made, a daughter of Re-Horakhty. It has been sent to you as a greeting from another country. Send your men to search the whole world for her. Look everywhere, but pay particular attention to the Valley of the Cedar. You can collect this treasure, and she shall be yours.'

And so it was done. The men set out to search the whole world and came back empty-handed; only the men sent to the Valley of the Cedar failed to return, for Bata had killed them, leaving just one alive. The king of Egypt tried again. This time he sent not only troops and chariots, but also an older, experienced woman who could tempt the unworldly younger woman with clothing, jewellery and feminine trinkets. The woman was successful in her mission, and the king of Egypt was delighted with his prize. He married the young woman, and made her his queen. Then he quizzed her about Bata, but all she would say was, 'Cut down and chop up the great cedar tree that grows outside his house.'

The king's troops returned to the Valley of the Cedar and hacked down the great tree that held Bata's heart. Instantly, Bata died.

The next day, in a land far away, Anubis came home from the fields. He washed his hands, then called for a jug of beer. But as soon as the beer was placed in his hands it started to foam and froth. Alarmed, Anubis called for a jug of wine which turned sour in his grasp. Then he understood what he must do. He packed his bag, laced his sandals, took up his staff and set off for the Valley of the Cedar. Here he soon found his brother's house and, inside, his brother lying dead on his bed. Anubis wept over Bata's body. Then he set to work. For three years he searched in vain for Bata's heart. Just as he was about to give up he found a pinecone, and somehow he knew that this was the thing he had been searching for. Anubis dropped the pinecone into a bowl of cool water, and then sat beside Bata's bier to watch what might happen.

As night fell the heart inside the cone absorbed the water and Bata's stiff body shuddered and jerked. Bata's dead eyes rolled towards his brother, and Anubis held out the bowl so that Bata might drink from it. Thus Bata's heart made its way to its proper place, and Bata was alive once again. The brothers embraced each other, and talked throughout the night. For Bata had a plan to revenge himself on those who had betrayed him:

'I shall transform myself into a bull, the most beautiful, multicoloured bull ever seen, and you can ride upon my back. By sunrise we will have reached the place where my wife is. You must present me to the king of Egypt. He will welcome the gift of the splendid bull, and you will receive a great reward of silver and gold. You can then return home, leaving me behind.'

The plan was carried out in every detail. The king of Egypt was enormously pleased with the magnificent gift, and Anubis was soon on his way home, a wealthy man. Meanwhile, Bata remained in the palace disguised as the multicoloured bull. As the king's favourite, he was permitted to roam from room to room.

One day the bull entered the kitchen where the king's beautiful young wife stood. And he began to talk to her:

'See, despite all your efforts, I am still alive.'

'Who are you?' gasped the queen, horrified.

'I am Bata. I know that it was you who told the king to chop down the cedar tree, and I know that you must have done this because you wanted me dead. But look, I am alive again. Not a man this time, but a bull.'

Hearing this, the queen was terrified.

The king of Egypt sat down to a splendid banquet with his beautiful young wife. She poured him many drinks, and he grew increasingly pleased with her. Then she murmured: 'Husband, will you promise me something before the gods?'

'Anything you want.'

'I want you to sacrifice the great multicoloured bull that wanders around the palace, and I want to eat his liver. After all, he is a beast with no practical use.'

The king heard these words with a heavy heart, for he was fond of his magnificent bull, but he had promised. So the next day he ordered his steward to make the sacrifice. The bull was killed, and as he died two drops of blood flew from his neck. One landed on the left doorpost of the palace, and one landed on the right. Instantly, two tall persea trees grew from the blood to stand straight and beautiful before the palace. This marvel caused great celebrations throughout the whole of Egypt, and the king himself rode out in his golden chariot to view the trees. The queen, too, came out to see the wonder. And as the king sat in the shade of one tree, she sat under the other.

Then Bata spoke again to his wife: 'Greetings, faithless one. I am your husband, Bata. In spite of all you have done, I am still alive. I know that it was you who told the king to chop down the cedar tree, and I know that it was you who told the king to sacrifice the magnificent bull.'

The desperate queen knew what she had to do. A few days later, as she again poured wine for her doting husband, she spoke in a sweet voice:

'Husband, will you promise me something before the gods?'

'Anything you want.'

'I want you to cut down the two great persea trees that stand at the portal of the palace, and I want you to use their wood to make exquisite furniture.'

The king listened with a heavy heart, for he was fond of his beautiful trees, but a promise was a promise. So the next day he ordered the carpenters to set to work. The queen stood watching as both trees crashed to the ground. And a splinter flew upwards and entered her mouth, and she became pregnant with Bata.

Nine months later the queen gave birth to a fine and healthy son. Delighted with the new arrival, the king decreed that there should be celebrations throughout the whole land. The king immediately appointed the boy viceroy of Kush. And eventually he became crown prince, his father's sole heir. When the old king died the prince took his place on the throne of Egypt. Then the new king spoke. 'Have all the high officials brought before me, so that I might tell them my story.' And it was done.

Next the faithless wife was brought in, and Bata judged her before the whole court. Finally Anubis appeared before the court. To reward his loyalty, Bata appointed his brother crown prince. And when Bata eventually died after thirty years on the throne, it was Anubis who ruled in his place. Thus everything ended happily.

THE TALE OF TRUTH AND FALSEHOOD[109]

Like Anubis and Bata, Truth and Falsehood are brothers. But theirs is a bitter, unhappy relationship more akin to the relationship between Osiris and Seth. Their story is an elaborate allegory dealing with the restoration of *maat*. It provides us with an interesting, if exaggerated, view of the Egyptian judicial system. In particular, it introduces us to the idea of compensation payments, and to the use of court-sanctioned physical punishments.

The lost beginning of this 19th Dynasty tale would have told us that Falsehood once lent his brother Truth a fantastic dagger. For some reason Truth failed to return the dagger, and so Falsehood denounced him before the court of the gods. As we join the trial, Falsehood is describing his lost property, the like of which has never been seen before. Clearly, Falsehood is exaggerating:

'All the copper of Mount El went into its blade; all the timber in the Koptos wood was carved into its haft. Its sheath was the size of a rock-cut tomb; its belt was sewn from all the hides of the herd of Kal. And Truth has lost this most precious blade. Let Truth now be brought before you, and let him be blinded in both eyes in punishment. Then let him serve as my doorkeeper as a permanent reminder of his crime.'

The Ennead, judging Truth guilty, did as Falsehood asked.

One day Falsehood suddenly realized how truly good his brother was. And this realization disturbed him. So Falsehood summoned Truth's servants. He ordered them to lead their blind master into the desert where he might be eaten by a wild lion with many hungry lionesses. The servants did as Falsehood commanded, and Truth was led away. But Truth realized what was happening and pleaded with his servants to let him go. This they did, because they loved Truth and hated Falsehood. The servants returned home and lied to Falsehood, telling him that they had actually watched as a hungry lion devoured Truth.

Many days later a lady came out of her house accompanied by her servants. The servants found Truth lying under a bush, and were impressed by his muscular physique. They suggested to the lady that he would make an excellent doorkeeper. The servants fetched Truth and showed him to the lady. Instantly, she desired him very much, for he was a handsome man. That very night blind Truth slept with the lady, and she conceived a son.

The son born to the lady was a wonderful child; he was tall, healthy and strong like the son of a god. At school he excelled at writing and fighting, so that he surpassed even the boys who were older than him. But his friends were jealous of his success, and they taunted him: 'Whose son are you? You don't have a father.'

The boy was wounded by his friends' words. He went to his mother, and asked her to name his father. Much to his surprise she told him that his father was a member of her household.

'You see that blind man who guards our door. He is your father.'

The boy was aghast, and rounded on his mother.

'You and all your family deserve to be fed to a crocodile, for treating my father with such disrespect.'

He went straight to his father, bringing him a comfortable

chair and a footstool. He gave him good food to eat, and beer to drink, and then he questioned him.

'Tell me who blinded you, so that I might avenge you.'

Truth told his son the whole story.

The son packed ten loaves of bread, a staff, a pair of sandals, a canteen of water and a sword. Then he fetched a beautiful ox, and drove it to his uncle's field. Here he spoke to the herdsman.

'Take my loaves, and my staff, my canteen, my sword and my sandals, for I do not need them. But look after my beautiful ox until I return.'

The beautiful ox was put among Falsehood's cattle, and thrived.

One day, while Falsehood was walking in the fields, he caught sight of the beautiful ox. He ordered the herdsman to bring the beast to him, for he wanted to kill it and eat it. But the herdsman refused.

'It is not my ox, sir, and so I cannot give it to you. That would not be right.'

'Surely I can have this one ox, and you can give one of my cattle to its owner, in its place?'

And so it was done.

The young boy heard that his uncle had taken his ox. He returned to the herdsman and demanded the return of his property. The herdsman, embarrassed, offered him the pick of Falsehood's cattle, but the boy would not be moved: 'None of these beasts is as big or as beautiful as my ox. My ox was as large as Egypt. If my ox stood on Amen's Isle its tail would brush the papyrus marshes while one horn rested on the eastern mountain, and one on the west.'

The herdsman laughed at the boy's exaggeration.

'Don't be silly. There is no ox as large as the one you describe. It is impossible.'

The boy seized the herdsman and marched him to confront Falsehood. He summoned Falsehood to appear before the council of the gods.

The gods were not impressed with the boy's claim.

'What you have described is impossible. We have never seen an ox as large as the one you describe. It is impossible for an ox to be as large as Egypt.'

But the boy persevered.

'So, you don't believe in my magnificent ox? Yet you had no trouble believing that there could have been a dagger as large as the one this man once described to you, with all the copper of Mount El in its blade, all the timber in the Koptos wood in its haft? Its sheath the size of a rock-cut tomb, and its belt sewn from all the hides of the herd of Kal? Now you must judge between Truth and Falsehood. For I am the son of Truth, and I have come to avenge my father for the wrong done to him.'

Falsehood swore an oath before the gods. 'Truth is dead. I swear before you all, that if you can find Truth alive I shall be blinded in both eyes and become his doorkeeper.'

Then the boy led the gods to his father, who was still sitting outside his mother's house, very much alive. So Falsehood was beaten one hundred times, cut with five open wounds, and blinded in both eyes. And thus Falsehood became the door-keeper in the house of Truth. In this way the young boy avenged his father, and the quarrel between Truth and Falsehood was settled.

THE VOYAGE OF WENAMUN[110]

Just one version of *The Voyage of Wenamun* has survived on a papyrus dating to the late 20th or early 21st Dynasty. Unfortunately the beginning of the story has significant gaps, and its end is missing. The tale is set during the reign of Ramesses XI, and tells of a trading mission sent from Thebes to buy wood from the Lebanon. This should be a simple transaction as a shortage of tall trees means that Egypt has been importing wood for many centuries. But Wenamun lives in turbulent times. The once glorious New Kingdom is rapidly nearing its end, the empire has vanished, and Egypt has little or no influence over her neighbours, who feel free to demand cash in advance for their goods and services. Back home things are no better. Ramesses XI, last of the Ramesside rulers, is king in name only and the true power is shared between two influential men. In the south there is Herihor, high priest of Amen, based at Thebes; in the north there is Smendes, based at the eastern Delta city of Tanis. Smendes will later become the first king of the 21st Dynasty.[111]

Experts are divided over the authenticity of this story. Is it an accurate, official report of a genuine trade mission, or is it a work of fiction set in a real historical time – the New Kingdom equivalent of *Sinuhe*? Certainly Herihor does claim, on the wall of the Theban Khonsu temple, to have built a boat for Amen 'from Lebanese wood, decorated with gold throughout'. However, while at first sight the story reads like a lengthy administrative document submitted by an inept and unduly pompous official with a strong devotion to Amen, the bizarre sequence of events, the lengthy conversations reported word for word and the (we assume) deliberate use of irony are a strong indication that it is likely to be fiction.

Day 16 of the second month of summer, Year 5

On this day Wenamun, elder of the Portal of the Temple of Amen, set off on his travels. His mission was to acquire the timber needed for the construction of the magnificent riverboat of Amen-Re, king of the gods. The name of the god's riverboat was 'Amen-Mighty-of-Prow'.

I arrived in Tanis, home to Smendes and his wife Tantamen. I handed over the letter from Amen-Re, king of the gods, and it was read out to them. The royal couple graciously agreed to do as Amen-Re, king of the gods, had asked. I stayed in Tanis until the fourth month of summer. Then Smendes and Tantamen waved me off in the care of the Syrian ship's captain Mengebet. On the first day of the first month of the inundation I sailed down to the great Syrian Sea.

Eventually I reached Dor, a Tjeker port. On hearing of my arrival Beder, prince of Dor, sent me fifty loaves, an amphora of wine and an ox haunch. Then a very bad thing happened. A member of my ship's crew ran away, taking with him a gold vessel worth 5 *deben*, four silver jars worth 20 *deben*, and a bag holding 11 *deben* of silver. In total he stole 5 *deben* worth of gold and 31 *deben* worth of silver from me.

The next morning, as soon as I awoke, I paid a visit on the prince. I spoke quite forcefully to him: 'I have just been robbed in your harbour. You are the prince of this land; you are responsible for its justice. You must find my missing money! For it is not my money. It belongs to Amen-Re, king of the gods. It belongs to Smendes, and to Herihor my lord and to the other magnates of Egypt. It belongs to you. Last but not least, it belongs to Tjeker-Baal, prince of Byblos.'

The prince of Dor was taken aback by my words. 'You must be joking! I don't understand your reasoning at all. If a thief from my land had crept down to your ship and stolen your goods, then of course I would compensate you from my own treasury until the thief had been caught and your property restored. But the thief who robbed you came from your ship. He has to be your responsibility. Nevertheless, stay here for a few days, so that I may search for him and find your property for you.'

I spent a fruitless nine days moored in his harbour. Then I

returned to the prince. 'Look here, you have failed to find the man who stole my property. Let me continue my journey.'

Here the text is fragmented. It seems that the prince of Dor attempts to persuade Wenamun to wait, but our hero is anxious to be on his way. He sails to the port of Byblos. There, just outside the harbour, perhaps following Beder's advice, he takes the law into his own hands. He confiscates 30 *deben* of silver from a ship belonging to the Tjeker. He tells the owners that their property will be returned only when his own goods are found. Not surprisingly, this act of piracy incenses the Tjeker people.

They went away, and I celebrated my triumph in a tent on the seashore of Byblos harbour. There I found a secure hiding place for Amen-of-the-Road and his property. But then the prince of Byblos sent an abrupt message: 'Get out of my harbour!'

My response was equally to the point: 'Where should I go? If you can find a ship that will carry me, I will return to Egypt. If not, I stay here.' I ended up spending twenty-nine days in his harbour, while he sent daily messages ordering me to leave.

Then one day, while the prince of Byblos was offering in his temple, the god possessed one of the boys in his entourage, and put him in a trance. The god spoke to the prince, through the voice of the boy: 'Summon the Egyptian god. And summon the envoy who escorts him. For he has been sent by the great god Amen-Re. It is Amen who has made him come to us.'

That very day, just as the boy entered his trance, I had managed to track down a ship heading for Egypt. I had already loaded all my goods on board, and was waiting until nightfall so that I might load the god secretly, under cover of darkness. The next thing I knew, the harbourmaster came hurrying towards me.

'The prince orders you to stay, at least until tomorrow.'

I couldn't believe my ears. 'What! Aren't you the one who has been sending me daily messages telling me to go home. And now, just as I have found a ship that will carry me to Egypt, you are telling me to stay. Presumably when the ship has sailed, you will start ordering me to go home again! No, my friend, it is too late, I am going. Goodbye.'

The harbourmaster rushed back to the prince of Byblos, and he sent word to the captain of the ship, telling him to delay his departure.

The next morning the prince of Byblos sent for me and I went to him, leaving the god resting in the tent on the seashore. I found the prince sitting in his imposing upper chamber, his back to the window. Behind him I could see the breaking waves of the great Syrian Sea.

I greeted the prince politely, as the occasion demanded. 'May the blessings of Amen be upon you.'

He, however, did not feel the need for politeness. Abruptly, he started to question me. 'How long is it since you left Thebes, home of Amen?'

'I have been travelling for exactly five whole months to this day.'

'But, if this is true, where is the letter from Amen-Re, king of the gods, which details your mission? Where is the letter of authority from the high priest of Amen?'

I explained all that had happened to me. 'I gave the letter of authority to Smendes and Tantamen in Tanis.'

This made him unaccountably angry. 'Now, try to look at this matter from my point of view. You landed on my shore without any form of official validation. Where is the great ship that Smendes gave you to transport the wood? Where is its Syrian crew? Surely Egypt has her own fleet. Or, when Smendes entrusted you to the care of a Syrian sea-captain, did he intend the captain to murder you and throw your body overboard?'

Controlling my temper, I replied: 'It was an Egyptian ship, not a Syrian one. Those who sail under Smendes are Egyptian crews.'

'I know what I am talking about. There are at least twenty ships here in my harbour that do business with Smendes.'

I fell silent. Then the prince spoke again.

'Why exactly have you come here? What is your business?'

'I have come in search of timber for the great boat of Amen-Re, king of the gods. Help me in my mission just as your father once helped Egypt's envoys, and your father's father before him.'

The prince smiled at last, but it was not a kind smile. 'This, at least, I know to be true. And, of course, if you pay me properly I will indeed help you. My ancestors did supply wood to Egypt, but only after they had been properly rewarded. The king of Egypt sent six boats loaded with valuable Egyptian products, and they were unloaded into our warehouses. Then, and only then, he received his goods. But you have arrived empty-handed and so deserve nothing.'

To emphasize his point the prince called for the palace daybooks and had the relevant entries read to me; the entries mentioned a thousand *deben* of silver, and other precious goods. Then he spoke to me again, warming to his theme:

'If the king of Egypt were lord of Byblos, and the prince of Byblos merely his servant, he would never have sent silver and gold in payment – he would simply have taken what he needed for the service of Amen-Re. He paid my father and his father before him properly, as an equal. I am not your servant nor am I the servant of your master, and I should therefore be paid for my wood and my labour.'

At this point, perceiving my inability to pay as an insult to his nation, he went off into a rather alarming rant: 'Of course,

I have only to shout out to the Lebanon, and the sky will open and the gods will drop the cut timber on to the beach. Give me the sails that you brought to move your ships loaded with timber back to Egypt. Give me the ropes that you brought to lash together the wood. Take your wood, and go! Ever since he placed Seth beside him, Amen has been able to thunder in the sky. We all know that Amen founded all the lands, and that he founded the land of Egypt first. We all know that crafts and learning started in Egypt, and travelled to Byblos. But now we have both crafts and learning in abundance – we require nothing from Egypt. And yet you have arrived. So, tell me, Wenamun, what exactly is the point of your pointless journey?'

'You are wrong! It is not a pointless journey. There is not a ship on the river that does not belong to Amen. He owns the sea and he owns the Lebanon, even though you claim it as your own. Amen-Re, king of the gods, told Herihor to send me on this quest, and he sent me with the great god. But you have made the great god waste twenty-nine days in your harbour. Did you not realize that he was here, and why?

'Now you have the audacity to haggle with him, the owner of the Lebanon! You keep telling me that the Egyptian kings of old sent your ancestors gifts of silver and gold. Perhaps they did. But if they had the gift of life and health they would not have sent those paltry goods – they would have sent life and health instead. Now Amen-Re, king of the gods, is the lord of life and health; it is he who was the lord of your fathers. They spent their lifetimes offering to Amen. You too are a servant of Amen. If you agree to do as he asks, you will live, prosper and be healthy. Your entire land will benefit. Do not covet the things that belong to Amen-Re, king of the gods. Instead send your scribe to me so that I may write to Smendes and Tantamen, the two pillars that Amen has set up in the north of his land. They will send you whatever payment you think necessary. I will explain matters to them; I will ask them to send you payment until I return to the south of Egypt, then my master Herihor will refund their expenses.'

The prince of Byblos gave my letter to his messenger, and he loaded the ship with the keel piece, the bow, the stern plus four great logs – a total of seven hewn logs – and he sent them to Egypt. I remained in Syria. The messenger returned to me in the first month of winter. Smendes and Tantamen had not let me down. Here is the list of the goods that they sent:

Four jars and one vessel of gold
Five silver bowls
Ten garments made from fine royal linen and ten sheets of fine
   linen
500 smooth linen mats
500 ox hides
500 ropes
20 sacks of lentils
30 baskets of fish

In addition the queen sent me a personal gift of five fine linen garments, five fine linen covers, one sack of lentils and five sacks of fish.

The sight of so many precious goods galvanized the prince of Byblos. Three hundred men and three hundred oxen set to work under the supervision of his personally chosen officials. They felled the timber that I needed, and it lay on the ground throughout the winter. In the third month of summer the logs were dragged to the seashore. The prince went to inspect them, and he summoned me. But when I had been ushered into his presence, an unfortunate thing happened. The shadow of his fan fell across me. Seeing this, Penamen, Egyptian butler to the prince of Byblos, made a big fuss: 'The shadow of the king of Egypt, your lord, has fallen on you.'

But the prince grew angry with Penamen, and told him to leave me alone. As I stood before the prince of Byblos, he spoke to me: 'Look, I have now done the same business with you that my father and grandfather did in the past, although you did not treat me as well as they were treated. The last of your timber has now been cut, and lies ready. Do as I wish, and load it on to your ship, for it has been given to you. But do not look at the terror of the sea. For if you look at the terror of the sea, you will see my very own terror. You should note that I have not treated you in the same way that the envoys sent by Khaemwaset were treated. They spent seventeen years in this land, and eventually died here.'

And turning to his butler, he ordered him to take me to the place where the envoys of Khaemwaset were buried so that I might see just how my unfortunate compatriots had fared.

'Do not make me see this terrible thing,' I cried, horrified. 'The envoys sent by Khaemwaset were mere men, just as Khaemwaset himself was a mere man. I am not one of his envoys – you can't tell me what to do. I am a mortal envoy, but I am sent by a great god. You should rejoice at my coming and have a magnificent stela carved in celebration. And on it you should proclaim, for all to read:

"Amen-Re, king of the gods, sent his divine messenger Amen-of-the-Road, and his mortal messenger Wenamun, to my land in search of the timber needed to build the riverboat of the great god Amen-Re. I felled the trees, and I loaded the logs on to the ships that I had supplied. I sent the wood to Egypt – and in exchange I asked that Amen grant me an extra fifty years of life beyond that which the fates had planned."

'Then, if it should ever happen that another Egyptian envoy comes to your land and he is able to read your stela, you will receive the water of the west like the gods who dwell there.'

The prince spoke to me again, thanking me with some irony for my unasked-for advice. And I assured him that all my debts to him would be repaid in full when I, and the ships, reached Thebes.

I went down to the seashore, where the logs lay ready and waiting. At least it seemed that my long mission was over and I could return home. But then I saw to my horror that eleven Tjeker ships had docked, and their sailors were roaming the shore looking for me.

'There he is! Arrest him! Under no circumstances allow his ship to sail for Egypt!'

There was nothing I could do to escape. I would never leave Byblos. I would never see my homeland again. I sat down and wept on the shore.

The scribe of the prince of Byblos came to me, concerned that I was weeping on what should have been a happy occasion. He asked me what was wrong. And I told him of my sorrow at being stranded far from home.

'Look into the sky – can you see the birds migrating? I have lived here for so long that I have already seen them fly twice to Egypt, and now am forced to watch as they journey north again to the cooler lands. When will I ever be able to fly away? Look, can't you see, those men have come to arrest me.'

The scribe went straight to the prince and told him of this new development. And the prince, moved to tears by my words, sent the scribe back to me bringing two jugs of wine and a sheep. He also sent Tentne, a famous Egyptian singer who worked at his court, and he told her to sing me cheerful songs that would take my mind off my problems. He sent a message with the scribe: 'Eat, drink and be merry if you can, Wenamun.

Don't worry about your situation. For tomorrow I will pronounce judgement on your case.'

In the morning Tjeker-Baal, prince of Byblos, summoned his court. He questioned the Tjeker closely: 'Why have you come here? What exactly do you want?'

'We demand the right to confiscate the ships that you are sending to Egypt with our enemy.'

The prince considered for a moment, then reached his decision.

'I cannot allow this to happen on my land. I cannot be responsible for arresting the envoy of the great god Amen-Re. I will send the envoy off to sea, and you must arrest him there.'

Hearing this, my heart sank. The prince made me board my ship, and I sailed from the harbour. The strong wind drove me towards Cyprus, and there I landed. I had gone from a bad situation to a worse. The townspeople rushed out of their houses, determined to kill me. But I forced my way into the presence of Hatiba, their princess. I ran to her as she left her palace and, in desperate fear of my life, asked if anyone could translate my words so that I might plead my cause. Most fortunately, there was a man in the crowd who could speak Egyptian very well. And so I was able to speak to the good lady.

'Madam. Living at Thebes, home of the great god Amen, I have heard many stories of injustices committed in other lands. But I never heard that the land of Cyprus was unjust. Now prove to me that your land is indeed a just one.'

She looked at me in surprise. 'What do you mean by that? Explain yourself, foreigner.'

And so I spoke at length. 'The great sea raged, and the strong wind blew me to your land against my will. Will you really allow your people to kill me, the envoy of Amen? Your people have determined that they will never let me go – they may well kill me. But think about this. If they kill the sailors from Byblos who crew my ship, the prince of Byblos will hunt down ten of your ships, and kill their crews in revenge.'

Hatiba saw the sense of my words. She summoned the people to her, and reprimanded them. Then she spoke to me. 'Stay the night, Wenamun . . .'

A DEVELOPING MYTHOLOGY

While kings enjoyed the luxury of commissioning their own myths and legends to decorate their temple walls, some commoners had mythology thrust upon them. Two even became nationally recognized gods. A statue base recovered from the Sakkara Step Pyramid complex of the 3rd Dynasty King Djoser introduces us to the first of these. He is 'The chancellor of the king of Upper and Lower Egypt, the first after the king of Upper Egypt, administrator of the great palace, hereditary lord, greatest of seers, Imhotep, the builder, the sculptor, the maker of stone vases'.[112]

IMHOTEP AND AMENHOTEP SON OF HAPU

Imhotep, vizier and high priest of Re, was respected during his lifetime as the polymath 'overseer of works' of the Sakkara Step Pyramid. One thousand years later he was widely esteemed as a sage whose sayings carried great authority. By the end of the New Kingdom he had evolved into a god with impressive healing powers and the ability to help barren women conceive. During the Ptolemaic Period, the sick travelled to his temple to spend the night 'incubated' – literally sleeping in a cubicle in the hope of receiving a dream-cure. Imhotep was now worshipped throughout

Egypt as Imouthes, a son of Ptah born to a beautiful human mother, Kherduankh, and acknowledged by his divine step-mother, Sekhmet. At Thebes, in the Ptolemaic temple of Ptah, the mortal Kherduankh took the form of the divine Hathor; in the Delta she was recognized as the daughter of the ram-headed Banebdjedet of Mendes. The deified Imhotep was an anthropo-morphic god who wore the skull cap associated with Ptah and the long kilt worn by priests. In dreams, however, he might appear to the faithful as a scarab beetle.

We have already seen Imhotep in impressive action on the Famine Stela, the Ptolemaic inscription that tells how Djoser, troubled by seven years of famine, received good advice from a priest of Imhotep. The Harris Stela[113] preserves the autobiography of Pasherenptah III, high priest of Ptah during the reign of Cleo-patra VII. From this we learn that Pasherenptah and his wife Taimhotep had three daughters but no son. The unhappy couple prayed to Imhotep and finally, when the 43-year-old priest had lost all hope, a healthy son was born who was named Imhotep in honour of the god.

Imhotep's own Sakkara tomb had been lost by the end of the Old Kingdom. Undaunted, the 26th Dynasty kings found him a replacement tomb which now served as the Asklepion, the cult centre where the faithful could appeal to their god for help and leave offerings of mummified ibises and model body-parts rep-resenting the organs and limbs in need of a cure.[114] Today the Asklepion is lost, and Imhotep's true tomb remains undiscovered, although it has been suggested that it might be the large, un-inscribed mastaba known as Sakkara 3518.

On a slightly smaller scale the deceased 18th Dynasty sage and architect Amenhotep son of Hapu, overseer of the many building projects of Amenhotep III, was worshipped as a divine healer alongside Imhotep in the Theban area. Images of Amenhotep the god show him, as we might expect, as an anthropomorphic scribe sitting cross-legged with a papyrus scroll stretched across his lap.

TUTHMOSIS III AND GENERAL DJEHUTY

While Imhotep and Amenhotep acquired divinity but a limited mythology, some individuals acquired legendary status without the supernatural interaction which would turn their stories into myths. This was, however, rarer than we might expect. Although all Egyptians were heroes in their own tomb autobiographies, there was only room for one hero – the king – in the public sphere. Large-scale images of the divinely inspired pharaoh smashing the enemies of Egypt dominated the outer temple walls, while the accompanying, exaggerated texts highlighted the heroism of kings who did not baulk at humiliating their troops in order to make themselves look better. As the king enforced *maat* on foreign chaos, as he emphasized his own valour at the expense of others, he reinforced both his own position and the position of the temple god. We have already read of the extreme bravery of Ramesses II who, despite what he obviously saw as the startling incompetence of his generals, was apparently able to fight off an entire army at the battle of Kadesh single-handed. One hundred and eighty years earlier, Tuthmosis III had developed and ruled an empire which extended from below the Third Nile Cataract in Nubia to the banks of the Euphrates in Syria. Tuthmosis ordered his scribes to record the minutiae of his campaigns in an official 'day book'. Later in his reign details of his eastern triumphs (regnal Years 22–42) were inscribed on the walls of two newly built halls in the Karnak temple. Today known as the 'Annals', this *Boys'-Own*-style account of foreign adventures allows us an unprecedented insight into Tuthmosis' military exploits.

One campaign in particular stands out. In Year 23 Tuthmosis

planned an advance eastwards, from Syria, across the Carmel mountain range to the fortified city of Megiddo (modern northern Israel), where he was to face a daunting coalition of enemies led by the king of Kadesh. As Tuthmosis himself tells us, there were three possible ways of approaching the city, one more dangerous than the other two. In a council of war, his cowardly generals made it clear which routes they preferred:

What will it be like to go on this path which keeps getting narrower? We have received reports that the enemy is waiting on the other side and that their numbers are constantly increasing. Will our horses not have to go in single file and our army and people likewise? Will our vanguard not have to fight while our rearguard is still standing here in Aruna unable to fight? But there are two other roads here. One of them is to our east – it comes out at Taanach. The other goes north of Djefti – and would lead us to the north of Megiddo. Our lord should go on whichever of these seems best, but he should not make us march along that difficult path.

Ignoring this advice, Tuthmosis led his troops – an estimated 10,000 men – on a three-day march in single file along a winding mountain pass. This daring move allowed him to creep up on the enemy camped outside the walls of Megiddo. As dawn broke over the mountains, the sun illuminated the high ground which, it was now obvious, was occupied by a massive Egyptian army. At the head of his troops stood Tuhmosis himself: 'Amen was protecting his body, the blood-lust and strength of Seth were flowing through his limbs.'

The battle was easily won. Then, however, things started to go wrong. As the defeated enemy ran back towards Megiddo the Egyptian soldiers defied their orders and paused to loot the abandoned camps. The city gates were slammed shut, and the

Egyptians watched in amazement as the kings of Megiddo and Kadesh were hauled up the city walls by their clothing, and 'sheets were lowered down to lift them into the town'. Refusing to panic, Tuthmosis simply built a thick wall around the city and waited. Seven months later the starving citizens surrendered. This great victory would linger in the folk memory for centuries. Over 1,000 years later, when the writer of the Biblical Book of Revelation described the horrors of the last battle of doomsday, he set it at Megiddo:[115] 'And he gathered them together into a place called in the Hebrew tongue Armageddon.'

Tuthmosis' army did produce one genuine non-royal hero. Djehuty was a general or 'overseer of the army' who, during Year 22, besieged the city of Joppa (modern Jaffa). A Ramesside papyrus tells us that the enterprising Egyptians broke the siege by smuggling 200 soldiers into the city, hidden inside large baskets which were presented as peace offerings to the somewhat gullible citizens.[116] Comparisons with the later tale of the siege of Troy, and with the Arabian tale of *Ali Baba and the Forty Thieves*, are obvious. For his part in this remarkable escapade Djehuty was rewarded with a hero's tomb in the Sakkara cemetery.[117]

THE PYRAMID BUILDERS

Princes who failed to succeed their fathers might develop legendary status. We last met the storytelling Prince Hardjedef at the 4th Dynasty court of Khufu, where he entertained his father by introducing him to the magician Djedi. Hardjedef never ruled Egypt but, clearly a person of great importance, he was accorded the honour of a large tomb near his father's Giza pyramid. In death he was celebrated as a sage with borderline supernatural knowledge. *The Instructions of Hardjedef*, a didactic text written by an anonymous scribe during the 5th Dynasty, became well respected as a guide to dynastic life, while *Book of the Dead* spell 30, a spell intended to stop the heart from betraying the deceased, was understood (almost certainly wrongly) to have been discovered by Hardjedef during the reign of his nephew Menkaure.

The anonymous author of *Papyrus Westcar* treats both Snefru and Khufu as genial monarchs whose worst vices were a mild voyeurism and an over-eagerness to witness advanced magic. But, while Snefru would always be remembered as a wise and good king, his son Khufu soon developed a less flattering reputation. Two thousand years after Khufu raised his pyramid, Herodotus recorded a potted biography of the king. As a Greek, Herodotus would have found it difficult to envisage a pyramid-building nation – indeed, any successful nation – able to function without slaves. His Khufu, whom he knows as Cheops, therefore becomes a blasphemous tyrant loathed by the people that he must have enslaved in order to build his pyramid. Furthermore, his Khufu is a king who abuses his daughter:[118]

> But no crime was too great for Cheops: when he was short of money, he sent his daughter to a brothel with instructions to charge a certain sum – they did not say how much. This she actually did, adding to it a further transaction of her own; for with the intention of leaving something to be remembered by after her death, she asked each of her customers to give her a block of stone, and of these stones (the story goes) was built the middle pyramid of the three which stand in front of the Great Pyramid.

This assessment is very unfair. A further 2,500 years on, archaeology has confirmed that Khufu's pyramid was built by professional craftsmen and respected labourers who were well fed, well housed and provided with good medical care. As to the king's character and his relationship with his daughter(s), we do not have enough evidence to make any sensible comment.

Khufu was not the only 4th Dynasty king to be accused of exploiting a daughter. Herodotus also tells of the daughter of Mycerinus (Menkaure), builder of the third Giza Pyramid, who, having died young, was entombed by her father in a gold-plated wooden cow. This cow, attended by ranks of colossal wooden statues, was displayed in the royal palace at Sais, where Herodotus was able to inspect it. He then tells a less salubrious version of the story, which sees Menkaure raping his daughter who, shamed, hangs herself. The queen, believing her daughter to have been betrayed by her serving maids, then exacts revenge by cutting off their hands. In spite of this story, Herodotus's Menkaure is a good man who has been unjustly condemned by fate to reign for just six years. The king is not prepared to accept this injustice, and he orders that the lamps be lit so that he can turn nights into days and so live twelve years in the space of six. This cunning plan clearly worked, as the real Menkaure reigned for somewhere between eighteen and twenty-eight years.

Herodotus mentions, but quickly dismisses, rumours that Menkaure's pyramid was built by Rhodophis, a courtesan of outstanding beauty and apparently unlimited earning powers. The Classical author Strabo based a Cinderella-like tale on this legend. As the rosy-cheeked Rhodophis was bathing in the Delta city of Naucratis, her sandal was stolen by an eagle. The eagle flew straight to Memphis and dropped the sandal into the king's lap. The king, seduced by the beauty and perfume of the sandal, ordered an immediate search for its owner. Rhodophis was found and brought to Memphis. In best fairy-tale tradition she then married the king, who built her a pyramid as a token of his love.

Menkaure's own pyramid might occasionally be assigned to Nitokris, the legendary female king whose death marked the end of the 6th Dynasty and the end of the Old Kingdom. Herodotus records the salient features of her reign: [119]

> Next, the priests read to me from a written record the names of three hundred and thirty monarchs, in the same number of generations, all of them Egyptians except eighteen, who were Ethiopians, and one other, who was an Egyptian woman. This last had the same name – Nitokris – as the queen of Babylon. The story was that she ensnared to their deaths hundreds of Egyptians in revenge for the king her brother, whom his subjects had murdered and forced her to succeed; this she did by constructing an immense underground chamber, in which, under the pretence of opening it by an inaugural ceremony, she invited to a banquet all the Egyptians whom she knew to be chiefly responsible for her brother's death; then, when the banquet was in full swing, she let the river in on them through a large concealed conduit-pipe. The only other thing I was told about her was that after this fearful revenge she flung herself into a room full of ashes to escape her punishment.

Even today the naked ghost of Nitokris is said to haunt the Giza Plateau, where it is occasionally glimpsed by susceptible men.

THE EXTRAORDINARY KING RHAMPSINITUS

Herodotus writes of a third abused princess. His 'King Rhampsinitus' is a mixture of the 19th Dynasty Ramesses II and the 20th Dynasty Ramesses III, yet his reign is set before that of Khufu.

Rhampsinitus was an extraordinarily wealthy monarch. To keep his treasure safe he designed a secure stone vault.

Unfortunately, Rhampsinitus employed a dishonest builder who incorporated a removable stone in the outer wall of the vault. On his deathbed the builder passed this secret on to his two sons, and they started to make regular visits to steal the king's treasure.

Rhampsinitus was puzzled: his treasure was gradually vanishing from a sealed room. How could this happen? Eventually he set a trap, which caught one of the thieves. Struggling in the trap, the doomed thief ordered his brother to cut off his head and take it away, so that his body might go unrecognized and the thefts might continue. This was duly done, and the second thief escaped with his life and his brother's head. The king, shocked to find a headless body in the sealed vault, ordered that the body be placed on public display. Anyone weeping over the body might be presumed to know the identity of the thief. However, the plan backfired, and the surviving thief was able to make off with his brother's corpse.

Rhampsinitus then sent his daughter to work in a brothel. She had strict instructions to sleep with as many customers as possible, but to ask each one what was the cleverest and most wicked thing that he had ever done. This also failed: the brother duly visited the princess in the brothel, but escaped leaving her clutching a hand cut from a corpse. Finally Rhampsinitus admitted defeat. A pardon was issued, and the thief made himself known to the king and married the princess.

A second story featuring Rhampsinitus tells of a visit to the land of the dead (Hades to Herodotus), where the king plays dice with the Greek goddess Demeter. Having won some games and lost some, Rhampsinitus returns to the land of the living with a precious golden cloth, the gift of the goddess.

PRINCE KHAEMWASET

Khaemwaset, the fourth-born son of Ramesses II by Queen Iset-Nofret, developed his own extensive mythology. Khaemwaset had served at Memphis as the *sem*-priest of Ptah, a position that allowed him to take responsibility for the sacred Apis bulls. Eventually he became high priest of Ptah and, as his older brothers died, his father's intended heir. But the long-lived Ramesses survived his first twelve sons, and it would be Khaemwaset's full brother, Merenptah, who eventually inherited the throne at over 60 years of age.

During his lifetime Khaemwaset was respected as a priest, a scholar and a restorer of Egypt's ancient ruins. In recognition of this work he is occasionally described as 'the first Egyptologist', although it seems likely that his archaeological zeal was primarily inspired by the desire to promote both himself and his father as the bringers of *maat* to chaos. In death Khaemwaset was transformed into the powerful magician Setne Khaemwaset, Setne being a corruption of his title *sem*-priest. Setne became the hero of a cycle of fantastic adventures, just two of which have survived. *Setne I* is written on a torn Ptolemaic papyrus, while *Setne II*, which we have already read in Chapter 6, comes from a Roman papyrus.[120] Unusually, the pages of *Setne I* are numbered: we can therefore tell that the first two pages of the six-page document are lost. The surviving story tells of Setne's desire to steal the magical *Book of Thoth* from its guardian, the dead priest Naneferkaptah. His magic proves an effective tool in his mission, but eventually Setne faces the realization that he will never be able to steal the secrets of the gods. Here I have reconstructed the introduction to the story.

Setne Khaemwaset, son of Ramesses II and high priest of Ptah at Memphis, was a wise man and a powerful magician. He spent his time studying the monuments of the ancestors, and reading ancient books. One day he learned of the book of magic written by the god Thoth, which was housed in the tomb of the long-dead Prince Naneferkaptah in the Memphite necropolis. After a long search, helped by his brother Inaros, Setne found the tomb of Naneferkaptah and entered it. He saw the *Book of Thoth*, which glowed with an eerie light, and he attempted to seize it. The ghosts of Naneferkaptah and his wife Ahwere then rose up to stop him. Ahwere and her son Merib were actually buried at Koptos, not Memphis, yet she travelled to stand beside her husband at this moment of crisis. Standing before Setne Khaemwaset she explained how she and her husband had lost their lives in their quest to acquire the *Book*.

Ahwere began her tale by explaining that she and Naneferkaptah were sister and brother, the only children of King Mernebptah. They loved each other very much, yet were forbidden to marry because the king wished to increase his family by marrying his son to the daughter of a general, and his daughter to the son of a general. Ahwere was eventually able to persuade her father that their union would be a good thing, and she married Naneferkaptah. Soon the young couple had a son, Merib. The king, delighted with his grandchild, rewarded the young couple with many beautiful and valuable gifts.

One day Naneferkaptah was wandering through the temple of Ptah, idly reading the ancient inscriptions. An old priest saw him, and laughed: 'You are reading words which are of no importance to anyone. But pay attention to me, and I will send you to the place where the *Book of Thoth* is stored; the *Book* that the god wrote with his own hand. There are just two spells in the *Book*. When you recite the first spell you will charm the sky, the earth, the netherworld, the mountains and the waters, you will understand what the animals are saying and will see all the fish in the river. When you recite the second spell, whether you are alive or dead, you will see Re appearing in the sky with the Ennead, and the rising Moon, and the stars in all their forms.'

This kind of information did not come cheap. Naneferkaptah agreed to pay a price of a hundred *deben* of silver and two tax-free stipends, and then the old priest spoke: 'The *Book* is in the middle of the waters of Koptos in an iron box. Inside the iron box is a copper box. Inside the copper box is a wooden box. Inside the wooden box is a box of ebony and ivory. Inside the box of ebony and ivory is a silver box. Inside the silver box is a gold box. And inside the gold box is the *Book of Thoth*. But be warned. A host of snakes, scorpions and reptiles guard the boxes which hold the *Book*, and an eternal serpent is wrapped around them.'

Stunned by this tale, Naneferkaptah left the temple and sought his wife. He told her everything that he had heard. Ahwere was reluctant to seek the *Book* – she cursed the old priest who had tempted her husband – yet she eventually agreed to accompany Naneferkaptah on the voyage to Koptos. The king, having heard the tale, provided a fine ship and crew to take his children to Koptos.

Having arrived at Koptos, Naneferkaptah, Ahwere and Merib offered an ox, a goose and some wine at the temple of Isis and Harpocrates. They then rested for four days with the priests and their families. On the fifth day Naneferkaptah fashioned a boat and its crew from pure wax. A spell made the wax model real and, embarking, Naneferkaptah ordered his oarsmen to take him to the place where the *Book* was hidden. Three days later the boat arrived. Naneferkaptah cast sand before him, forming an island in the river. He discovered the snakes, scorpions and reptiles guarding the place where the *Book* was, and slaughtered them. Then he fought and killed the eternal serpent three times until, hacked into pieces, it was permanently dead.

Naneferkaptah opened the iron box and discovered the copper box. He opened the copper box and discovered the wooden box. He opened the wooden box and discovered the box of ebony and ivory. He opened the box of ebony and ivory and discovered the silver box. He opened the silver box and discovered the gold box. And inside the gold box he discovered the *Book of Thoth*. Reading from the *Book* he recited the spells, and all was as the old priest had foretold. Then he ordered his oarsmen to take him back to his wife and child.

Ahwere greeted her husband with relief. She too read from the *Book* and recited the spells, and again all was as the old priest had foretold. Then Naneferkaptah copied the spells on to a sheet of new papyrus. He dissolved the papyrus in beer and drank it, and so he absorbed all the magic of the *Book*. Finally, Naneferkaptah, Ahwere and Merib began their return journey. They reached a point on the river six miles to the north of Koptos.

When Thoth learned what had happened to his *Book* and its guardians he was filled with rage. He rushed to report the matter to Re, demanding that the family be punished for their crime. Immediately, the young boy Merib fell overboard and drowned. As the crew wailed, Naneferkaptah raised his dead son to the surface of the river and recited a spell over his body. Merib was able to tell his father what Thoth had demanded of Re. Merib was embalmed and buried in a tomb in Koptos.

Then Naneferkaptah and Ahwere boarded their boat again. But when they reached the place where Merib had died, Ahwere fell overboard and she too drowned. As before, Naneferkaptah was able to raise his dead wife to the surface of the river and speak to her. And Ahwere was able to tell her husband what

Thoth had demanded of Re. Ahwere was embalmed and buried in Koptos alongside Merib.

Naneferkaptah boarded his ship, and the oarsmen set to work. When they reached the place, six miles to the north of Koptos, where Merib and Ahwere had drowned he tied the *Book of Thoth* to his body with a linen scarf. When, as he had anticipated, Naneferkaptah too fell overboard and drowned, the *Book* went with him. The boat continued its journey to Memphis with none of the crew knowing what had happened to their master's body. When the king came down to the ship to mourn his lost family, he found the body of his son clinging to the rudder. They raised his body and found the *Book of Thoth*. And the king buried the *Book* with Naneferkaptah in the Memphite cemetery.

Ahwere concluded her tale of woe: 'These are the evil things that befell my family when we tried to claim the *Book*. Now you say that you wish to take it from us. But you have no right to it whatsoever, whereas our lives were forfeit on account of it.'

Setne Khaemwaset still desired the *Book*: 'Let me take it, or I will seize it by force!'

Hearing this Naneferkaptah rose from his coffin and proposed that the matter be settled over the *senet* board. Setne agreed: 'I am ready.'

The *senet* pieces were laid on the board and they started to play. During the first game Naneferkaptah recited a magical spell, struck Setne on the head with the game box, and caused him to sink into the ground up to his knees. Thus Naneferkaptah won the first game. During the second game Setne sank into the ground up to his penis and Naneferkaptah won the game. During the third game Setne sank into the ground up to his ears and Naneferkaptah won again.

Setne called to his brother Inaros: 'Hurry back to the land

of the living and tell the king all that has happened to me. Bring me my books of sorcery and the amulets of my father Ptah.'

Inaros did as he was bidden. Returning to the tomb of Naneferkaptah he placed the amulets on his brother's body, and Setne was freed. Snatching the *Book of Thoth*, Setne and Inaros ran from the tomb. Behind him, Ahwere wept and Naneferkaptah comforted his grieving wife: 'Do not mourn. I will make him return the *Book*, with a forked stick in his hand and a burning brazier on his head.'

Hearing this tale the king advised Setne to return the *Book of Thoth* to the tomb of Naneferkaptah. But, deaf to reason, Setne unrolled the *Book* and settled down to read.

Some time after this adventure, Setne Khaemwaset was strolling in the public court of the temple of Ptah when he saw the most beautiful woman in the world. She wore fine golden jewellery, and was accompanied by a maid and two menservants. Overwhelmed by the woman's beauty, Setne sent his own servant to question her maid: 'Who is your mistress?'

'She is Tabubu, the daughter of the priest of Bastet. She has come to this temple to worship the great god Ptah.'

Setne issued a new order: 'Tell the maid to tell her mistress that Setne Khaemwaset, son of Ramesses II, will give her ten pieces of gold if she spends an hour with him. Or he will settle a difficult lawcase for her, or will take her to a hidden place where no one will ever find her . . .'

Insulted by the message, the maid cried out. Then the beautiful Tabubu spoke directly to Setne's servant: 'Stop communicating via this foolish maid, and talk directly to me.'

The servant repeated Setne's message, and Tabubu frowned: 'Tell Setne Khaemwaset that I am a person of the highest rank. If he desires to do what he wishes with me, he must visit me in my house, in my home town of Bubastis. There he can do whatever he likes with me, without anyone seeing, and without my having to act like a low-born woman of the street.'

Besotted, Setne ordered a boat, and sailed at once to Bubastis. Here he found Tabubu's house, an impressive residence with a walled garden and a seat by the door. Tabubu took him by the hand and led him up the stairs into a luxurious room filled with couches and fine linen. A golden goblet was placed in his hand, and he drank thirstily. As the room filled with a power-fully scented incense, Setne turned to the beautiful Tabubu: 'Let us now do what I have come here for.'

But Tabubu demurred: 'Remember, I am not a low-born woman of the streets. If you are to do all you wish with me, you must first show your goodwill by giving me a deed of maintenance, granting me all your possessions.'

Setne needed no persuading. He sent for the schoolmaster, and the deed was drawn up.

Then a messenger entered the room to announce that Setne's children had arrived, and were waiting for their father down-stairs. Hearing this, Tabubu dressed herself in a robe of linen so fine that her beautiful limbs could be glimpsed through its folds. Seeing her veiled body, Setne was inflamed with desire. He pleaded with her: 'Tabubu, now please let me accomplish what I came here to do.'

Again Tabubu demurred: 'Remember, I am not a low woman of the streets. If you are to do all you wish with me, you must show your goodwill by killing your children. Do not leave them alive to dispute with my children over your property.'

Driven mad with lust, Setne agreed. Tabubu had the children killed in front of their father. Their bodies were thrown down to the dogs and cats, who ate their flesh as Setne drank with Tabubu.

Setne pleaded: 'Tabubu, I have done all you asked. Now let me accomplish what I came here to do.'

Tabubu led him to a storehouse in the garden. He lay down on a couch of ivory and ebony, and the beautiful Tabubu lay beside him. But, just as he stretched out his hand to touch her, she opened her mouth wide and gave a terrible cry.

Setne awoke from his dream sweating. He was hot and aroused, and he had no clothes to hide his shame. At that moment his father the king passed by in his litter. Astonished, Ramesses ordered his servants to stop: 'Setne, what has happened to you?'

'It is Naneferkaptah who has done this to me.' And Setne told his father all that had happened in the house of the beautiful Tabubu.

The wise king smiled: 'Setne, here are some clothes. Go to Memphis where your children are still alive and waiting for you.'

Taking his father's advice, Setne decided to return the *Book of Thoth* to the tomb of Naneferkaptah. As Naneferkaptah had predicted, he did this with a forked stick in his hand and a burning brazier on his head. He then arranged for the bodies of Ahwere and Merib to be brought from Koptos, so that the family might rest in peace together.

We recognized the connection between board games and life beyond death in Chapter 3, when we considered the coiled snake Mehen and the board game of the same name. The link is more obvious in the case of *senet* ('the passing game' or 'thirty squares'), a popular backgammon-like game for two players. *Senet* was played on a rectangular board with three parallel, adjoining rows of ten squares or 'houses'. Each player had either seven (Old Kingdom) or five (New Kingdom) playing pieces known as 'dancers'; the object of the game was to guide the dancers through the houses, reversing direction on every row, and blocking, diverting and passing over the opponent's pieces wherever possible. Occasional decorated houses representing good or bad luck made the journey around the board more exciting. The earliest images of the game, included among tomb scenes of daily life, show two living opponents playing while the deceased watches. By the 6th Dynasty the deceased sits at the board to play a live opponent, suggesting that the game has become a conduit that will enable the dead to communicate with the living. During the New Kingdom the deceased often plays an invisible opponent – death, perhaps? By now *senet* has become equated with the idea of resurrection and the struggle of the soul to reach the security of eternal life, and *senet*-playing scenes are frequently used to illustrate the lengthy *Book of the Dead* spell 17.

CLEOPATRA AND HER SNAKE

Ancient Egypt's most modern legend, a legend which developed at the very end of the dynastic age and so just squeezes into this book, returns to the connection between divine kingship and protective snakes. On 12 August 30 BC, Cleopatra VII committed suicide. Our understanding of her death is derived from the accounts preserved by the Roman historians Plutarch, in his *Life of Antony*, and Cassius Dio, in his *Roman History*.[121] As both authors wrote well over a century after the queen's death, neither account can be considered entirely reliable. The agreed facts are, however, simple. Antony and Cleopatra were defeated by the Roman Octavian at the Battle of Actium. Antony later committed suicide, and was buried in Alexandria. Having visited his tomb, Cleopatra returned to her palace, bathed and ate a final meal which may, or may not, have included a basket of figs. She then sent a sealed message to Octavian. Octavian received and opened the message, and realized that Cleopatra, too, was about to commit suicide. Roman soldiers ran to her palace but they were too late to stop her. Cleopatra was already dead. Dio sums up the evidence:

> No one knows clearly in what way she perished, for the only marks on her body were slight pricks on the arm. Some say she applied to herself an asp which had been brought in to her in a water jar, or perhaps hidden in some flowers. Others declare that she had smeared a pin, with which she was wont to fasten her hair, with some poison possessed of such a property that in ordinary circumstances it would not injure the body at all, but if it came into contact with even a drop of blood it would destroy the body very quietly and painlessly; and that previous to this time she had worn it in her hair as usual, but now had made a slight scratch on her arm and had dipped the pin in the blood.

In support of the death-by-snake theory, he adds that Octavian summoned Libyan snake-charmers but they arrived too late to help. Plutarch gives more detail:

> It is said that the asp was brought with those figs and leaves and lay hidden beneath them, for thus Cleopatra had given orders, that the reptile might fasten itself upon her body without her being aware of it. But when she took away some of the figs and saw it, she said: 'There it is, you see', and baring her arm she held it out for the bite. But others say that the asp was kept carefully shut up in a water jar, and that while Cleopatra was stirring it up and irritating it with a golden distaff it sprang and fastened itself upon her arm. But the truth of the matter no one knows; for it was also said that she carried about poison in a hollow comb and kept the comb hidden in her hair; and yet neither spot nor other sign of poison broke out upon her

body. Moreover, not even was the reptile seen within the chamber, though people said they saw some traces of it near the sea, where the chamber looked out upon it with its windows. And some also say that Cleopatra's arm was seen to have two slight and indistinct punctures; and this Caesar (Octavian) *also seems to have believed. For in his triumph an image of Cleopatra herself with the asp clinging to her was carried in the procession.*

For a person kept under armed guard in a city palace, suicide by snakebite is no easy matter. But for a member of Egypt's royal family, a dramatic death by snakebite is a highly suitable end. As such, it is a death with a huge appeal to authors and artists. Soon after her suicide Horace, Virgil and Propertius each wrote about Cleopatra's demise, each incorporating the 'twin snakes of death' in his tale. Later writers, Shakespeare included, accepted the idea of the two snakes but transferred their bites from the arm to the breast. Today it is almost impossible to think of Cleopatra without thinking of the snake (or snakes) which might never have existed, yet which has become her defining symbol.

POSTSCRIPT

This book has covered the myths and legends told by the Dynastic Egyptians between the unification of the country in approximately 3100 BC and the death of Cleopatra VII, and Egypt's absorption by Rome, in 30 BC. It has included Egyptian tales recorded by Classical authors, but excluded the tales told about Egypt by other cultures. The Biblical story of Moses in the bullrushes and the Exodus from Egypt, for example, is omitted because, although it concerns Egypt, it is neither a historically documented event nor an Egyptian legend.

In the 2,000 years since Cleopatra's death, Egypt's myths and legends have continued to evolve. The more orthodox of the post-dynastic myths concern the established pantheon and, in particular, the mythology of Isis who is still worshipped today. The more spectacular – tales of royal curses, booby-trapped tombs and supernatural revenge – have tended to centre on the 1922 discovery of the tomb of Tutankhamen. Regretfully, these tales belong to a different book.

DRAMATIS PERSONAE
A GLOSSARY OF THE MAJOR GODS AND HEROES MENTIONED IN THIS BOOK

Their propensity to separate and combine makes it difficult to count Egypt's gods, but it has been estimated that there were approximately 1,500 named deities during the 3,000 years of the dynastic period. Given that some gods claimed a different name for every day of the year this is, if anything, an underestimate. Already large at the start of the dynastic age, the pantheon slowly but surely expanded as foreign deities were welcomed into the fold. Meanwhile, the state gods waxed and waned in popularity. Horus (Early Dynastic Period), Re (Old Kingdom) and Amen (New Kingdom) each served for a time as Egypt's principal god. Only once, during the short-lived Amarna Age, was there any attempt to restrict the number of gods; this experiment lasted for less than twenty years.

Agathoi Daemones: the 'good spirits' who took the form of snakes to protect the city of Alexandria and bless its inhabitants.

Ahwere: the dead heroine of the Late Period tale of *Setne I*.

Akar: an ancient earth god whose two sphinx-like heads faced away from each other.

Akhenaten: the 18th Dynasty pharaoh whose devotion to the Aten led him to ban many of Egypt's traditional gods and myths.

Alexander the Great: the conqueror who developed his own legends both within and outside Egypt.

Amaunet: the female counterpart and consort of Amen, and one of the Ogdoad of Hermopolis Magna.

Amen: 'the hidden one'. An extremely powerful creator deity and member of the Ogdoad of Hermopolis Magna, who became the god of Egypt's New Kingdom empire.

Amenemhat I: a murdered 12th Dynasty pharaoh, who appears to have left a helpful account of his own assassination.

Amenhotep III: the divine son of Amen-Re, who told the story of his own divine birth in the Luxor temple.

Amenhotep son of Hapu: an 18th Dynasty sage and architect, who was worshipped after death as a divine healer in the Theban area.

Amen-Kematef: the first primeval god, who took the form of a snake to fertilize the first egg.

Amen-Min: an ithyphallic fertility god of awesome potency.

Amen-Re: the immensely powerful fusion of the northern sun god Re and the southern warrior god Amen.

Ammit: the 'eater of the damned', equipped with the head of a crocodile, the foreparts and body of a lion or leopard and the hindparts of a hippopotamus.

Anath: the daughter of the Canaanite god El, who arrived in Egypt during the late Middle Kingdom. As 'the woman who acts like a warrior' she became a loyal daughter who protected both Re and all of Egypt's kings with her axe, spear and shield.

Andjety: the obscure god of Busiris, whose tale of resurrection was usurped by Osiris.

Ani: the deceased owner of a beautifully decorated *Book of the Dead*.

Anti: a falcon-headed god, who committed an awful crime and suffered severe punishment.

Anubis: (1) the elder of the eponymous 'Two Brothers' in a 19th Dynasty tale of lust, betrayal and wicked women; (2) the jackal-headed guardian of the cemeteries; and (3) the scientist who developed the art of mummifiction.

Anukis: a divine huntress, who wears a distinctive feathered headdress.

Apis bull: the earthly representative of Ptah.

Apophis: a malevolent serpent, who threatened to stop the night-boat of Re.

Astarte: the equivalent of the Babylonian goddess Ishtar and the Sumerian Inanna, associated with horses and chariots.

Aten: the mythless solar disk worshipped by Akhenaten and (perhaps under duress) his court.

Atum: 'lord of totality'. The creator god of Heliopolis, who became the ageing sun.

Babi: a baboon god, who both feasted off the entrails of the dead and helped the deceased to regain their sexual powers.

Banebdjedet: a ram god of great sexual prowess, who represented the souls of Osiris, Re-Atum, Shu and Geb.

Bastet: 'lady of the *bas*', or perfume jar. Initially the fierce lioness who nursed the dead king, Bastet later became a mild-mannered cat or cat-headed deity who protected mothers and pregnant women.

Bat: 'female spirit'; an early cow goddess.

Bata: the younger of the eponymous 'Two Brothers' in a 19th Dynasty tale of lust, betrayal and wicked women.

Benu: a shining solar bird with a phoenix-like ability to regenerate.

Bes: a dwarf demi-god, who brought comfort and protection to mothers and children, and who also offered protection against snakes.

Bestet: the female counterpart of the dwarf Bes.

Buchis bull: the earthly representative of Montu.

Cleopatra VII: Egypt's last queen. During her lifetime she was worshipped as the living incarnation of Isis; after death she developed (and still continues to develop) her own legends.

Dionysos: an eastern god offering a promise of resurrection to the faithful, who may be equated with the Egyptian Osiris.

Djadja-em-Ankh: a priest and magician who features in the *Papyrus Westcar*.

Djedi: a powerful living magician who visited the 4th Dynasty court of Khufu to perform the awesome feats of magic related in *Papyrus Westcar*.

Djehuty: an 'overseer of the army' of Tuthmosis III, who is credited with bringing a surprising and successful end to the siege of Joppa.

Djehuty-Nakht: the unscrupulous villain in the *Tale of the Eloquent Peasant*.

Djoser: a real 3rd Dynasty king who features in the fictional *Papyrus Westcar* and in the fictitious *Famine Stela*.

Doomed Prince: the hero of an 18th or 19th Dynasty fantasy, who married the beautiful daughter of the Prince of Naharin.

Eye of Atum (or **Eye of Re**): the fierce daughter of the creator god, who took the form of the uraeus to protect her father. This role may be played by any one of several solar goddesses.

Eye of Re: *see* Eye of Atum.

Falsehood: the villain in the *Tale of Truth and Falsehood*.

Four Sons of Horus: the deities who guarded the organs removed from the body during mummification. They are the human-headed Imseti (guardian of the liver), the baboon-headed Hapy (lungs), the dog-headed Duamutef (stomach) and the falcon-headed Qebehsenuef (intestines).

Geb: the earth god and one of Egypt's first kings.

Gengen: the celestial goose.

Great Tom Cat of Re: a knife-wielding feline who killed Apophis under the *ished* tree of Heliopolis.

Hapy: the plump god of the inundation.

Hardjedef: a real prince who features in the fictional *Papyrus Westcar* as a storyteller and friend of the magician Djedi. After his death Hardjedef was celebrated as a sage with some supernatural knowledge.

Harkhuf: a real-life Old Kingdom adventurer who brought the young Pepi II the precious gift of a dancing dwarf.

Harpocrates: the infant son of Isis and Serapis.

Hathor: an ancient bovine deity with strong solar connections and some stellar and lunar aspects. As *Hwt Hor* she is literally the 'house of Horus'. She had many diverse roles, but is perhaps best celebrated as the goddess associated with motherhood, sexual pleasure and drinking.

Hatmehit: 'she who is before the fishes', Egypt's only entirely piscine (or, perhaps, dolphin) deity.

Hatshepsut: an 18th Dynasty female pharaoh who tells the story of her own divine conception and birth on the walls of her Deir el-Bahri mortuary temple.

Hauhet: a primeval being; one of the Ogdoad of Hermopolis Magna.

Heh: a primeval being; one of the Ogdoad of Hermopolis Magna.

Heka: magic, or creative energy.

Heket: the frog midwife.

Heryshef: a god who emerged from the waters of Nun to serve as the 'lord of blood and butchery', and who protected the weak against evil.

Hesat: 'the wild one'; a cow goddess whose milk had strong healing powers.

Horakhty: 'Horus of the two horizons', an aspect of Horus specifically linked to the vigorous rising sun.

Horemakhet: 'Horus in the horizon', an aspect of Horus.

Horus (Horus-the-Elder or **Harwer; Haroeris** to the Greeks): both the lord of the sky and a sun god who represents living kingship.

Horus Khenty-en-irty: the eyeless Horus who relieved his anger by tormenting the evil dead.

Horus Khenty-irty: the calm and sighted counterpoint to the angry Horus Khenty-en-irty.

Horus-the-Child: the weak and accident-prone son of Isis; a permanent infant in need of constant protection.

Hu: authoritative speech.

Iah: the personification of the moon.

Ihy: the son of Hathor, who bears the titles 'lord of bread' and 'master of brewing'.

Imhotep: the 3rd Dynasty architect of Djoser's Sakkara step pyramid, who, after death, was worshipped as a wise man and accomplished healer.

Isis: the devoted sister-wife of Osiris and mother of Horus-the-Child. A member of the Ennead of Heliopolis, Isis became one of Egypt's most powerful and long-lasting deities.

Iusaas: the personification of the hand that Atum used to masturbate.

Kauket: a primeval being; one of the Ogdoad of Hermopolis Magna.

Kek: a primeval being; one of the Ogdoad of Hermopolis Magna.

Khaefre (Chephren): a real 4th Dynasty king who features in the fictional *Papyrus Westcar*.

Khentamentiu: 'foremost of the westerners'; the original canine god of the Abydos cemetery and patron of its Old Kingdom temple.

Khepri: the beetle who represented the young and vigorous morning sun.

Khepri-Re-Atum: a compound solar deity.

Khnum: the ram-headed craftsman who moulded mankind on his potter's wheel.

Khonsu: the lunar, perpetually young son of Amen.

Khufu (Cheops): a real 4th Dynasty king who is featured in the fictional *Papyrus Westcar* and who is given an unjustifiably bad press by the historian Herodotus.

Khun-Anup: the Eloquent Peasant, the talkative hero of a Middle Kingdom tale.

Lord of Punt: the snake who told his tale to the Shipwrecked Sailor.

Maat: the personification of the concept of truth, justice, the status quo and 'rightness'.

Mehen: the coiled snake who protects the night-boat of Re.

Mehet-Weret: a cow goddess who, born from the first waters, gave birth to Re in the primeval marsh and raised him into the sky on her horns.

Menhyt: an obscure lioness goddess.

Meretseger: the 'Peak of the West' who guarded the Theban necropolis.

Meskhenet: a midwife goddess who determined the status of the new-born.

Min: an ithyphallic creator god with a strong liking for lettuce.

Min-Amen-Kamutef: the 'bull of his mother'; a god who fornicated with his mother and so fathered himself.

Mnevis bull: the earthly representative of Re-Atum.

Montu: a falcon-headed warrior who served as principal state god during the Middle Kingdom.

Mut: the politically powerful consort of Amen and the mother or adoptive mother of Khonsu.

Mycerinus (Menkaure): the builder of the third Giza Pyramid, who has attracted a host of minor legends.

Naneferkaptah: the dead husband of Ahwere, heroine of the tale of *Setne I*.

Narmer: a real person recognized as the first king of unified Egypt, and the hero of the myths illustrated on the Narmer Palette.

Naunet: a primeval being; one of the Ogdoad of Hermopolis Magna.

Nebethetepet: a version of Iusaas who represents abundance.

Nebka: a real 3rd Dynasty king who is featured in the fictional *Papyrus Westcar*.

Nectanebo II: Egypt's last native king who, after vanishing, developed into a semi-legendary character.

Neferkare: the 6th Dynasty King Pepi II, who was suspected of an illicit relationship with a general.

Nefertem: the personification of the blue lotus.

Nehebu-Kau: a benign snake god.

Neith: one of Egypt's oldest goddesses; a warrior, weaver and creator.

Nekhbet: the vulture goddess of southern Egypt who was closely associated with the white crown.

Nemty: the ferryman in the *Contendings of Horus and Seth*, who defied orders and was punished severely for his disobedience.

Neper: a corn god, son of Renenutet.

Nephthys: the shadowy sister of Isis, Osiris and Seth.

Nitokris: the legendary, almost certainly fictional female king, whose dramatic death marks the end of the Old Kingdom.

Nun: the genderless, boundless primeval waters which carry the potential for life. Nun can be personified in the form of a human-form god who is often shown holding Re's solar boat in his raised arms.

Nut: the sister wife of Geb, who became the sky and the protector of the dead.

Onuris: a hunter god who tracked down and eventually married the fleeing daughter of Re.

Opet: 'the nurse', a hippopotamus goddess.

Osiris: the brother-husband of Isis, who first ruled Egypt and then, after his vicious murder, was brought back to a semblance of life to serve as king of the dead.

Ouroboros: a long, straight snake who swallowed his own tail to form an unbroken circle symbolizing eternity.

Pakhet: 'she who scratches'; a wild lioness who hunted by night in the deserts of Middle Egypt.

Ptah: the craftsman-creator god of Memphis.

Ptah-Sokar-Osiris: a triple deity representing the cycle of life.

Ramesses II: (in his own estimation) a great hero, who told the story of his own divine conception and birth.

Ramesses III: a murdered 20th Dynasty pharaoh.

Rat-tawi: a version of Hathor.

Re: the sun god; one of Egypt's oldest and most powerful beings.

Redjedet: the mother of divine triplets in *Papyrus Westcar*.

Re-Horakhty: a manifestation of Re as the strong rising sun.

Renenutet: 'she who nourishes'; the cobra goddess of the harvest. A divine nurse, Renenutet suckled babies in general and the king in particular.

Rhampsinitus: a mixture of the 19th Dynasty Ramesses II and the 20th Dynasty Ramesses III, who features in the writings of Herodotus.

Rhodophis: a courtesan of outstanding beauty; the forerunner of Cinderella.

Ruty: the twin or opposing lions who guarded the eastern and western horizons.

Sah: the constellation of Orion, and consort of Sothis.

Satis: the goddess guardian of Egypt's southern border.

Sekhmet: the 'powerful one', an uncompromising, fire-breathing lioness armed with an arsenal of plagues and pestilence.

Serapis: a Ptolemaic combination of Osiris and the Greek deities Dionysos, Hades, Asklepios, Helios and Zeus. Serapis personifies divine kingship, healing, fertility and the afterlife.

Serket: the scorpion, 'she who causes the throat to breathe', is another Eye of Re with strong healing powers.

Seshat: the patroness of mathematics, recording, architecture and astronomy.

Seth: the brother of Osiris, Isis and Nephthys, who murdered Osiris in a bid to become king of Egypt, but who later lost his crown to his nephew Horus.

Setne Khaemwaset: the hero of a cycle of Late Period tales, based on the real-life *sem*-priest Khaemwaset, son of Ramesses II.

Seven Hathors: seven aspects of Hathor who, at the birth of a child, could look into the future to see the timing and manner of that child's death.

Shai: the personification of destiny.

Shed: 'saviour'; an aspect of Horus-the-Child who might appear armed with a bow or sword to ward off wild animals.

Sheshmetet: a lioness goddess who stood with Sekhmet, Wadjet and Bastet to guard the dead Osiris.

Shipwrecked Sailor: an anonymous hero who had an exciting marine adventure and talked to a giant snake.

Shu: the atmosphere. The husband-brother of Tefnut, who separated his children Geb and Nut.

Sia: perception.

Sinuhe: the hero of a Middle Kingdom story who fled Egypt only to discover that there was no place like home.

Si-Osiri: a powerful magician who takes his father, Setne, on a visit to the halls of the afterlife.

Snefru: a bored 4th Dynasty king who features in *Papyrus Westcar*.

Sobek: the crocodile who is both a life-enhancing fertility god closely linked with kingship and royal power, and the merciless one 'who takes women from their husbands whenever he wishes'.

Sokar: an ancient craftsman deity associated with metalwork, the cemetery and the afterlife.

Sothis: Soped, or Sirius the Dog Star. The heliacal rising of Sothis on the eastern horizon at dawn, after an absence of seventy days, heralded the start of the agricultural year.

Tabubu: the irresistible but thoroughly evil daughter of the priest of Bastet, who tempted Setne Khaemwaset.

Tatenen: the personification of Egypt emerging from the annual inundation.

Taweret: a pregnant hippopotamus who protects women and babies in childbirth.

Tefen: a large, bold scorpion who featured in the myth of Isis and the seven scorpions.

Tefnut: the moist sister-wife of Shu, mother of Geb and Nut.

Thoth: the wise scribe of the gods, who may take the form of either an ibis or a baboon.

Truth: the good brother in the *Tale of Truth and Falsehood*.

Tutankhamen: the restorer of the traditional mythologies following the brief 18th Dynasty 'Amarna heresy'.

Tuthmosis III: a heroic king, the victor of the battle of Megiddo.

Tuthmosis IV: the dream-inspired restorer of the sphinx.

Two Ladies: the goddesses Wadjyt and Nekhbet.

Universal Lord: Re-Atum-Horakhty-Atum, a powerful combination of all the aspects of the sun god.

Wadjet: the cobra goddess of northern Egypt, who was associated with the red crown and who acted as the protector of the king.

Webaoner: a skilled magician with an unfaithful wife, featured in *Papyrus Westcar*.

Wenamun: hero of a fictional Late Period voyage.

Wepwawet: Lord of Abydos, an ancient cemetery jackal.

Weret-Hekau: 'Great in Magic', a cobra or lioness who personified the magic of the royal crowns and served as the uraeus.

CHRONOLOGICAL TABLE

PREDYNASTIC PERIOD *c.*5300–3100 BC

Various prehistoric cultures including, in the Nile Valley:
Badarian cultural phase
Nagada I cultural phase (also known as the Amratian)
Nagada II cultural phase (also known as the Gerzean)

EARLY DYNASTIC PERIOD *c.*3100–2686 BC

Nagada III cultural phase / Dynasty 0 c.3200–3050 BC
Ending with:
Narmer

1st Dynasty c.3050–2890 BC
Aha
Djer
Djet
Den
Meritneith (female pharaoh)
Anedjib
Semerkhet
Qa'a

2nd Dynasty c.2890–2686 BC

Hetepsekhemwy

Raneb

Ninetjer

Weneg

Sened

Peribsen

Khasekhemwy

OLD KINGDOM *c.2686–2181* BC

3rd Dynasty c.2686–2613 BC

Nebka/Sanakht?

Netjerikhet Djoser

Sekhemkhet

Khaba

Nebka/Sanakht?

Huni

4th Dynasty c.2613–2494 BC

Snefru

Khufu

Djedefre

Khaefre

Menkaure

Shepseskaf

5th Dynasty c.2494–2345 BC

Userkaf

Sahure

Neferirkare-Kakai

Shepseskare

Raneferef

Niuserre
Menkauhor
Djedkare-Isesi
Unas

6th Dynasty c.2345–2181 BC
Teti
Userkare?
Pepi I
Merenre I
Pepi II
Merenre II ?
Nitokris? (female, possibly fictitious, pharaoh)

FIRST INTERMEDIATE PERIOD c.2181–2055 BC

7th–8th Dynasties c.2181–2160 BC
A series of ephemeral pharaohs named Neferkare

9–10th Dynasties c.2160–2025 BC
A series of ephemeral pharaohs from Herakleopolis Magna

11th Dynasty (first part) c.2151–2055 BC
A series of increasingly influential local Theban rulers overlapping
with Dynasties 9 and 10

MIDDLE KINGDOM c.2055–1650 BC

11th Dynasty (second part) c.2055–1985 BC
Montuhotep II
Montuhotep III
Montuhotep IV

12th Dynasty c.1985–1773 BC
Amenemhat I
Senwosret I
Amenemhat II
Senwosret II
Senwosret III
Amenemhat III
Amenemhat IV
Sobeknofru (female pharaoh)

13th Dynasty c.1773–1650 BC
A series of short-lived kings of diminishing national importance

SECOND INTERMEDIATE PERIOD *c.*1650–1550 BC

14th Dynasty
A line of ephemeral rulers of uncertain date contemporary with
Dynasties 13 and 15

15th Dynasty c.1650–1550 BC
Foreign 'Hyksos' kings rule northern Egypt

16th Dynasty c.1650–1580 BC
Theban kings descended from Dynasty 13 and contemporary
with Dynasty 15 rule southern Egypt

17th Dynasty c.1580–1550 BC
A line of strong Theban pharaohs ending with:
    Senakhtenre Taa I
    Sekenenre Taa II
    Kamose

NEW KINGDOM *c.*1550–1069 BC

18th Dynasty c.1550–1295 BC
Ahmose I
Amenhotep I
Tuthmosis I
Tuthmosis II
Tuthmosis III
Hatshepsut (female pharaoh)
Amenhotep II
Tuthmosis IV
Amenhotep III
Amenhotep IV/Akhenaten
Neferneferuaten?
Tutankhamen
Ay
Horemheb

19th Dynasty c.1295–1186 BC
Ramesses I
Seti I
Ramesses II
Merenptah
Amenmessu
Seti II
Siptah
Tawosret (female pharaoh)

20th Dynasty c.1186–1069 BC
Sethnakht
Ramesses III
Ramesses IV
Ramesses V
Ramesses VI

Ramesses VII
Ramesses VIII
Ramesses IX
Ramesses X
Ramesses XI

THIRD INTERMEDIATE PERIOD *c.*1069–715 BC

21st Dynasty c.1069–945 BC
Smendes
Amenemnisu
Pasebkhanut (Psusennes) I
Amenemope
Osorkon the Elder
Siamun
Psusennes II

22nd (Libyan) Dynasty c.945–715 BC
Sheshonk I
Osorkon I
Sheshonk II
Takeloth I
Osorkon II
Takeloth II
Sheshonk III
Pimay
Sheshonk V
Osorkon IV

23rd Dynasty c.818–715 BC
Contemporary with the 22nd and 24th Dynasties. The precise
order and dates of the kings are uncertain

24th Dynasty c.724–715 BC
Bakenrenef

LATE PERIOD *c.715–332* BC

25th (Nubian) Dynasty c.715–672 BC
(Piye)
Shabaqo
Shebitqo
Taharka
Tanutamani

26th (Saite) Dynasty 672–525 BC
Nekau I
Psamtek I (Psammetichus)
Nekau II
Psamtek II
Wahibre (Apries)
Ahmose II (Amasis)
Psamtek III

27th (First Persian) Dynasty 525–404 BC
Egypt ruled by remote Persian kings

28th Dynasty 404–399 BC
Amyrtaios

29th Dynasty 399–380 BC
Nefarud I
Hakor
Nefarud II

30th Dynasty 380–343 BC
Nectanebo I

Djedhor (Teos)
Nectanebo II

31st (Second Persian) Dynasty 343–332 BC
Egypt ruled by remote Persian kings

MACEDONIAN AND PTOLEMAIC PERIODS 332–30 BC

Macedonian Dynasty 332–304 BC
Alexander III 'The Great'
Philip Arrhidaeos
Alexander IV

Ptolemaic Dynasty 304–30 BC
Ptolemy I Soter I
Ptolemy II Philadelphos
Ptolemy III Euergetes I
Ptolemy IV Philopator
Ptolemy V Epiphanes
Ptolemy VI Philometor
Ptolemy VIII Euergetes II
Ptolemy IX Soter II
Ptolemy X Alexander I
Berenice III Thea Philopator and Ptolemy XI Alexander II
Ptolemy XII Neos Dionysos
Cleopatra VII Thea Philopator and Ptolemy XIII
Cleopatra VII Thea Philopator and Ptolemy XIV
Cleopatra VII Thea Philopator and Ptolemy XV Caesar Theos
  Philopator Philometor

ACKNOWLEDGEMENTS AND PERMISSIONS

I first explored some of the themes developed in this book while writing *Tales from Ancient Egypt* (2004, Bolton), a limited edition book published to support the ongoing fieldwork by Liverpool University at the Ramesside fortress site of Zawiyet Umm el-Rakham. I am grateful to the directors of Rutherford Press Limited for permission to revisit themes presented in that work, and to Steven Snape for permission to reuse his translation of the *Great Hymn to the Aten*.

In most cases I have chosen to retell the ancient stories rather than provide a straight translation of the surviving texts. However, where it seemed appropriate that the Egyptians should be allowed to speak for themselves, I have used direct translations. Dr Patricia Spencer, Director of the Egypt Exploration Society, kindly gave permission to quote from the *Journal of Egyptian Archaeology*, and Penguin Books gave permission for me to quote from the A. de Sélincourt translation of Herodotus (1954, revised 1996). Permission to use extracts from the beautiful translations given in Miriam Lichtheim's *Ancient Egyptian Literature* (3 volumes, 1973–80) was given by the Regents of the University of California. Oxford University Press gave permission to quote from R. O. Faulkner's translations of the *Pyramid Texts* (1969) and Oxbow Books gave permission to quote from R. O. Faulkner's translations of the *Coffin Texts* (three volumes, 1973–8). The author and publishers have made every attempt to trace the copyright holders of quoted material. Any omissions will be rectified on notification.

I would like to thank Richard Duguid and the staff at Penguin for all their hard work. Janet Tyrrell worked extremely hard on the text. My editor, Georgina Laycock, deserves my particular gratitude as she has exhibited enthusiasm, encouragement and patience far beyond the call of duty while working with me. It is entirely due to her that the forces of *maat* managed to triumph over the sea of chaos that threatened at times to overwhelm me.

The students and staff of the KNH Centre for Biomedical Egyptology, the Manchester University online Certificate Course in Egyptology and the Manchester Museum have all, in various ways, opened my eyes a little bit wider to the frequent delights and occasional horrors of studying the ancient world. Philippa Snape has contributed stimulating discussion and the loan of several books. I owe a huge and hitherto unacknowledged debt to Professor Christopher Eyre, whose lectures so many years ago inspired my interest in ancient Egypt. I am not sure if he will be amused or horrified to be mentioned here – but I thank him anyway.

Finally, as always, I must thank my family – my husband Steven, daughter Philippa, son Jack and mother Anne – for their continued encouragement and support.

NOTES

INTRODUCTION

1 From the Late Period *Papyrus Insinger*, Instruction 24. Translation by Lichtheim (1980: 209–11).

2 Singular, ostracon: an inscribed flake of stone or piece of broken pottery.

3 Singular, stela: a carved and/or painted stone slab.

4 Translation by Lichtheim (1976: 113).

5 Translation by Ebbell (1937: 70–71). *Papyrus Ebers* is housed in the University of Leipzig Library.

6 Translation by Breasted (1930: I, 474). *Papyrus Edwin Smith* is housed in the New York Academy of Medicine.

7 Edwards (1877, revised 1888: 434).

8 Blackman (1927, revised 2000: 268).

9 El-Shamy (1980: 3).

10 The *Ramesseum Dramatic Papyrus* is the script of a play or ritual to be performed in honour of King Senwosret I by actors who not only took the roles of gods, but who also executed set actions, such as eating a meal, using specific props.

11 The extracts from the *Pyramid Texts* quoted throughout this book are based on the translations of R. O. Faulkner (1969) and the spell numbers follow his system. Although now somewhat dated, these translations remain the most immediately

accessible for non-specialist readers. Those with an interest in this branch of Egyptian literature/theology should also consult the recent translations and commentaries presented in Allen (2005).

12 Translation by Faulkner (1969: 124).

13 To establish consistency with the *Pyramid Texts*, and for ease of access to the entire published corpus, the extracts from the *Coffin Texts* quoted throughout this book are based on the translations given in Faulkner (1973–8).

14 Chests which held the preserved viscera of the deceased.

15 Translation by Faulkner (1973: 111).

16 The majority of the extracts from the *Book of the Dead* quoted throughout this book come from the *Book* prepared for the funeral of Ani (British Museum). This 78-foot-long, illustrated papyrus allows us an intimate glimpse of the determined Ani and his pale wife Tutu, who have dressed in their finest white garments to face their destiny. Translation by Faulkner (1972: Plate 17).

17 *Histories* 2: 35. Translation by de Sélincourt (1996: 98).

18 Hierakonpolis Tomb 100: this tomb is now lost.

19 As both Maat and the queen consort are the constant female companion of the king, it is not surprising that their roles, duties and even appearance came to be somewhat confused, so that, for example, Tiy, beloved wife of the 18th Dynasty King Amenhotep III, could be described as 'in the following of the king just as Maat is in the following of [the sun god] Re'.

1 SUNRISE: THE NINE GODS OF HELIOPOLIS

20 British Museum 10188.

21 Plutarch, *Isis and Osiris*, Moralia V: 74. Translation by Babbitt (1936).

22 Translation by Faulkner (1969: 198).

23 Translation by Faulkner (1973: 77–8).

24 Discussed with translation in J. J. Janssen (1988), Marriage Problems and Public Reactions, in J. Baines et al. (eds.), *Pyramid Studies and Other Essays Presented to I. E. S. Edwards*, London: 134–7.

25 Uraeus (plural uraei) is a non-Egyptian word derived from the Greek *ouraios*, meaning 'risen one'. In the living Egypt the uraeus was worn by kings from the 1st Dynasty reign of Den onwards; later, queens and gods, too, might be protected by the rearing cobra on the brow. While kings generally wore one uraeus, queens might wear two or three on the brow, or might wear a circle of uraei as the base of a more elaborate crown.

26 In the short period between Nut giving birth at first light and the sun appearing on the horizon, the young sun is able to develop strength and 'become effective'.

2 ALTERNATIVE CREATION

27 The compass being unknown to the ancient Egyptians, the cardinal points were determined by reference to the river and the sky.

28 Translation by Lichtheim (1980: 45–8: 47).

29 Translation by Lichtheim (1976: 109–10).

30 Louvre Museum E 17110.

31 British Museum 498.

32 The story that Shabaqo preserves is the 'Logos' doctrine – creation through the spoken word. This, foreshadowing the Bible by many years – 'And God said, "Let there be light" ' (Genesis 1:3); 'In the Beginning was the Word, and the Word was with God, and the Word was God' (John 1:1) – is an abstract and sophisticated story, which confirms not only the creation of man by gods, but the establishment of the political structure by Ptah.

33 Translation by Lichtheim (1973: 51–7: 55).

34 *Histories* 3: 29. Translation by de Sélincourt (1996: 165).

35 Dorman (1999: 83–99: 82).

36 Translation by Lichtheim (1980: 111–15: 112).

37 These statues are now displayed in the Ashmolean Museum, Oxford.

3 SUNSET

38 This tale, although loosely based on a muddle of events occurring during the reigns of Amenhotep III and Ramesses II, has no historical validity.

39 An abbreviated version of the Khonsu Cosmogony. Translation by L. H. Lesko (1991: 105).

40 The *Brooklyn Snake Papyrus* in Brooklyn Museum 47.218.48 and 47.218.85; the papyrus has two museum numbers because it has been cut in half.

41 Translation by Faulkner (1977: 65).

42 Translation by Faulkner (1937: 168).

43 Some 26th Dynasty tomb walls do include *mehen* scenes in their deliberately archaic decoration, but there is no evidence to suggest that the game was actually being played at this late date.

44 *Papyrus Leningrad* 1115, housed in the Hermitage Museum, St Petersburg.

4 THE DEATH OF OSIRIS

45 Louvre Museum C286. Translation by Lichtheim (1976: 83).

46 *Library of History*, 1:21. Translation by Oldfather (1933: 65).

47 Plutarch, *Moralia: Concerning Isis and Osiris*.

48 Natron is a naturally occurring salt used by the ancient

Egyptians to desiccate the body during the mummification process.

49 Plutarch, *Isis and Osiris*, Moralia V: 18. Translation by Babbitt (1936).

50 For a translation of this stela see Lichtheim (1973: 124–5). The stela is currently housed in the Berlin Museum.

51 Today it is housed in Ismailiya Museum.

52 See J. J. Janssen and P. W. Pestman (1968), Burial and Inheritance in the Community of the Necropolis Workmen at Thebes, *Journal of the Economic and Social History of the Orient* 11:137–170: 140.

5 *THE CONTENDINGS OF HORUS AND SETH*

53 Just one copy of the lengthy story known today as *The Contendings of Horus and Seth* has survived on a papyrus which originally belonged to the Theban clerk of works Qenherkhepshef. *Papyrus Chester Beatty I* (Chester Beatty Library and Gallery, Dublin) is dated to the 20th Dynasty reign of Ramesses V, but it tells a far more ancient tale, and we can already identify disjointed elements of the myth in the spells of the *Pyramid Texts*. The back of the papyrus preserves a cycle of love songs.

54 *Ostracon Oriental Institute 12073*: discussed in J. Cerny (1973), *A Community of Workmen at Thebes in the Ramesside Period*, Cairo: 282–3; A. G. McDowell (1990), *Jurisdiction in the Workmen's Community at Thebes*, Leiden: 180–81.

55 *Papyrus Jumilhac* (Louvre Museum) explains how Anubis buried the eyes of Horus on a mountainside; when Isis watered the ground they were re-animated, and the first grapevine was created.

56 British Museum 10042.

57 Translation by Griffiths (1960: 33–4). *Papyrus Hearst* is today

housed in the Bancroft Library, University of California.

58 Neferkare's story survives in two Late Period forms – a writing-board in the Oriental Institute (Chicago 13539) and *Papyrus Chassinat I* (Louvre Museum).

59 Griffith (1898): PL3, VI 12, 1.31–6.

6 AT THE END OF TIME

60 *Histories* 2: 86. Translation by de Sélincourt (1996: 115).

61 The decorated tombs in the Valley of the Kings generally show twelve portals, each bearing the name of a goddess and each protected by a guardian and a fire-spitting snake.

62 *Book of the Dead,* ch. 125. Spell 14, in contrast, admits the possibility that the deceased may have done some inadvertent wrong, and seeks to diminish Osiris' anger.

63 Ch. 30A. Translation by Faulkner (rev. edn 1994: 103).

64 Extract from the funerary stela of Taimhotep, British Museum 147. Translation by Lichtheim (1980: 63).

65 Kemp (2007: 44).

66 *Setne Khamwas and Si-Osire* (*Setne II*), British Museum papyrus 604.

67 Translation by Faulkner (1978: 168).

68 Translation by Faulkner (1972, rev. edn, 1994: Plate 29).

7 THE GOLDEN ONE

69 Archaeological evidence suggests that Egypt's prehistoric pastoralists felt a strong, even spiritual, link to the bulls and cows that played such an important role in their daily lives. Images of cattle, and small carved cattle figurines, were produced throughout the Predynastic Age and included among the grave-goods of the elite. While the Neolithic Western Desert herders of Nabta Playa buried disarticulated cattle, and at least

one articulated cow, under tumuli, the Badarian peoples of the Nile Valley buried their cattle (and occasional sheep, antelopes, cats and dogs) apart from, beside or even within human graves. A more specific association between cattle and human burials is apparent as early as 10,000 BC, when the horn-cores of wild cattle were used as grave markers at the Nubian-Egyptian site of Tushka. This linking of cattle with human mortuary rituals continued into the dynastic period, so that the 1st Dynasty tomb of the official Sekhemka (Sakkara Tomb 3504) was provided with a low bench for the display of 300 model bull heads fitted with real horns.

70 The goddess Soped, the personification of the Dog Star, certainly started life as a cow, although later she would be identified with Isis.

71 The *menyt* is technically the counterpoise to a heavy, beaded necklace.

72 Mortal kings are frequently depicted suckling from Hathor in either cow or human form.

73 The *Book of the Cow of Heaven* is a collection of spells preserved in varying degrees of completeness on the walls and furnishings of the New Kingdom rock-cut tombs of Tutankhamen, Seti I and Ramesses II, III and VI in the Valley of the Kings. As the story is written in Middle Egyptian language, it is likely that it was actually composed during the Middle Kingdom.

74 *Papyrus Harris 500*, British Museum.

75 *Histories* 2: 60. Translation by de Sélincourt (1996: 108).

76 *Pyramid Texts* spell 508 makes Bastet's role clear.

8 ISIS: GREAT OF MAGIC

77 See, for example, *Papyrus Ebers* recipe 69; *Book of the Dead* spell 156.

78 Translation by Faulkner (1936: 122).

79 This is made most obvious in the 18th Dynasty Deir el-Bahri mortuary temple built by the female King Hatshepsut on a site already sacred to Hathor. Hatshepsut, who felt a strong devotion to the goddess, included a Hathor temple within her mortuary complex and this became Khemmis, with Hathor playing the role of mother of Horus. Images of Hathor taking the form of a cow to lick and suckle Hatshepsut reflect the tradition that Hathor acted as wet-nurse to Horus-the-Child. See E. Naville (1895–1908), *The Temple of Deir el-Bahari* IV, London: 4.

80 *Histories* 2: 156. Translation by de Sélincourt (1996: 144–5).

81 Metropolitan Museum of Art, New York, 50.85.

82 A full translation with commentary is given in Griffiths (1960: 51–2). The initial interpretation of this text had the roles of Horus and Seth reversed.

9 WARRIORS AND WISE WOMEN

83 *Vienna Demotic Papyrus* 6165.

84 Translation by Lichtheim (1976: 107–9: 108). We previously met Neferabu in Chapter 2, where he was bemoaning his stupidity in offending Ptah. Clearly, Neferabu was not a man to learn from past experience.

85 Carter and Mace (1923: 119–20).

86 Experts who have studied and interpreted the shrine include, among others, Bosse-Griffiths (1973), Eaton-Krauss and Graefe (1985) and Roberts (2008).

87 In animal form Neith may be either a cow or a snake.

88 Plutarch, *Isis and Osiris*, Moralia V: 9. Translation by Babbitt (1936).

89 Alongside Neith, Tayet was a goddess of weaving and Renenutet could also supply funerary bandages.

90 The same vulture headdress was worn by most of Egypt's queens from the 4th Dynasty onwards but, for some unknown reason, was not worn during the Middle Kingdom.

91 They are mentioned in *The Contendings of Horus and Seth* as the daughters of the Universal Lord and potential brides for Seth.

92 British Museum ESA 10687.

93 The story of *Astarte and the Insatiable Sea* is recorded on the badly fragmented *Papyrus Amhurst 9* (Pierpont Morgan Library, New York; the first page is now recognized as *Papyrus Bibliothèque Nationale 202*, Paris). This abbreviated version has been heavily reconstructed.

10 DIVINE KINGS

94 Berlin Museum 3033. Analysis of the language employed indicates that the papyrus was written during the Second Intermediate Period, but the stories themselves appear to be Middle Kingdom in origin.

95 *Histories* 2: 111. Translation by de Sélincourt (1996: 123–4).

96 Translation by Faulkner (1969: 99).

97 *Papyrus Leningrad 1116B*.

98 The mask is housed in Manchester Museum. The figure of a naked, lion-headed woman figure – Bestet? – was recovered from the same house, but is today lost.

99 For a full translation with commentary of the autobiographical inscription of Harkhuf, consult Lichtheim (1973: 23–7).

100 *Papyrus Leiden 344*.

101 This small Dendera temple is now reconstructed in the atrium of Cairo Museum.

102 For a full publication of the temple see Naville (1895–1908). The scenes and texts detailing Hatshepsut's birth myth are published in volume 2.

103 The male Egyptian sphinx should not be confused with the female Greek sphinx, who famously guarded the Greek city of Thebes and set riddles for Oedipus (and, more recently, for Harry Potter).

104 Translation by Kitchen (1996: 99–110).

105 Translation by S. Snape (Tyldesley, 1998: 86–7).

11 TALES OF GODS AND MEN

106 *Papyrus Berlin* 3024.

107 *Papyrus Berlin* 3023, 3025 and 10499, and *Papyrus British Museum* ESA 10274.

108 *Papyrus d'Orbiney*, British Museum 10183.

109 *Papyrus Chester Beatty* II, British Museum 10682.

110 *Papyrus Moscow* 120.

111 As a southerner, Wenamun dates the key events of his adventure using the 'Renaissance Era' dates introduced by Herihor. Year 5 mentioned by Wenamun therefore equates to Year 23 of Ramesses XI. But the dates he gives have no chronological logic. Following Lichtheim (1976: 229) I have amended his first date, 'day 16 of the fourth month of summer, Year 5', so that it reads 'second month of summer' – this makes better sense if Wenamun stays in Tanis 'until the fourth month of summer'. Similarly, it is likely that Wenamun sails down to the great Syrian Sea on the 'first day of the first month of the inundation' rather than the 'first day of the first month of summer'.

12 A DEVELOPING MYTHOLOGY

112 Translation by Ray (2002: 15).

113 British Museum 886. We have already considered the funerary stela of Pasherenptah's wife Taimhotep.

114 Later, the Asklepion would be identified as the prison where the Old Testament Joseph was briefly incarcerated.

115 Revelation 16:16.

116 British Museum EA 10060.

117 The sad history of the discovery and plundering of Djehuty's tomb is detailed in Reeves (2000: 30–31). Today, Djehuty's tomb is once again lost, his mummy is presumably destroyed and his grave-goods are scattered, largely unidentified, through-out various collections, including the Louvre.

118 *Histories* 2: 126. Translation by de Sélincourt (1996: 132–3).

119 ibid: 2: 100. Translation by de Sélincourt (1996: 120).

120 *Setne I*, Cairo Museum 30646; *Setne II*, British Museum 604.

121 Plutarch, *The Parallel Lives: Life of Antony* 85–6, translation by Perrin (1920); Cassius Dio, *Roman History* 51: 13–14, translation by Cary (1914–27).

BIBLIOGRAPHY AND
FURTHER READING

Allam, S. (1992) Legal Aspects in the 'Contendings of Horus and Seth', in A. Lloyd (ed.), *Studies in Pharaonic Religion and Society in Honour of J. Gwyn Griffiths*, London: 137–45.

Allen, J. P. (1988) *Genesis in Egypt: the Philosophy of Ancient Egyptian Creation Accounts*, New Haven.

—— (2005) *The Ancient Egyptian Pyramid Texts*, Atlanta.

Arnold, D. (1999) *Temples of the Last Pharaohs*, Oxford and New York.

Assmann, J. (2001) *The Search for God in Ancient Egypt*, trans. D. Lorton, New York.

Baines, J. (1982) Interpreting Sinuhe, *Journal of Egyptian Archaeology* 68: 31–44.

—— (1990) Interpreting the Story of the Shipwrecked Sailor, *Journal of Egyptian Archaeology* 76: 55–72.

—— (1991) Egyptian Myth and Discourse: Myth, Gods, and the Early Written and Iconographic Record, *Journal of Near Eastern Studies* 50 (2): 81–105.

—— et al.(eds)(1988) *Pyramid Studies and Other Essays Presented to I. E. S. Edwards*, London.

Berman, L. M. (1998) Overview of Amenhotep III and his Reign, in D. O'Connor and E. Cline (eds), *Amenhotep III: Perspectives on his Reign*, Ann Arbor: 1–26.

Blackman, W. S. (1927, revised 2000) *The Fellahin of Upper Egypt*, ed. S. Ikram, Cairo.

Borghouts, J. F. (1973) The Evil Eye of Apopis, *Journal of Egyptian Archaeology* 59: 114–49.

—— (1978) *Ancient Egyptian Magical Texts*, Leiden.

Bosse-Griffiths, K. (1973) The Great Enchantress in the Little Golden Shrine of Tutankhamun, *Journal of Egyptian Archaeology* 59: 100–108.

—— (1976) Further Remarks on *Wrt Hkw*, *Journal of Egyptian Archaeology* 62: 181–2.

Breasted, J. H. (1930) *The Edwin Smith Surgical Papyrus*, 2 vols, Chicago.

Buck, A. de (1935–56) *The Egyptian Coffin Texts*, Chicago.

Carter, H. and Mace, A. C. (1923) *The Tomb of Tut.ank.Amen: Search, Discovery and Clearance of the Antechamber*, London.

Cassius Dio, *Roman History*, trans. E. Cary (1914–27), 9 vols, Cambridge, Mass. and London.

Clark, R. T. Rundle (1959) *Myth and Symbol in Ancient Egypt*, London.

Cline, E. H. and O'Connor, D. (eds) (2006) *Thutmose III: A New Biography*, Ann Arbor.

David, A. R. (1982) *The Ancient Egyptians: Religious Beliefs and Practices*, London.

Diodorus Siculus, *Library of History*, Book I, trans. C. H. Oldfather (1933), vol. I, Cambridge, Mass. and London.

Dorman, P. F. (1999) Creation on the Potter's Wheel at the Eastern Horizon of Heaven, in E. Teeter and J. A. Larson (eds), *Gold of Praise: Studies on Ancient Egypt in Honor of Edward F. Wente*, Chicago: 83–99.

Eaton-Krauss, M. and Graefe, E. (1985) *The Small Golden Shrine from the Tomb of Tutankhamun*, Oxford.

Ebbell, B. (1937) *The Papyrus Ebers: the Greatest Egyptian Medical Document*, Copenhagen.

Edwards, A. B. (1877, revised 1888) *A Thousand Miles up the Nile*, London.

El-Daly, O. (2005) *Egyptology: the Missing Millennium; Ancient Egypt in Medieval Arabic Writings*, London.

El-Din, S. B. (2006) *A Guide to the Reptiles and Amphibians of Egypt*, Cairo.

El-Hawary, A. (2007) New Findings about the Memphite Theology, in J.-C. Goyon and C. Cardin (eds), *Proceedings of the Ninth International Congress of Egyptologists* 1: 567–74.

El-Shamy, H. (1980) *Folktales of Egypt*, Chicago.

Erman, A. (1911) *Hymnen an das Diadem der Pharaonen*, Berlin.

—— (1927) *The Literature of the Ancient Egyptians,* trans. A. M. Blackman, London. (Also published as *Ancient Egyptians: a Sourcebook of Their Writings*, New York, 1966.)

Eyre, C. J. (1976) Fate, Crocodiles and Judgement of the Dead: Some Mythological Allusions in Egyptian Literature, *Studien zur Altägyptischen Kultur* 4: 103–14.

—— (1992) Yet Again the Wax Crocodile, *Journal of Egyptian Archaeology* 78: 280–81.

—— (1999) Irony in the Story of Wenamun: the Politics of Religion in the 21st Dynasty, in J. Assmann and E. Blumenthal (eds), *Literatur und Politik im Pharaonischen und Ptolemäischen Ägypten*, Institut Français d'Archéologie Orientale: 235–52.

—— (2002) *The Cannibal Hymn: A Cultural and Literary Study*, Liverpool.

Faulkner, R. O. (1933) *The Papyrus Bremner-Rhind*, Brussels.

—— (1936) The Bremner-Rhind Papyrus – I, *Journal of Egyptian Archaeology* 22 (2): 121–40.

—— (1937) The Bremner-Rhind Papyrus – III, *Journal of Egyptian Archaeology* 23 (2): 166–85.

—— (1938) The Bremner-Rhind Papyrus – IV, *Journal of Egyptian Archaeology* 24 (1): 41–53.

—— (1969) *The Ancient Egyptian Pyramid Texts*, Oxford.

—— (1973) *The Ancient Egyptian Coffin Texts I: Spells 1–354*, Warminster.

—— (1977) *The Ancient Egyptian Coffin Texts II: Spells 355–787*, Warminster.

—— (1978) *The Ancient Egyptian Coffin Texts III: Spells 788–1185*, Warminster.

—— (rev. edn, 1994) *The Egyptian Book of the Dead: the Book of Going Forth by Day*, with contributions by J. Wasserman, C. A. R. Andrews and O. Goelet, San Francisco. (First published 1972.)

Foster, J. L. (1992) *Echoes of Egyptian Voices: an Anthology of Ancient Egyptian Poetry*, Norman and London.

Frankfort, H. (1948) *Kingship and the Gods: a Study of Near Eastern Religion as the Integration of Society and Nature*, Chicago and London.

Germond, P. (1981) *Sekhmet et la Protection du Monde*, Basle and Geneva.

Gillam, R. A. (1995) Priestesses of Hathor: Their Function, Decline and Disappearance, *Journal of the American Research Center in Egypt* 32: 211–37.

—— (2005) *Performance and Drama in Ancient Egypt*, London.

Goelet, O., Jr (1991) The Blessing of Ptah, in E. Bleiberg and R. Freed (eds), *Fragments of a Shattered Visage: the Proceedings of the International Symposium of Ramesses the Great*, Memphis: 28–37.

Goodison, L. and Morris, C. (eds) (1998) *Ancient Goddesses*, London.

Griffith, F. Ll. (1890) *The Antiquities of Tell el Yahudiya and Miscellaneous Work in Lower Egypt During the Years 1887–1888*, London.

—— (1898) *Hieratic Papyri from Kahun and Gurob*, London.

Griffiths, J. G. (1960) *The Conflict of Horus and Seth from Egyptian and Classical Sources*, Liverpool.

—— (1970) *Plutarch's De Iside et Osiride*, Cardiff.

Hart, G. (2003) *Egyptian Myths*, London. (Published both as an individual title and as part of a compilation volume entitled *World of Myths*.)

Herodotus, *The Histories*, trans. A. de Sélincourt (1996), revised edn with introduction and notes by J. Marincola, London. (First published 1954.)

Hollis, S. T. (1990) *The Ancient Egyptian 'Tale of Two Brothers': the Oldest Fairy Tale in the World*, Norman.

—— (1998) Otiose Deities and the Ancient Egyptian Pantheon, *Journal of the American Research Center in Egypt* 35: 61–72.

Hornung, E. (1982) *Conceptions of God in Ancient Egypt: the One and the Many*, trans. J. Baines, New York.

—— (1999) *The Ancient Egyptian Books of the Afterlife*, trans. D. Lorton, New York and London.

Johnson, S. B. (1990) *The Cobra Goddess of Ancient Egypt: Predynastic, Early Dynastic and Old Kingdom Periods*, London and New York.

Kemp, B. J. (2007) *How to Read the Ancient Egyptian Book of the Dead*, London.

Kirk, G. S. (1970) *Myth: Its Meaning and Function in Ancient and Other Cultures*, Cambridge and Berkeley.

Kitchen, K. A. (1982) *Pharaoh Triumphant: the Life and Times of Ramesses II*, Warminster.

—— (1996) *Ramesside Inscriptions Translated and Annotated 2: Ramesses II Royal Inscriptions*, Oxford.

—— (1999) *Ramesside Inscriptions Translated and Annotated 2: Notes and Comments*, Oxford.

—— (1999) *Poetry of Ancient Egypt*, Gothenburg.

Leibovitch, J. (1953) Gods of Agriculture and Welfare in Ancient Egypt, *Journal of Near Eastern Studies* 12 (2): 73–113.

Lesko, B. (1999) *The Great Goddesses of Egypt*, Norman.

Lesko, L. H. (1991) Ancient Egyptian Cosmogonies and

Cosmology, in B. E. Shafer (ed.), *Religion in Ancient Egypt: Gods, Myths and Personal Practice*, New York.

Lichtheim, M. (1973) *Ancient Egyptian Literature I: The Old and Middle Kingdoms*, Berkeley and London.

—— (1976) *Ancient Egyptian Literature II: The New Kingdom*, Berkeley and London.

—— (1980) *Ancient Egyptian Literature III: The Late Period*, Berkeley and London.

Loprieno, A. (ed.) (1996) *Ancient Egyptian Literature: History and Forms*, Leiden, New York and Köln.

Manniche, L. (1981) *The Prince Who Knew His Fate: an Ancient Egyptian Tale Translated from Hieroglyphs and Illustrated*, New York.

—— (1987) *Sexual Life in Ancient Egypt*, London.

Monserrat, D. (2000) *Akhenaten: History, Fantasy and Ancient Egypt*, London.

Morenz, L. D. (2004) Apophis: on the Origin, Name and Nature of an Ancient Egyptian Anti-god, *Journal of Near Eastern Studies* 63 (3): 201–5.

Morenz, S. (1973) *Egyptian Religion*, trans. A. Keep, London.

Naville, E. (1895–1908) *The Temple of Deir el-Bahari*, 7 vols, London.

Nunn, J. F. (1997) *Ancient Egyptian Medicine*, London.

O'Connor, D. (2009) *Abydos: Egypt's First Pharaohs and the Cult of Osiris*, London.

Parkinson, R. B. (1991) *Voices from Ancient Egypt: an Anthology of Middle Kingdom Writings*, London.

—— (1997) *The Tale of Sinuhe and Other Ancient Egyptian Poems 1940–1640 BC*, Oxford.

—— (2002) *Poetry and Culture in Middle Kingdom Egypt: a Dark Side to Perfection*, London and New York.

Piccione, P. A. (1990) Mehen, Mysteries, and Resurrection from the Coiled Serpent, *Journal of the American Research Center in Egypt* 27: 43–52.

Pinch, G. (2002) *Egyptian Mythology: a Guide to the Gods, Goddesses and Traditions of Ancient Egypt*, Oxford.

Plutarch, *The Parallel Lives: Life of Antony*, trans. B. Perrin (1920), vol. IX, Cambridge, Mass. and London.

—— *Isis and Osiris, Moralia* V, trans. F. C. Babbitt (1936), Cambridge, Mass. and London.

Quibell, J. E. (1896) *The Ramesseum*, with translations and comments by W. Spiegelberg, London.

Quirke, S. (1992) *Ancient Egyptian Religion*, London.

—— (2001) *The Cult of Ra: Sun Worship in Ancient Egypt*, London.

Ray, J. (2002) *Reflections of Osiris*, London.

Redford, D. B. (1984) *Akhenaten: the Heretic King*, Princeton.

—— (ed.) (2002) *The Oxford Essential Guide to Egyptian Mythology*, Oxford.

Reeves, N. (2000) *Ancient Egypt: the Great Discoveries*, London.

—— (2001) *Akhenaten: Egypt's False Prophet*, London.

Ritner, R. K. (1990) O. Gardiner 363: a Spell Against Night Terrors, *Journal of the American Research Center in Egypt* 27: 25–41.

Roberts, A. (1995) *Hathor Rising: The Serpent Power of Ancient Egypt*, Totnes.

—— (2000) *My Heart My Mother: Death and Rebirth in Ancient Egypt*, Rottingdean.

—— (2008) *Golden Shrine, Goddess Queen: Egypt's Anointing Mysteries*, Rottingdean.

Scott, N. E. (1951) The Metternich Stela, *Metropolitan Museum of Art Bulletin* 9 (8): 201–17.

Shafer, B. E. (ed.) (1991) *Religion in Ancient Egypt: Gods, Myths and Personal Practice*, New York.

Simpson, W. K. (ed.) (2003) *The Literature of Ancient Egypt: an Anthology of Stories, Instructions, Stelae, Autobiographies, and Poetry*, 3rd edn, New Haven and London.

Snape, S. (1996) *Egyptian Temples*, Princes Risborough.

Stewart, H. M. (1971) A Crossword Hymn to Mut, *Journal of Egyptian Archaeology* 57: 87–104.

Strudwick, N. C. (2005) *Texts from the Pyramid Age*, Atlanta.

Szpakowska, K. (2003) Playing with Fire: Initial Observations on the Religious Uses of Clay Cobras from Amarna, *Journal of the American Research Center in Egypt* 40: 113–22.

Te Velde, H. (1977) *Seth, God of Confusion: a Study of His Role in Egyptian Mythology and Religion*, Leiden.

Tobin, V. A. (1988) Mytho-Theology in Ancient Egypt, *Journal of the American Research Center in Egypt* 25: 169–83.

—— (1993) Divine Conflict in the Pyramid Texts, *Journal of the American Research Center in Egypt* 30: 93–110.

Troy, L. (1986) *Patterns of Queenship in Ancient Egyptian Myth and History*, Uppsala Studies in Ancient Mediterranean and Near Eastern Civilizations 14, Uppsala.

Tyldesley, J. A. (1998) *Nefertiti: Egypt's Sun Queen*, London.

—— (2000) *Judgement of the Pharaoh: Crime and Punishment in Ancient Egypt*, London.

—— (2004) *Tales from Ancient Egypt*, Bolton.

—— (2005) *Stories from Ancient Egypt*, Bolton.

Vandier, J. (1961) *Le Papyrus Jumilhac*, Paris.

Wilkinson, R. H. (2003) *The Complete Gods and Goddesses of Ancient Egypt*, London.

Wilkinson, T. A. H. (1999) *Early Dynastic Egypt*, London and New York.

Witt, R. E. (1971) *Isis in the Ancient World*, Baltimore and London. (Originally published as *Isis in the Graeco-Roman World*.)

INDEX

He just wanted a decent book to read ...

Not too much to ask, is it? It was in 1935 when Allen Lane, Managing Director of Bodley Head Publishers, stood on a platform at Exeter railway station looking for something good to read on his journey back to London. His choice was limited to popular magazines and poor-quality paperbacks – the same choice faced every day by the vast majority of readers, few of whom could afford hardbacks. Lane's disappointment and subsequent anger at the range of books generally available led him to found a company – and change the world.

'We believed in the existence in this country of a vast reading public for intelligent books at a low price, and staked everything on it'
Sir Allen Lane, 1902–1970, founder of Penguin Books

The quality paperback had arrived – and not just in bookshops. Lane was adamant that his Penguins should appear in chain stores and tobacconists, and should cost no more than a packet of cigarettes.

Reading habits (and cigarette prices) have changed since 1935, but Penguin still believes in publishing the best books for everybody to enjoy. We still believe that good design costs no more than bad design, and we still believe that quality books published passionately and responsibly make the world a better place.

So wherever you see the little bird – whether it's on a piece of prize-winning literary fiction or a celebrity autobiography, political tour de force or historical masterpiece, a serial-killer thriller, reference book, world classic or a piece of pure escapism – you can bet that it represents the very best that the genre has to offer.

Whatever you like to read – trust Penguin.